RAPE

BLAME IT ON PATRIARCHY AND CONSERVATISM IN INDIA

JAYEETA ROY

To all women who are silenced.

Contents

Prologue

Rape.

Section 375 of the Indian Penal Code defines Rape as;

"sexual intercourse with a woman against her will, without her consent, by coercion, misrepresentation or fraud or at a time when she has been intoxicated or duped, or is of unsound mental health and in any case if she is under 18 years of age."

CHAPTER ONE

Introduction

Overview of Rape Culture Globally

Rape culture is a sociological concept that describes a setting in which rape is pervasive and normalised due to societal attitudes about gender and sexuality. It is a culture that encourages male sexual aggression and supports violence against women. In a rape culture, women perceive a continuum of threatened violence that ranges from sexual remarks to physical abuse. A culture that trivialises, excuses, or condones sexual violence creates an environment in which rape and other forms of sexual violence are more likely to occur.

Globally, rape culture manifests in various ways, including media representations that glamorise or trivialise sexual violence, legal systems that fail to protect victims or punish perpetrators adequately, and social norms that blame victims for their assaults. In many parts of the world, gender inequality and misogyny are deeply embedded in societal structures, reinforcing the power dynamics that underlie rape culture.

Media Representations and Their Impact

Media plays a significant role in perpetuating rape culture by shaping societal attitudes toward gender and sexuality. In many countries, films, television shows, music, and advertisements often depict women as sexual objects and normalise male aggression. These portrayals contribute to a desensitisation of violence against women and reinforce harmful stereotypes.

For example, in the United States, a study by the Geena Davis Institute on Gender in Media found that women are often depicted in subordinate roles and are more likely to be shown in sexually suggestive content compared to men. These media representations can influence public perceptions and contribute to a culture that excuses or trivialises sexual violence. Similarly, in India, Bollywood movies have been criticised for glamorising stalking and non-consensual advances, which can contribute to a normalisation of such behaviours in real life.

Legal Systems and Their Failures

Legal systems worldwide often fail to adequately protect victims of sexual violence or to hold perpetrators accountable. This failure can be attributed to various factors, including insufficient laws, inadequate implementation, and a lack of sensitivity and training among law enforcement and judicial personnel.

In the United States, the handling of the Brock Turner case highlighted significant issues within the legal system. Turner, a Stanford University student, was convicted of sexually assaulting an unconscious woman but received a lenient six-month jail sentence, of which he served only three months. The case sparked outrage and underscored the need for stricter penalties and more victim-centred approaches within the judicial system.

In Europe, the treatment of sexual violence cases has varied widely. Countries like Sweden and Germany have progressive laws and relatively higher reporting rates, but challenges remain, particularly in addressing sexual violence within migrant communities. The influx of refugees and asylum seekers has brought attention to issues of integration and cultural differences, which can complicate the prosecution of sexual violence cases.

Cultural Practices and Gender Inequality

In many parts of the world, cultural practices that devalue women and girls contribute to a cycle of violence and rape culture. In Africa and South Asia, practices such as child marriage, female genital mutilation (FGM), and dowry-related violence are prevalent and have deep cultural roots.

Child marriage, for instance, remains a significant issue in countries like Nigeria, India, and Bangladesh. According to UNICEF, nearly 12 million girls are married before the age of 18 each year, which increases their vulnerability to sexual violence and limits their opportunities for education and economic independence.

Female genital mutilation, a practice that involves the partial or total removal of the external female genitalia for non-medical reasons, is still prevalent in many African and Middle Eastern countries. The World Health Organization estimates that over 200 million girls and women alive today have undergone FGM, which has severe physical and psychological consequences and reflects deep-rooted gender inequalities.

Global Statistics and Trends

Understanding the global scope of rape culture requires examining data on sexual violence and its impact. The World Health Organization (WHO) estimates that one in three women worldwide have experienced either physical and/or sexual intimate partner violence or non-partner sexual violence in their lifetime. This statistic underscores the pervasive nature of gender-based violence and the need for comprehensive strategies to address it.

In the European Union, a 2014 survey by the European Union Agency for Fundamental Rights (FRA) revealed that 33% of women had experienced physical and/or sexual violence since the age of 15. The survey also highlighted significant variations between countries, with Denmark reporting the highest prevalence (52%) and Poland the lowest (19%).

In sub-Saharan Africa, data from the United Nations Population Fund (UNFPA) indicates that gender-based violence is widespread, with countries like South Africa reporting exceptionally high rates. In South Africa, a study by the Medical Research Council found that one in four men admitted to having committed rape, highlighting the urgent need for societal and legal reforms.

Efforts to Combat Rape Culture

Efforts to combat rape culture require a multifaceted approach that includes legal reforms, education, and shifts in societal attitudes towards gender and sexuality. Several countries have made significant strides in addressing these issues through legislation, public awareness campaigns, and grassroots activism.

Legal reforms are crucial in providing a framework for protecting victims and prosecuting perpetrators. In India, the Criminal Law (Amendment) Act of 2013, also known as the Nirbhaya Act, was introduced in response to the 2012 Delhi gang rape. The act included harsher penalties for sexual violence, a broader definition of rape, and measures to improve the handling of sexual assault cases by law enforcement and the judiciary.

Public awareness campaigns play a vital role in changing societal attitudes and breaking the silence around sexual violence. The #MeToo movement, which began in the United States, has had a global impact, encouraging survivors to speak out and hold perpetrators accountable. The movement has also prompted discussions about consent, power dynamics, and the need for systemic change in various sectors, including entertainment, media, and politics.

Grassroots activism is another essential component in combating rape culture. Organisations like the Women's Global Network for Reproductive Rights (WGNRR) and Equality Now work internationally to advocate for women's rights and provide support to survivors of sexual violence. These organisations often collaborate with local groups to address specific cultural and societal issues that contribute to rape culture.

Rape culture is a pervasive issue that affects societies globally, manifesting in various forms such as media representations, legal system failures, and harmful cultural practices. The common denominator is the devaluation of women and the normalisation of sexual violence. Addressing rape culture requires comprehensive strategies that include legal reforms, education, public awareness campaigns, and grassroots activism. By understanding the global context and learning from international efforts, societies can work towards creating a safer and more equitable world for all individuals, regardless of gender.

Synopsis of the Case Studies discussed and analysed

1. Nirbhaya Case (2012)

On the night of December 16, 2012, a 23-year-old physiotherapy intern, later known as Nirbhaya, and her male friend boarded a private bus in Delhi after watching a movie. They were unaware that the bus was off-duty and occupied by six men, including the driver. The men, who were from economically disadvantaged backgrounds, attacked the couple. Nirbhaya's friend was beaten unconscious, and she was gang-raped and brutally assaulted with an iron rod, causing severe internal injuries. The perpetrators then threw both victims out of the bus. Despite undergoing multiple surgeries, Nirbhaya succumbed to her injuries on December 29, 2012, in a Singapore hospital. The case sparked massive protests across India and led to changes in the country's laws on sexual assault. All six attackers were apprehended; four were sentenced to death and executed in March 2020, one committed suicide in prison, and the juvenile was sentenced to three years in a reform facility. The case is now closed. 〔BBC〕

2. Unnao Rape Case (2017)

On June 4, 2017, in Unnao, Uttar Pradesh, a minor girl was abducted and raped by Kuldeep Singh Sengar, a BJP MLA with considerable political influence in the region. The victim, from a lower-middle-class family, initially faced significant delays in justice due to Sengar's political power. The case gained national attention in April 2018 when the victim attempted self-immolation outside the Chief Minister's residence, protesting the lack of action against Sengar. This public outcry led to Sengar's arrest and eventual conviction. In December 2019, he was sentenced to life imprisonment. The case highlights the intersection of political power and judicial processes in India and underscores the challenges faced by victims seeking justice against influential perpetrators. The case is now closed. 〔 The Hindu 〕

3. Hathras Gang Rape Case (2020)

On September 14, 2020, a 19-year-old Dalit woman from a poor family in Hathras, Uttar Pradesh, was gang-raped and fatally injured by four upper-caste men from her village. Despite her serious injuries, the initial police response was inadequate, influenced by caste dynamics and local pressures. The victim was eventually transferred to a Delhi hospital, where she succumbed to her injuries two weeks later. The incident led to widespread protests and criticism of the authorities' handling of the case. The trial is ongoing, and there have been continuous allegations of police negligence and caste-based discrimination. The case remains a significant point of discussion regarding caste, gender, and justice in India. 〔 The Indian Express 〕

4. Kathua Rape Case (2018)

In January 2018, an 8-year-old girl from a nomadic Muslim community was kidnapped, drugged, raped, and murdered in a temple in Kathua, Jammu and Kashmir. The perpetrators included a temple custodian and police officers, and their motive was to drive the victim's community out of the area. The crime, fueled by communal tensions, drew national and international outrage. The investigation revealed severe lapses by local police and attempts to cover up the crime. Three of the accused were sentenced to life imprisonment, and three others received five-year sentences. The case highlighted the interplay of communal politics and justice in India and brought to light the systemic issues within the judicial system. The case is now closed. 〔 Al Jazeera 〕

5. Shakti Mills Gang Rape Case (2013)

On August 22, 2013, a 22-year-old photojournalist was gang-raped by five men in the abandoned Shakti Mills compound in Mumbai. The victim was on assignment with a male colleague when they were attacked. The assailants, who were jobless young men from economically disadvantaged backgrounds, tied up the colleague and took turns raping the victim. The incident, occurring in the wake of the Nirbhaya case, led to significant media coverage and public outrage. The case was fast-tracked, resulting in the conviction of the perpetrators. Three were initially sentenced to death, later commuted to life imprisonment, and the juvenile received a three-year sentence in a reform facility. The case underscored the impact of media and public pressure on the judicial process. The case is closed. [The Guardian]

6. Jisha Rape and Murder Case (2016)

On April 28, 2016, Jisha, a 30-year-old law student from a lower-middle-class Dalit family, was found brutally raped and murdered in her home in Perumbavoor, Kerala. She had been subjected to severe physical trauma. The perpetrator, Ameerul Islam, a migrant laborer from Assam, was arrested based on forensic evidence linking him to the crime. The case highlighted the vulnerability of Dalit women and the systemic issues they face. Islam was convicted and sentenced to death, bringing some closure to the victim's family. This case emphasized the broader social issues related to caste and gender violence in India. The case is closed. [India Today]

7. Badaun Gang Rape Case (2014)

On May 27, 2014, in Badaun, Uttar Pradesh, two teenage cousins from a lower-caste family were found hanging from a tree after allegedly being gang-raped. Five men, including two police officers, were initially implicated. The case was marked by allegations of police involvement and a subsequent cover-up, leading to significant public outcry. The Central Bureau of Investigation (CBI) later concluded that the girls were not raped, attributing their deaths to suicide. This controversial conclusion led to further public outrage and criticism. The case highlighted the deep-rooted issues of caste-based violence and corruption within the law enforcement system. The case is closed controversially. [BBC]

8. Bilaspur Rape Case (2006)

On March 18, 2006, in Bilaspur, Chhattisgarh, a 24-year-old nurse was raped and murdered by a local politician with a criminal background. The victim, from a middle-class family, faced delays in justice due to the political influence of the perpetrator. Persistent media coverage and public pressure eventually led to the politician's conviction and life imprisonment. This case illustrated the significant challenges faced by victims of sexual violence when the perpetrators are influential individuals, and it underscored the importance of media and public advocacy in the pursuit of justice. The case is closed. [The Hindu]

9. Gudia Rape Case (2012)

On August 15, 2012, a 16-year-old girl named Gudia was abducted and gang-raped by three men in a moving car in Barmer, Rajasthan. The perpetrators, from influential local families, initially used their status to delay justice. However, persistent legal efforts by the victim's family and public support eventually led to the conviction of the three men, who were sentenced to life imprisonment. This case demonstrated the difficulties in securing justice in the face of local influence and highlighted the importance of community support and legal perseverance. The case is closed. [Times of India]

10. Guwahati Molestation Case (2012)

On July 9, 2012, a teenage girl was molested by a mob of around 20 men outside a pub in Guwahati, Assam. The incident was filmed by a journalist, and the footage went viral, causing national outrage. The video facilitated the identification and arrest of several perpetrators. The incident drew significant attention due to its public nature and the role of media in highlighting the crime. Sentences for the convicted men varied, reflecting the complexities of mob violence and public accountability. This case underscored the role of media in bringing attention to crimes against women and the impact of public scrutiny on legal proceedings. The case is closed. [NDTV]

11. Suryanelli Rape Case (1996-2012)

In January 1996, a 16-year-old girl from Suryanelli, Kerala, was abducted and raped by 42 men over 40 days. The case involved numerous influential individuals and saw multiple trials and retrials over the years. The victim, from a lower-middle-class family, faced significant social stigma and prolonged legal battles. Despite initial delays and political interference, multiple convictions were eventually secured, although the case remains ongoing with appeals and legal battles. This case highlighted the systemic issues in addressing sexual violence and the prolonged struggle for justice that victims often face. [The Hindu]

12. Park Street Rape Case (2012)

On February 5, 2012, in Kolkata, West Bengal, a woman was gang-raped in a moving car after leaving a nightclub. The victim, an Anglo-Indian woman working in the service industry, hailed a taxi after spending the evening at a popular nightclub. Unbeknownst to her, the taxi driver and his accomplices planned to assault her. After driving to a secluded area, the men attacked and raped her. Despite the victim immediately reporting the crime, initial police skepticism and derogatory comments by political figures, including the Chief Minister of West Bengal, complicated the case. The police initially dismissed her complaint as fabricated. However, media attention and public outrage pressured authorities to act. The main accused were eventually arrested, and after a protracted legal battle, they were convicted and sentenced to prison. This case underscores the societal prejudices and victim-blaming attitudes that survivors of sexual violence often face, as well as the critical role of media and public pressure in ensuring justice. The case is now closed. [The Telegraph]

13. Noida Double Murder Case (2008)

On May 16, 2008, 14-year-old Aarushi Talwar was found murdered in her bedroom in her family's home in Noida, Uttar Pradesh. The next day, the body of Hemraj, the family's domestic worker, was discovered on the terrace. The initial investigation was marred by police missteps and media sensationalism. Aarushi's parents, Dr. Rajesh and Nupur Talwar, both affluent professionals, were accused of the murders. The case was heavily covered by the media, with various theories and accusations being publicly debated. The parents were convicted in 2013, but the High Court later acquitted them in 2017 due to insufficient evidence, highlighting the flaws in the investigative process and the impact of media pressure on high-profile cases. This case is a stark example of how media can influence public perception and judicial proceedings, and it remains a significant point of study for understanding the complexities of the Indian judicial system. The case is now closed. 〔 The Hindu 〕

14. Ajmer Rape Case (1992)

In the early 1990s, a series of rapes and sexual assaults came to light in Ajmer, Rajasthan, involving several schoolgirls who were blackmailed and gang-raped by a group of influential men. The perpetrators were from prominent families in Ajmer, including members of a well-known political and religious group. The case was revealed in 1992 when photographs of the victims, taken during the assaults, began circulating. Many of the victims were from middle to lower-middle-class families and were coerced into silence through threats and blackmail. The influential status of the accused led to significant delays in justice, as they used their power to obstruct investigations and intimidate witnesses. After prolonged legal battles, several of the accused were convicted, although some cases remain under appeal. This case highlights the intersection of power, politics, and gender-based violence, demonstrating the systemic challenges in prosecuting influential offenders. 〔 India Today 〕

15. Madurai Rape Case (2013)

On August 10, 2013, a 20-year-old college student was gang-raped by four men in Madurai, Tamil Nadu. The victim, a middle-class college student, was returning home when she was abducted by the perpetrators, who were from economically disadvantaged backgrounds. They took her to a remote area where they assaulted her. The case drew significant public attention and prompted swift action by the police. The trial proceeded without major delays, and all four men were convicted and sentenced to life imprisonment. This case is noted for the relatively prompt judicial process and serves as an example of effective law enforcement response in cases of sexual violence, emphasizing the importance of timely and unbiased investigation and prosecution. The case is now closed. 〔 The Hindu 〕

CHAPTER THREE

Specific Context within India

India presents a unique and complex case when it comes to rape culture. The country has been grappling with high levels of gender-based violence, which have sparked national and international outrage. Incidents such as the 2012 Delhi gang rape, also known as the Nirbhaya case, brought global attention to the severity of the issue in India. This case highlighted not only the brutality of sexual violence in India but also the pervasive societal attitudes that contribute to rape culture.

Deeply Rooted Patriarchal Norms

In India, several factors contribute to the entrenchment of rape culture, including deeply rooted patriarchal norms. Patriarchy in India is reinforced by traditional practices and beliefs that subordinate women to men. These patriarchal norms dictate every aspect of a woman's life, from education and employment opportunities to marriage and family roles.

From a young age, girls are often taught to conform to gender-specific roles and to prioritise family honour over their own well-being. This social conditioning perpetuates a cycle of dependency and subordination. Educational opportunities for girls are frequently limited, with many families prioritising the education of boys. According to the Annual Status of Education Report (ASER) 2018, while enrolment rates for girls in primary school are high, dropout rates increase significantly at the secondary level, particularly in rural areas.

Employment opportunities for women are also constrained by patriarchal norms. The World Bank's 2020 report highlights that female labour force participation in India stands at a mere 20.8%, one of the lowest in the world. This economic dependence on men further limits women's autonomy and ability to escape abusive situations.

In marriage, the concept of the "ideal woman" as a dutiful wife and mother reinforces gender stereotypes and perpetuates inequality. Marital rape remains a contentious issue, as Indian law does not recognise it as a criminal offence unless the wife is under 18 years old. This legal gap underscores the deep-seated patriarchal belief that a wife is the property of her husband.

Caste Dynamics and Sexual Violence

The caste system further complicates the issue, as women from lower castes, particularly Dalit women, are disproportionately affected by sexual violence. The intersectionality of caste and gender creates a compounded form of discrimination and vulnerability. Dalit women often face barriers in accessing justice, as perpetrators from higher castes are protected by social and economic power.

Dalit women are subjected to both caste-based and gender-based violence, making them one of the most marginalised groups in India. According to the National Crime Records Bureau (NCRB) 2019 report, crimes against Dalits increased by 7.3% from the previous year, with many of these crimes involving sexual violence against Dalit women.

The socio-economic status of Dalit women also contributes to their vulnerability. Many are employed in low-paying, informal jobs, making it difficult for them to access resources and support systems. Additionally, social ostracisation and fear of retaliation often deter Dalit women from reporting incidents of sexual violence.

Religious and Cultural Conservatism

Religious and cultural conservatism also play a significant role in perpetuating rape culture in India. Traditional views on female chastity and honour place the burden of sexual violence on the victims rather than the perpetrators. This victim-blaming mentality discourages many women from reporting incidents of sexual violence due to fear of social stigma and ostracisation.

Cultural norms often dictate that a woman's honour is tied to her sexual purity, and any violation is seen as a stain on her family's reputation. This belief system not only stigmatises survivors of sexual violence but also deters them from seeking justice. The fear of being labelled as "impure" or "dishonoured" can be so powerful that many women choose to remain silent about their experiences.

Religious teachings can also reinforce these conservative attitudes. In many communities, religious leaders hold significant influence and often propagate patriarchal interpretations of religious texts that subordinate women. These interpretations can perpetuate gender discrimination and justify violence against women.

Impact of Media and Public Perception

The media in India plays a dual role in shaping public perception of rape and sexual violence. On one hand, media coverage of high-profile cases like the Nirbhaya incident has raised awareness about the prevalence of sexual violence and spurred public outcry. On the other hand, sensationalist reporting and victim-blaming narratives often dominate media coverage, reinforcing harmful stereotypes and attitudes.

For instance, media outlets frequently focus on the character and behaviour of the victim, questioning their attire, actions, or lifestyle choices. This type of reporting shifts the blame from the perpetrator to the victim and perpetuates the idea that women are responsible for preventing their own victimisation.

Legal and Judicial Challenges

The Indian legal system has made significant strides in addressing sexual violence, particularly following the Nirbhaya case. The Criminal Law (Amendment) Act of 2013 introduced stricter penalties for sexual violence, expanded the definition of rape, and implemented measures to improve the handling of sexual assault cases by law enforcement and the judiciary.

Despite these legal advancements, challenges remain in the implementation and enforcement of these laws. The judicial process is often slow, and there is a lack of sensitivity and training among law enforcement officials in handling cases of sexual violence. According to the NCRB, the conviction rate for rape cases in India was only 27.8% in 2019, highlighting the gaps in the judicial system.

Moreover, there is a significant backlog of cases in the Indian courts, which delays justice for survivors. The lack of adequate support services, such as counselling and legal aid, further exacerbates the challenges faced by survivors in seeking justice.

Grassroots Movements and Activism

Grassroots movements and activism have played a crucial role in challenging rape culture in India. Women's rights organisations and activists have been at the forefront of advocating for legal reforms, raising awareness about gender-based violence, and providing support to survivors.

The #MeToo movement gained significant traction in India, with women from various sectors coming forward to share their experiences of sexual harassment and assault. This movement has sparked important conversations about consent, power dynamics, and the need for systemic change in workplaces and institutions.

Organisations such as the All India Democratic Women's Association (AIDWA) and the Centre for Women's Development Studies (CWDS) work tirelessly to address issues of gender violence and support survivors. These organisations often operate at the grassroots level, providing legal assistance, counselling, and advocacy services to women in need.

A complex interplay of patriarchal norms, caste dynamics, religious and cultural conservatism, media representations, legal challenges, and grassroots activism shapes the specific context of rape culture in India. Addressing rape culture in India requires a multifaceted approach that includes legal reforms, education, shifts in societal attitudes, and robust support systems for survivors. Understanding these contextual factors is essential for developing effective strategies to combat rape culture and promote gender equality in India. The following chapters will delve deeper into these aspects, exploring the role of patriarchy, conservatism, and rigid social structures in perpetuating rape culture and proposing strategies for change.

Historical Perspective on Gender Violence in India

The historical context of gender violence in India is crucial to understanding the current landscape of rape culture. Historically, Indian society has been deeply patriarchal, with gender roles strictly defined and enforced. Ancient texts and laws, such as the Manusmriti, codified the subjugation of women and prescribed their roles within the household and society. Women's rights and autonomy were severely restricted, and practices such as child marriage, sati (widow immolation), and purdah (seclusion of women) were prevalent.

Ancient and Medieval Periods

Manusmriti and Codification of Patriarchy

The Manusmriti, an ancient legal text, laid the foundation for the patriarchal structure of society. It prescribed strict roles for women, emphasising their subordination to men. Women were considered the property of their fathers, husbands, and sons, and their primary roles were confined to domestic duties and procreation. The Manusmriti explicitly stated that a woman should never be independent:

"In childhood, a female must be subject to her father; in youth, to her husband; and when her lord is dead, to her sons. A woman must never be independent." - Manusmriti 5.148

Practices such as Sati and Purdah

Practices such as sati, where a widow was compelled or expected to immolate herself on her husband's funeral pyre, and purdah, which involved the seclusion of women from public observation, further entrenched gender inequality. Sati was seen as a means of maintaining family honour and ensuring the widow's fidelity even after her husband's death. Purdah, prevalent among both Hindus and Muslims, restricted women's mobility and their participation in public life.

Child Marriage

Child marriage was another practice that reflected the low status of women. Girls were married off at a very young age, often before they reached puberty, to ensure their chastity and secure alliances between families. This practice curtailed their education and personal development, reinforcing their dependence on male relatives.

Colonial Period

British Reforms

During the colonial period, the British administration introduced legal reforms aimed at addressing some of these oppressive practices. The Regulation XVII of 1829 banned sati, largely due to the efforts of social reformers like Raja Ram Mohan Roy. The Age of Consent Act of 1891 raised the age of consent for girls from ten to twelve years, a small but significant step towards protecting young girls from early marriage and sexual exploitation.

Resistance to Reforms

However, these reforms were often met with resistance from conservative elements within Indian society. Many viewed the British efforts as an attack on traditional values and customs. The backlash against these reforms highlighted the deep-rooted patriarchal norms and the societal reluctance to change the status quo regarding women's roles and rights.

Social Reform Movements

Despite the resistance, social reformers continued to advocate for women's rights. Reformers such as Jyotirao Phule and Savitribai Phule worked tirelessly to promote women's education and fight against caste and gender discrimination. The Indian women's movement gained momentum with the establishment of organisations like the Women's Indian Association (WIA) in 1917, which campaigned for women's suffrage and legal rights.

Post-Independence Period

Constitutional Guarantees

The post-independence period saw significant strides in women's rights, beginning with the adoption of a constitution that guarantees equality and non-discrimination. Article 15 of the Indian Constitution prohibits discrimination on the grounds of religion, race, caste, sex, or place of birth, while Article 39 directs the state to ensure that men and women have an equal right to an adequate means of livelihood.

Legal Reforms

Legal reforms continued with the introduction of laws aimed at protecting women's rights and addressing gender-based violence. The Dowry Prohibition Act of 1961 sought to eliminate the practice of dowry, which often led to domestic violence and dowry-related deaths. The Protection of Women from Domestic Violence Act of 2005 provided a comprehensive framework to address domestic abuse, including physical, emotional, and economic violence.

Following the Nirbhaya case in 2012, the Criminal Law (Amendment) Act of 2013 was enacted, introducing stricter penalties for sexual violence, expanding the definition of rape, and implementing measures to improve the handling of sexual assault cases by law enforcement and the judiciary.

Challenges in Enforcement

Despite these legal advancements, the enforcement of these laws remains a challenge due to societal attitudes and systemic issues within the judicial and law enforcement systems. Victim-blaming, inadequate sensitivity training for law enforcement, and judicial delays often hinder the effective implementation of these laws. The conviction rate for rape cases in India remains low, underscoring the gaps in the judicial process.

Feminist Movement and Grassroots Activism

Role of Feminist Movement

The feminist movement in India has played a crucial role in raising awareness about gender violence and advocating for women's rights. Grassroots organisations and activists have been instrumental in challenging patriarchal norms and providing support to survivors of sexual violence. The feminist movement in India gained significant momentum during the 1970s and 1980s, with the formation of groups like the Self-Employed Women's Association (SEWA) and the All India Democratic Women's Association (AIDWA).

#MeToo Campaign

Movements such as the #MeToo campaign have gained momentum in India, highlighting the prevalence of sexual harassment and assault in various sectors, including entertainment, media, and politics. The #MeToo movement in India saw high-profile cases being exposed, leading to greater awareness and dialogue about workplace harassment and the need for systemic change.

Grassroots Organizations

Grassroots organisations continue to play a vital role in combating gender violence. Groups such as Jagori, Swayam, and the Centre for Enquiry into Health and Allied Themes (CEHAT) provide crucial support services, including legal aid, counselling, and advocacy for survivors of violence. These organisations often work at the community level, engaging with local leaders and stakeholders to change societal attitudes and promote gender equality.

Ongoing Struggle and Need for Change

Despite the progress made, the struggle against gender violence in India is ongoing. The deep-seated cultural and social norms that perpetuate rape culture require sustained efforts to change. Education and awareness campaigns are essential to challenge and transform these norms. Programs that promote gender sensitivity and equality from a young age can help shift societal attitudes and reduce the prevalence of gender-based violence.

Legal reforms must continue to evolve to address emerging challenges and gaps in the existing framework. Ensuring effective implementation of these laws requires training and sensitisation of law enforcement and judicial personnel, as well as adequate resources for support services for survivors.

The historical context of gender violence in India provides a critical backdrop to understanding the current landscape of rape culture. From ancient practices codified in texts like the Manusmriti to the colonial and post-independence legal reforms, the journey towards gender equality has been long and arduous. While significant progress has been made through legal reforms and the efforts of the feminist movement, the persistence of patriarchal norms and societal attitudes continues to pose challenges.

Addressing rape culture in India necessitates a comprehensive approach that includes continued legal reforms, education, and shifts in societal attitudes towards gender equality. The following chapters will delve deeper into these aspects, exploring the role of patriarchy, conservatism, and rigid social structures in perpetuating rape culture and proposing strategies for change.

Current Statistics and Trends in India

Understanding the current state of rape culture in India requires an analysis of available data and trends. According to the National Crime Records Bureau (NCRB), India reported over 32,000 cases of rape in 2019, which translates to an average of nearly 88 cases per day. However, these numbers are likely an underestimation due to underreporting driven by stigma and fear of retribution.

Underreporting and Societal Stigma

The underreporting of rape cases in India is a significant issue. Social stigma, fear of retribution, and a lack of trust in the legal system discourage many victims from coming forward. A survey conducted by the Thomson Reuters Foundation in 2018 ranked India as the most dangerous country for women due to the high risk of sexual violence and harassment. Many women who do report incidents face further victimisation and are often blamed for the assault, which perpetuates a culture of silence.

Vulnerability of Minors

The NCRB data also reveals that a significant proportion of rape cases involve victims who are minors, highlighting the vulnerability of young girls to sexual violence. According to the NCRB 2019 report, over 16,000 cases of child rape were reported under the Protection of Children from Sexual Offences (POCSO) Act. The Act, enacted in 2012, aims to address this issue by providing a legal framework for the protection of children. Despite this, the implementation of POCSO has faced challenges, including a backlog of cases and insufficient resources for law enforcement and judicial bodies.

Case Study: The Kathua Rape Case

In January 2018, an eight-year-old girl from the nomadic Bakarwal community was brutally raped and murdered in Kathua, Jammu and Kashmir. The incident shocked the nation and drew attention to the vulnerabilities of minor girls, especially from marginalised communities. The investigation revealed that the crime was premeditated and involved multiple perpetrators, including a retired government official and local police officers. The case highlighted not only the brutality of the crime but also the involvement of individuals in positions of power, which complicated the pursuit of justice.

Increase in Gang Rapes and Brutality

Another concerning trend is the increase in gang rapes and the brutality of such crimes. High-profile cases have exposed the deep-rooted societal issues that perpetuate sexual violence. These incidents have sparked widespread protests and calls for justice, but they also reveal the systemic failures in protecting victims and holding perpetrators accountable.

Case Study: The Nirbhaya Case

The 2012 Delhi gang rape, commonly known as the Nirbhaya case, involved the brutal gang rape and murder of a 23-year-old physiotherapy intern on a moving bus in Delhi. The incident triggered nationwide protests and led to significant legal reforms, including the Criminal Law (Amendment) Act, 2013. Despite these reforms, the persistence of gang rapes continues to highlight the gaps in the legal and social systems.

Case Study: The Hathras Gang Rape

In September 2020, a 19-year-old Dalit woman was allegedly gang-raped by four men in Hathras, Uttar Pradesh. She succumbed to her injuries two weeks later, sparking outrage across the country. The case was marred by allegations of police mishandling, a hasty cremation without the family's consent, and a narrative of caste-based violence. This incident underscored the intersection of caste and gender, where Dalit women face heightened risks of sexual violence and systemic injustice.

Regional Variations and Urban-Rural Divide

The prevalence of rape and sexual violence in India also shows significant regional variations. States like Uttar Pradesh, Maharashtra, and Rajasthan report high numbers of rape cases. The urban-rural divide is another important factor, with rural areas often experiencing higher levels of underreporting due to stronger community norms and less access to legal resources.

Data from Uttar Pradesh

Uttar Pradesh, India's most populous state, consistently reports high numbers of rape cases. In 2019, the state recorded over 3,065 cases of rape. The state's socio-economic disparities, coupled with deep-rooted patriarchal norms, contribute to the prevalence of sexual violence.

Data from Maharashtra

Maharashtra reported 2,299 cases of rape in 2019. The state has urban centres like Mumbai, which have higher reporting rates due to greater awareness and access to legal resources. However, rural areas in Maharashtra continue to grapple with underreporting and inadequate legal infrastructure.

Legislative and Judicial Responses

Following the Nirbhaya case, India introduced significant legal reforms aimed at addressing sexual violence. The Criminal Law (Amendment) Act, 2013, introduced stricter penalties for sexual violence, expanded the definition of rape, and included provisions for fast-track courts to handle rape cases. Despite these legal advancements, challenges in implementation remain.

Challenges in Legal Implementation

The judicial process in India is often slow, with a significant backlog of cases. According to the National Judicial Data Grid, over 140,000 cases of sexual offences were pending in Indian courts as of 2020. The conviction rate for rape cases is also low, at around 27.8% in 2019, highlighting the need for more efficient judicial processes and better support for victims.

Specialised Courts and Police Units

In response to the growing concerns, some states have established specialised courts and police units to handle cases of sexual violence. For instance, Maharashtra has set up dedicated police units for investigating crimes against women, and Delhi has introduced fast-track courts for rape cases. These measures aim to improve the speed and sensitivity with which cases are handled.

Grassroots and Civil Society Responses

Grassroots organisations and civil society play a crucial role in addressing rape culture and supporting survivors. Organisations such as Jagori, Swayam, and the Centre for Enquiry into Health and Allied Themes (CEHAT) provide essential services, including legal aid, counselling, and advocacy.

Community-Based Programs

Community-based programs that engage men and boys in conversations about gender equality and respect are crucial in changing societal attitudes. Programs like the "Men Against Violence and Abuse" (MAVA) initiative work to challenge traditional notions of masculinity and promote gender-sensitive behaviours.

Public Awareness Campaigns

Public awareness campaigns are also vital in changing societal attitudes and encouraging victims to come forward. Campaigns like "Beti Bachao, Beti Padhao" aim to improve the status of girls and women in society by promoting education and gender equality.

Support for Survivors

Providing support for survivors is critical in addressing the long-term impact of sexual violence. Shelters, counselling services, and legal aid are essential components of a comprehensive support system for survivors. Organisations like RAHI (Recovering and Healing from Incest) focus on providing psychological support to survivors of sexual violence, helping them to rebuild their lives.

The current state of rape culture in India is characterised by a complex interplay of social, cultural, and legal factors. While significant progress has been made in terms of legal reforms and public awareness, challenges remain in implementation and societal attitudes. High-profile cases and data from the NCRB underscore the pervasive nature of sexual violence and the need for continued efforts to combat it. Addressing rape culture in India requires a multifaceted approach that includes legal reforms, education, societal attitude shifts, and robust support systems for survivors. The following chapters will explore these aspects in greater detail, proposing strategies for change and highlighting successful initiatives.

CHAPTER FOUR

Statement of the Problem

Definition of Rape Culture

Rape culture is a sociological concept that describes a setting in which rape, sexual assault, and other forms of gender-based violence are normalised and excused in society. It is a culture that trivialises, excuses or condones sexual violence, making it pervasive and systemic. The term "rape culture" was coined by feminists in the 1970s to draw attention to the way in which societal norms, media portrayals, and institutional practices contribute to the acceptance of sexual violence against women and other marginalised groups.

Normalisation of Sexual Violence in India

Rape culture in India, like in many parts of the world, is underpinned by the normalization of sexual violence. This normalization is perpetuated through various societal mechanisms, including media representations, language and humour, victim-blaming, and institutional responses. Understanding these mechanisms within the Indian socio-political and cultural context provides deeper insights into the challenges and necessary interventions to address rape culture.

Media Representations

Bollywood and Television

Bollywood, the Indian film industry, plays a significant role in shaping societal norms and attitudes. Many Bollywood films depict aggressive courtship as romantic, often portraying male persistence and dominance as desirable traits. This can normalize the idea that relentless pursuit and crossing boundaries are acceptable forms of expressing love. For example, in the movie "Raanjhanaa," the male protagonist's obsessive pursuit of the female lead, despite her clear disinterest, is depicted as a romantic gesture. Such portrayals can desensitize audiences to the severity of sexual harassment and aggression, leading to real-life consequences where stalking and harassment are trivialized, and aggressive behaviour is misinterpreted as genuine affection.

Music and Advertisements

Music videos and advertisements also contribute to the normalization of sexual violence by often depicting women in objectifying and submissive roles. Item songs in Bollywood films frequently portray women as objects of male desire, reinforcing gender stereotypes and the commodification of women. These representations perpetuate the notion that women's primary value lies in their physical appearance and their ability to attract male attention, further entrenching gender biases and contributing to a culture that diminishes the seriousness of sexual violence.

Language and Humour

Everyday Language

Everyday language in India often includes phrases and idioms that trivialize sexual violence or place the blame on the victim. Phrases like "ladki ke kapde aise the" (the girl's clothes were such) imply that a woman's attire invites harassment. Terms like "eve-teasing" are used to describe street harassment, minimizing the seriousness of the act. Such language reinforces the idea that victims are responsible for the violence they experience, discouraging them from reporting incidents and perpetuating a cycle of silence.

Humour in Popular Culture

Rape jokes and sexist humour are common in Indian comedy, perpetuating harmful stereotypes and trivializing serious issues. The backlash against Indian comedian AIB for their roast show in 2015, which included inappropriate jokes about women, highlights the societal debate over what constitutes acceptable humour. While some defended it as free speech, others condemned it for perpetuating misogyny. Jokes about rape and sexual violence contribute to a culture of impunity, where such acts are not taken seriously, and perpetrators feel emboldened.

Victim-Blaming

Cultural Attitudes

Victim-blaming is pervasive in Indian society, where traditional norms often dictate that women are responsible for upholding family honour and purity. Public reactions to rape cases often involve questioning the victim's behaviour, attire, or choices rather than focusing on the perpetrator's actions. A study published in the "Journal of Interpersonal Violence" (2017) found that victim-blaming attitudes were prevalent among Indian respondents, with many believing that victims could have prevented their assaults by behaving differently. This discourages survivors from coming forward and reporting their experiences, perpetuating a cycle of silence and impunity.

Case Study: Nirbhaya Case

The infamous Nirbhaya case in 2012 saw significant victim-blaming from various societal quarters, including politicians and public figures. Some leaders suggested that the victim should not have been out late at night or questioned her choice of clothing. Despite the eventual legal reforms, the initial victim-blaming underscored deep-seated cultural biases that hinder the fight against sexual violence.

Institutional Responses

Law Enforcement

The response of law enforcement agencies often reflects and reinforces societal attitudes towards sexual violence. Police reluctance to file FIRs (First Information Reports), victim harassment, and insensitive handling of cases are common issues. In the Hathras gang rape case of 2020, the local police were accused of mishandling the investigation and coercing the victim's family. Such actions discourage victims from reporting crimes and erode trust in the justice system.

Judicial System

The judicial system's handling of rape cases often reflects broader societal biases. Lenient sentences and delayed trials contribute to a culture of impunity. While the Brock Turner case in the United States sparked outrage due to the lenient sentencing, similar issues are seen in India. The case of a prominent Indian religious leader, Gurmeet Ram Rahim Singh, who was convicted of raping his followers, highlighted the delays and difficulties in securing justice against powerful individuals. Inadequate judicial responses can embolden perpetrators and further victimize survivors.

Educational Institutions

Educational institutions also play a crucial role in either perpetuating or challenging rape culture. Failure to address sexual harassment on campuses and inadequate support for victims reflect broader societal issues. Cases of sexual harassment in Indian universities often go unreported due to fear of retaliation and lack of institutional support. This creates an unsafe environment for students and normalizes the presence of sexual violence in educational settings.

The normalization of sexual violence in India is a multifaceted issue deeply rooted in socio-political and cultural contexts. Media representations, everyday language, victim-blaming, and institutional responses collectively contribute to a culture that trivializes and perpetuates sexual violence. Addressing these issues requires comprehensive strategies, including legal reforms, educational initiatives, and shifts in societal attitudes. By tackling the normalization of sexual violence, India can move towards a more equitable and safe society for all its citizens.

Power Dynamics and Gender Inequality

Rape culture is deeply rooted in power dynamics and gender inequality. It reflects and reinforces the power imbalance between men and women, where men are often seen as dominant and entitled to exert control over women's bodies. This entitlement can manifest in various forms of sexual harassment, assault, and violence.

Patriarchy

Patriarchy, a social system in which men hold primary power and dominate in roles of political leadership, moral authority, social privilege, and control of property, is a fundamental component of rape culture. Patriarchal societies often value male dominance and female submissiveness, creating an environment where sexual violence is more likely to occur and be tolerated. Ancient texts like the Manusmriti in India codified gender roles and subjugated women, stating that women should always be under the authority of men (father, husband, son).

Toxic Masculinity

Toxic masculinity refers to cultural norms that define manhood as involving dominance, aggression, and sexual prowess. These norms encourage men to view women as objects for their gratification and to use violence to assert their masculinity. Toxic masculinity can pressure men to conform to harmful behaviours, including sexual aggression, to prove their manhood. The prevalence of phrases like "man up" or "don't be a sissy" in popular culture reinforces the notion that showing aggression and dominance is integral to male identity.

Objectification of Women

The objectification of women, where women are treated as objects for male pleasure rather than as full human beings, is a central aspect of rape culture. This objectification is prevalent in media, advertising, and everyday interactions. It dehumanises women and justifies their mistreatment. Studies, such as those by Fredrickson and Roberts (1997), highlight how objectification theory explains the societal tendency to view and treat women as objects, leading to higher rates of sexual harassment and assault.

Third Gender Recognition in India

Gender inequality remains a pervasive issue globally, and in India, it is further complicated by the recognition and rights of the third gender. The landmark Supreme Court judgment in 2014 legally recognised transgender individuals as a third gender, marking a significant step towards inclusivity. However, despite legal recognition, third-gender individuals continue to face substantial socio-economic challenges and discrimination. This essay explores the landscape of gender inequality in India with a focus on the third gender, examining the socio-political and cultural contexts that shape their experiences.

Nalsa v. Union of India (2014)

In 2014, the Supreme Court of India delivered a landmark verdict in the case of Nalsa v. Union of India, recognizing transgender people as a third gender. This historic judgment was a significant step in the fight for transgender rights in India. The court affirmed the rights of transgender individuals to self-identify their gender, moving away from the binary understanding of gender and acknowledging the spectrum of gender identities. The judgment directed the central and state governments to ensure that transgender individuals are treated equally and have access to social welfare schemes. It also mandated that transgender persons be included in the OBC (Other Backward Classes) category to avail reservations in education and employment. The ruling underscored the need for societal recognition and acceptance of transgender individuals, aiming to eliminate the stigma and discrimination they face.

The impact of the Nalsa judgment was profound, as it legally validated the existence and rights of transgender individuals in India. It paved the way for further legal and policy reforms aimed at promoting equality and inclusion for the third gender. The judgment also highlighted the importance of dignity, autonomy, and the right to live without fear of persecution for transgender individuals. By recognizing the right to self-identification, the Supreme Court set a precedent that personal identity should be respected and protected under the law. This ruling was celebrated as a major victory for transgender activists and human rights advocates, who had long been fighting for legal recognition and equal rights.

Transgender Persons (Protection of Rights) Act, 2019

Following the 2014 Supreme Court judgment, the Indian government enacted the Transgender Persons (Protection of Rights) Act in 2019. This Act aims to provide comprehensive protections for transgender individuals, prohibiting discrimination in various domains including employment, education, healthcare, and housing. It mandates that government and private establishments ensure non-discriminatory treatment of transgender persons and that necessary steps are taken to provide them with adequate facilities and opportunities. The Act also calls for the establishment of a National Council for Transgender Persons to monitor the implementation of policies and address issues faced by the transgender community.

The Transgender Persons (Protection of Rights) Act of 2019 represents a significant legislative effort to translate the principles laid out in the Nalsa judgment into actionable laws and policies. It seeks to address the systemic challenges and discrimination that transgender individuals face on a daily basis. By outlining specific prohibitions against discrimination and stipulating the need for welfare measures, the Act aims to create a more inclusive society where transgender persons can enjoy their rights fully and equally.

Despite its progressive intentions, the Act has faced considerable criticism from the transgender community and human rights advocates. One of the most contentious aspects of the Act is the requirement for transgender individuals to obtain a certificate of identity from a district magistrate to legally change their gender. Critics argue that this provision violates the right to self-identification, which was a cornerstone of the Nalsa judgment. The requirement for medical and psychological examinations as part of the process is seen as intrusive and demeaning, undermining the autonomy and dignity of transgender persons. Many activists feel that the Act, while well-intentioned, falls short in its implementation and perpetuates bureaucratic hurdles that complicate the lives of transgender individuals rather than simplifying them.

The Act's approach to gender recognition and the bureaucratic process involved has sparked debates about the true extent of its inclusivity and respect for transgender rights. While the legal framework is a step in the right direction, the on-ground realities and experiences of transgender individuals reveal the gaps and challenges in fully realizing the intended protections and rights. Addressing these criticisms and refining the Act to better align with the principles of self-identification and dignity will be crucial in ensuring that the transgender community can live with equality and respect.

The legal recognition of the third gender in India through the Nalsa v. Union of India judgment and the subsequent Transgender Persons (Protection of Rights) Act, 2019, marks significant milestones in the journey towards equality for transgender individuals. The Supreme Court's acknowledgment of the right to self-identification was a groundbreaking affirmation of transgender rights. However, the practical implementation of these rights, particularly through the 2019 Act, has faced challenges and criticisms. Ensuring that the legal framework truly respects and facilitates the rights of transgender individuals requires ongoing dialogue, reforms, and a commitment to upholding the principles of dignity and equality enshrined in the Nalsa judgment.

Socio-Economic Challenges

Education

Third-gender individuals in India often face significant barriers to accessing education, leading to widespread economic marginalization. Transgender students frequently experience bullying, harassment, and discrimination in educational institutions, creating a hostile environment that impedes their academic progress. These negative experiences contribute to high dropout rates, as many transgender students feel unsafe and unsupported in their schools. A 2018 study by the National Human Rights Commission (NHRC) found that a majority of transgender individuals in India have not completed secondary education. The lack of educational qualifications severely limits their opportunities for higher education and gainful employment, perpetuating a cycle of poverty and exclusion.

Employment

Discrimination in the workplace is rampant, with many employers reluctant to hire transgender individuals. This pervasive bias leads to high rates of unemployment and underemployment within the transgender community. Transgender individuals often encounter prejudice during job interviews, where their qualifications and skills are overshadowed by their gender identity. Even when employed, they may face hostile work environments, harassment from colleagues, and limited opportunities for career advancement. Consequently, many transgender people are forced into informal or precarious employment, such as begging or sex work, to survive. This economic marginalization not only affects their financial stability but also undermines their dignity and social inclusion.

Healthcare Access

Access to healthcare is another major issue for transgender individuals in India, who often face stigma and discrimination from healthcare providers. There is a pervasive lack of awareness and sensitivity among medical professionals regarding transgender health issues, including gender-affirming procedures and mental health support. Many transgender individuals report being denied medical treatment or receiving substandard care due to their gender identity. For instance, transgender patients may experience misgendering, invasive questioning, or outright refusal of care, further exacerbating their health disparities. The lack of specialized healthcare services for transgender people, including hormone therapy and surgical options, limits their ability to access necessary medical interventions. Additionally, mental health support tailored to the unique challenges faced by transgender individuals is often inadequate or unavailable, contributing to higher rates of depression, anxiety, and suicide within the community.

Housing

Housing discrimination is prevalent, with many transgender individuals being denied rental accommodations or facing eviction due to their gender identity. Landlords may refuse to rent to transgender tenants based on prejudiced beliefs or fears of social stigma. This discrimination forces many transgender individuals into unsafe living conditions or homelessness, as they struggle to find stable and affordable housing. In some cases, transgender people are confined to informal settlements or marginalized communities where they face additional risks of violence and exploitation. The lack of secure housing exacerbates their vulnerability and limits their ability to access other essential services, such as healthcare and employment.

Social Exclusion

Transgender individuals are frequently ostracized by their families and communities, leading to profound social isolation. Family rejection is a common experience for many transgender people, who may be disowned or forced to leave home due to their gender identity. This exclusion extends to public spaces, where transgender individuals are often subjected to harassment, violence, and discrimination. In many instances, they are denied entry to public facilities, such as restrooms, schools, and public transportation, based on their gender identity. The social stigma attached to being transgender isolates them from broader social networks and support systems, making it difficult to build meaningful relationships and integrate into society. This social exclusion not only affects their mental and emotional well-being but also limits their opportunities for personal and professional growth.

The socio-economic challenges faced by third-gender individuals in India are multifaceted and deeply entrenched in societal attitudes and institutional biases. Barriers to education and employment, inadequate healthcare access, and housing discrimination significantly contribute to the economic marginalization and social exclusion of transgender individuals. Addressing these challenges requires comprehensive and inclusive policies that promote equal opportunities and protections for transgender people. Efforts to raise awareness and sensitivity among educators, employers, healthcare providers, and the general public are crucial in creating a more inclusive and equitable society. By ensuring that transgender individuals have access to education, employment, healthcare, and safe housing, India can take significant steps towards reducing marginalization and promoting the dignity and rights of all its citizens.

Cultural and Social Context

Traditional Roles and Stigma

In Indian culture, there is a complex relationship with gender variance. Historically, hijras, a traditional transgender community, have held a unique position in society. Hijras have often been called upon to bless births and marriages, believed to possess special powers to confer fertility and good fortune. This cultural role has given them a certain degree of visibility and significance within Indian traditions. However, despite this unique cultural role, hijras and other transgender individuals have also faced significant marginalization and stigma. They are often viewed through a lens of pity or as subjects of ridicule rather than as equal members of society. This duality highlights the deep-seated prejudices that persist even in the face of historical recognition.

The general societal attitude towards transgender individuals is largely characterized by stigma and discrimination. Transgender people are frequently marginalized, facing exclusion from mainstream society. They are often ridiculed or viewed with contempt, making it difficult for them to find acceptance and integration into the broader community. This stigmatization is evident in various aspects of life, from education and employment to healthcare and housing. The pervasive discrimination they face contributes to their economic and social marginalization, perpetuating a cycle of poverty and exclusion.

Intersectionality with Caste and Religion

The experiences of transgender individuals in India are further complicated by intersections with caste and religion. Lower-caste transgender individuals, in particular, face compounded discrimination that affects their socioeconomic status and access to resources. The intersectionality of caste and gender identity means that lower-caste transgender people often face multiple layers of prejudice and exclusion. This dual marginalization can limit their opportunities for education, employment, and social mobility, exacerbating their vulnerability and economic hardship.

Religious contexts also play a significant role in shaping attitudes towards gender variance. Different religious communities in India have varied attitudes towards gender diversity. Some communities, such as certain Hindu sects, have historical recognition of gender diversity and may offer some level of acceptance. For example, hijras have been mentioned in ancient Hindu texts and have been integrated into certain religious rituals. However, other religious communities may be more rigid in their gender norms and less accepting of transgender individuals. This variation in religious attitudes can influence the level of acceptance and the challenges faced by transgender people within different cultural and religious contexts.

Political Inclusion

Political representation of transgender individuals has been limited in India, but there have been notable strides in recent years. Transgender activists have increasingly run for public office, and some have been elected to local government positions. These political milestones are significant as they provide visibility and a platform for transgender voices in governance. For example, in 2015, Madhu Bai Kinnar became the first openly transgender mayor in India, elected in Raigarh, Chhattisgarh. Her election was a significant milestone for transgender political representation, highlighting the potential for transgender individuals to influence policy and advocate for their rights within the political system.

Advocacy and Activism

Transgender activists and organizations have been at the forefront of advocating for their rights and fighting against discrimination. Their efforts have led to increased visibility and awareness of transgender issues in Indian society. Organizations like the Humsafar Trust and the National Network of Transgender Persons work tirelessly to support transgender individuals and advocate for their rights at both the local and national levels. These organizations provide essential services such as healthcare, legal aid, and educational support, while also campaigning for policy changes and social acceptance. The advocacy and activism of these groups have been instrumental in advancing the rights of transgender people in India, challenging societal norms, and pushing for greater inclusion and equality.

The recognition of the third gender in India has been a crucial step towards addressing gender inequality. However, significant challenges remain in ensuring that transgender individuals can enjoy their rights fully and equally. Socio-economic barriers, healthcare access issues, cultural stigma, and intersectional discrimination continue to impede progress. Addressing these challenges requires sustained efforts from the government, civil society, and the community itself. By fostering an inclusive environment and implementing effective policies, India can move closer to achieving true gender equality for all its citizens, regardless of their gender identity. Ensuring that transgender individuals have equal opportunities and protections is essential for building a just and equitable society.

Impact on Society

Impact on Survivors

Rape culture has devastating effects on survivors of sexual violence, impacting their physical, emotional, and psychological well-being. Survivors often endure significant trauma, which is compounded by societal attitudes that blame and stigmatize them rather than supporting their recovery. The normalization of rape culture can exacerbate their suffering by invalidating their experiences and denying them justice. Survivors may experience long-term effects such as depression, anxiety, PTSD, and difficulties in relationships and daily functioning. According to the National Centre for PTSD, approximately 94% of women who are raped experience symptoms of PTSD during the two weeks following the rape, and about 30% report these symptoms nine months later. These statistics underscore the profound and lasting impact that sexual violence has on individuals, necessitating a more supportive and empathetic societal response.

Shaping Attitudes

Rape culture shapes societal attitudes towards gender and violence, perpetuating harmful beliefs and behaviours. It teaches individuals that sexual violence is an inevitable part of life and that women are responsible for preventing their own victimization. This mindset places an unjust burden on women, implying that they must alter their behaviour, dress, or demeanour to avoid being assaulted. It also reinforces the idea that men have a right to control women's bodies. These attitudes contribute to cycles of violence and inequality, normalizing gender-based violence and perpetuating patriarchal norms. In many traditional societies, virginity and chastity are highly prized attributes for women, placing the burden of maintaining family honour on their behaviour and making them responsible for preventing sexual violence. This cultural expectation further entrenches gender inequality and victim-blaming.

Influence on Policy and Practice

Rape culture significantly influences public policy and institutional practices, often resulting in inadequate responses to sexual violence. Policies and procedures may fail to address sexual violence effectively, providing insufficient support services for survivors and lacking comprehensive education on consent and healthy relationships. Institutions operating within a rape culture framework may prioritize protecting their reputation over supporting survivors and holding perpetrators accountable. For instance, many universities worldwide have faced criticism for their handling of sexual assault cases, often prioritizing the institution's reputation over justice for survivors. The 2015 documentary "The Hunting Ground" highlighted numerous cases of mishandled sexual assault reports in U.S. colleges, illustrating the widespread institutional failure to address and prevent sexual violence adequately.

Data and Historical Texts

Historical and religious texts across cultures have often codified gender inequality, contributing to systemic gender-based violence. For example, the Manusmriti in India and certain passages in the Bible and Quran have been interpreted in ways that justify the subordination of women. These interpretations have historically reinforced patriarchal structures and normalized gender-based violence. Modern data also reflects the systemic failures in addressing sexual violence. According to the United Nations Office on Drugs and Crime (UNODC), globally, only 11% of sexual assault cases are reported, and of those, a fraction result in conviction. This highlights the widespread issue of underreporting and the systemic barriers that prevent survivors from obtaining justice.

Rape culture is a pervasive and systemic issue that normalizes and excuses sexual violence through various societal mechanisms. It is deeply rooted in power dynamics and gender inequality, affecting individuals and society as a whole. Addressing rape culture requires a comprehensive approach that includes legal reforms, education, public awareness campaigns, and grassroots activism. By challenging the normalization of sexual violence and promoting gender equality, societies can work towards creating a safer and more just environment for all individuals. The following chapters will delve deeper into these aspects, exploring the role of patriarchy, conservatism, and rigid social structures in perpetuating rape culture and proposing strategies for change. Through concerted efforts and systemic change, it is possible to dismantle the structures that support rape culture and foster a culture of respect, equality, and justice.

CHAPTER FIVE

Role of Religion in Contributing to Rape Culture in India

Religion has historically played a significant role in shaping societal norms and attitudes towards gender and sexuality in India. Different religions, including Hinduism, Islam, Sikhism, and Christianity, have influenced the cultural landscape in various ways. These religious teachings and practices can contribute to the perpetuation of gender-based violence, including rape, by reinforcing patriarchal norms and gender inequality. The first four major religions are considered for this.

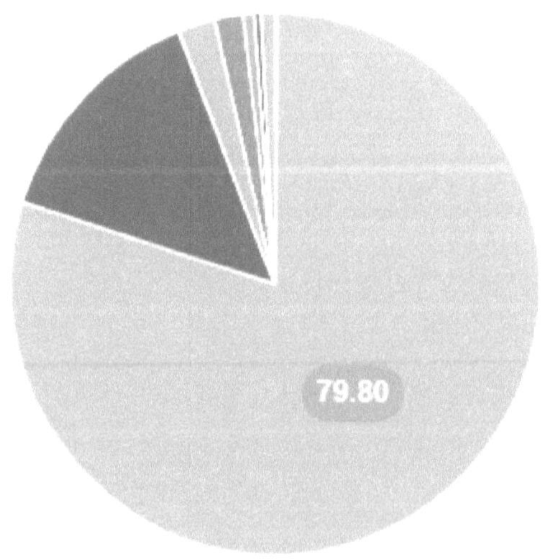

Source: Census of India 2011, Office of the Registrar General & Census Commissioner, India

Hinduism

Historical Context and Texts

Hinduism, the predominant religion in India, has deeply influenced societal norms and gender roles throughout the centuries. One of the most significant ancient texts that codified these roles is the Manusmriti, which dates back to approximately 200 BCE to 200 CE. The Manusmriti laid down strict guidelines for the behaviour and roles of women, advocating for their subjugation and perpetual dependency on male figures in their lives. It dictates that women should be under the control of their fathers during childhood, their husbands during youth, and their sons during widowhood. A key verse from the Manusmriti states, "In childhood, a female must be subject to her father; in youth, to her husband; and when her lord is dead, to her sons. A woman must never be independent" (Manusmriti 5.148). This textual evidence illustrates the deeply ingrained patriarchal norms that have historically influenced and restricted the autonomy and rights of women within Hindu society.

Cultural Practices

Several cultural practices in Hinduism, such as child marriage, dowry, and the emphasis on female chastity, further entrench gender inequality and contribute to a culture that can marginalize and victimize women. Child marriage, although illegal today, has historical roots in Hindu traditions and continues to affect many young girls, depriving them of education and childhood. The dowry system, another entrenched practice, places a significant financial burden on the bride's family and can lead to severe consequences, including dowry-related violence and harassment. The cultural emphasis on female chastity and purity places immense pressure on women to uphold family honour through their behaviour and sexual conduct. This often results in victim-blaming and the stigmatization of rape survivors, who are seen as having tarnished the family's honour. These cultural norms and practices contribute to a societal environment where women's rights and autonomy are severely limited, and their roles are confined within patriarchal structures.

Data and Trends

The influence of Hindu cultural and religious practices on gender norms is reflected in the data on sexual violence in India. According to the National Crime Records Bureau (NCRB), Hindu women constitute the majority of reported rape cases, which is reflective of the demographic distribution in India where Hindus form the largest religious group. However, specific data segregating rape incidents by religion is not readily available in public databases, making it challenging to analyse the full extent of the issue across different religious communities. The available data highlights the pervasive nature of sexual violence among Hindu women, influenced by deeply rooted cultural and religious norms that often marginalize them and exacerbate their vulnerability to such crimes.

The historical and cultural context of Hinduism has significantly shaped the gender norms and roles in Indian society, often perpetuating practices that marginalize women and contribute to rape culture. Ancient texts like the Manusmriti have codified the subjugation of women, while cultural practices such as child marriage, dowry, and the emphasis on female chastity continue to influence societal attitudes and behaviours. The data from the NCRB underscores the prevalence of sexual violence against Hindu women, reflecting the broader demographic trends but also pointing to the need for addressing the cultural and religious factors that perpetuate these crimes. Comprehensive efforts are required to challenge and change these deep-seated norms, promoting gender equality and protecting the rights and dignity of women in all spheres of life.

Islam

Historical Context and Texts

Islamic teachings in India are primarily derived from the Quran and Hadiths, which emphasize modesty, gender roles, and the segregation of genders. Islamic law, or Sharia, aims to protect women's rights and ensure their welfare, yet cultural interpretations and practices can often lead to gender discrimination. The Quran, being the central religious text of Islam, contains verses that have been variously interpreted in ways that influence gender dynamics. For example, Surah An-Nisa (4:34) has been interpreted by some to justify male authority over women: "Men are the protectors and maintainers of women because Allah has made one of them to excel the other, and because they spend from their means." This verse has sparked considerable debate among scholars, with some arguing that it reinforces patriarchal norms, while others advocate for a contextual interpretation that emphasizes mutual responsibility and care.

Cultural Practices

In many Muslim communities, practices such as purdah (the seclusion of women) and the enforcement of strict dress codes, including the hijab, niqab, or burqa, can significantly limit women's autonomy and contribute to gender inequality. Purdah, which involves the physical segregation of women from men and restricting their presence in public spaces, can curtail women's opportunities for education, employment, and social interaction. These practices are often justified in the name of modesty and protection but can result in the social isolation and economic dependence of women. Additionally, the cultural emphasis on female chastity and the fear of dishonour plays a significant role in the underreporting of sexual violence. Women who experience sexual assault may be blamed for bringing dishonour to their families, leading to social ostracism and further victimization. This societal pressure discourages many victims from seeking justice or speaking out about their experiences, perpetuating a cycle of silence and impunity.

Data and Trends

The National Crime Records Bureau (NCRB) does not specifically segregate rape cases by religion, making it challenging to obtain precise statistics on sexual violence against Muslim women. However, various studies and reports suggest that Muslim women, particularly those from marginalized communities, face significant barriers in reporting sexual violence due to cultural and social stigma. These barriers include fear of social ostracism, economic dependence, and a lack of trust in law enforcement. Marginalized

Muslim women, often residing in poorer, less secure environments, are particularly vulnerable to sexual violence and exploitation. The intersection of gender, economic status, and religious identity exacerbates their marginalization and limits their access to justice and support services.

Islamic teachings in India, while advocating for the protection and welfare of women, are often overshadowed by cultural practices and interpretations that perpetuate gender inequality. Historical and religious texts like the Quran have been interpreted in ways that reinforce patriarchal authority, though these interpretations are contested. Cultural practices such as purdah and strict dress codes further restrict women's autonomy and contribute to their marginalization. The fear of dishonour and emphasis on female chastity discourage many Muslim women from reporting sexual violence, perpetuating a cycle of silence and impunity. Addressing these issues requires a nuanced understanding of both religious teachings and cultural practices, alongside efforts to promote gender equality and protect women's rights within Muslim communities. By challenging discriminatory practices and fostering inclusive interpretations of religious texts, it is possible to create a more equitable and supportive environment for Muslim women in India.

Sikhism

Historical Context and Texts

Sikhism, founded in the 15th century by Guru Nanak and further developed by subsequent Gurus, fundamentally promotes gender equality and condemns discrimination. The teachings of Sikhism emphasize the equal status of women, challenging the deeply entrenched patriarchal norms prevalent during its inception and even today. Guru Nanak, the founder of Sikhism, preached that all humans are equal regardless of gender. This revolutionary perspective is reflected in the Sikh holy scripture, the Guru Granth Sahib. A notable verse from the Guru Granth Sahib states, "From woman, man is born; within woman, man is conceived; to woman he is engaged and married. Woman becomes his friend; through woman, the future generations come. When his woman dies, he seeks another woman; to woman he is bound. So why call her bad? From her, kings are born." (Guru Granth Sahib, p. 473). This verse celebrates the pivotal role of women in the cycle of life and asserts their fundamental dignity and respect, laying a strong foundation for gender equality within Sikhism.

Cultural Practices

Despite the egalitarian teachings of Sikhism, cultural practices within some Sikh communities can still reflect the broader patriarchal norms present in Indian society. The influence of these societal norms means that issues such as dowry and honour -related violence, although less prevalent in Sikh communities compared to others, still exist. The dowry system, where the bride's family is expected to provide substantial gifts to the groom's family, continues to be practiced by some, perpetuating gender inequality and financial burdens. Moreover, the pressure to uphold family honour can lead to violence and discrimination against women who are perceived to transgress cultural norms. For instance, honour -related violence, although not widespread, does occur in certain conservative Sikh families, particularly in rural areas. These practices stand in stark contrast to the teachings of Sikhism, which advocate for the dignity and equality of all individuals, irrespective of gender.

Data and Trends

There is limited specific data on rape incidents within Sikh communities, as most national crime statistics, including those from the National Crime Records Bureau (NCRB), do not segregate data by religion. However, general NCRB statistics suggest that gender-based violence affects all communities in India, including Sikhs. Cultural factors influencing reporting and support systems vary across different communities. In Sikh communities, the emphasis on family honour and reputation can sometimes discourage victims of sexual violence from reporting incidents to the authorities. Additionally, while Sikhism's teachings promote equality, societal norms and the influence of broader Indian culture can result in inadequate support systems for survivors of sexual violence. The lack of specific data makes it challenging to gauge the full extent of gender-based violence within Sikh communities, but it is clear that, like all communities, they are not immune to these issues.

Sikhism, with its foundational principles of gender equality and condemnation of discrimination, provides a progressive framework for the treatment of women. The teachings of Guru Nanak and subsequent Gurus, as enshrined in the Guru Granth Sahib, celebrate the vital role of women and advocate for their respect and equality. However, despite these teachings, cultural practices within some Sikh communities can still reflect broader patriarchal norms prevalent in Indian society. Issues such as dowry and honour -related violence, although less common, persist and challenge the egalitarian principles of Sikhism. The limited specific data on rape incidents within Sikh communities highlights the need for more comprehensive research and support systems. Addressing these challenges requires a concerted effort to align cultural practices with the progressive teachings of Sikhism, promoting gender equality and ensuring the safety and dignity of women within Sikh communities.

Christianity

Historical Context and Texts

Christianity was introduced to India primarily through colonial influence and missionary activities starting from the early Christian era and later intensified during European colonial rule. The teachings of Christianity, as outlined in the Bible, emphasize love, respect, and equality among all believers. However, interpretations of biblical texts have historically been influenced by patriarchal norms, shaping gender roles within Christian communities. For instance, passages such as Ephesians 5:22-24, which state, "Wives, submit yourselves to your own husbands as you do to the Lord. For the husband is the head of the wife as Christ is the head of the church," have been used to justify male authority over women. These interpretations have sparked considerable debate, with many modern scholars and denominations advocating for a contextual and egalitarian understanding of these texts, emphasizing mutual respect and equality.

Cultural Practices

In Indian Christian communities, cultural practices often blend with local traditions, which can include patriarchal norms. This syncretism means that while Christian teachings might promote equality and respect, local customs and societal expectations can still enforce traditional gender roles.

Practices such as the emphasis on chastity and family honour, which are prevalent in broader Indian society, also influence Christian communities. This cultural emphasis can contribute to the stigmatization of rape survivors, who may be seen as having tarnished the family's honour. Such attitudes can lead to victim-blaming, where the focus is on the victim's behaviour rather than the perpetrator's actions, discouraging survivors from reporting sexual violence and seeking justice.

Data and Trends

Specific data on rape incidents within Christian communities in India is not widely available, as national crime statistics typically do not segregate data by religion. However, reports and anecdotal evidence suggest that Christian women, like their counterparts in other religious groups, face challenges related to victim-blaming and social stigma. These challenges can be compounded by the interplay of religious teachings and local cultural norms. In many cases, the fear of social ostracism and the potential impact on family honour can discourage Christian women from reporting sexual violence or seeking support. Additionally, the influence of patriarchal interpretations of religious texts can affect how communities respond to and support survivors of sexual violence.

Christianity in India, while rooted in teachings of love, respect, and equality, is influenced by both its biblical texts and the local cultural context. The introduction of Christianity through colonial influence brought with it interpretations of the Bible that have been shaped by patriarchal norms. Passages such as Ephesians 5:22-24 have historically been used to justify male authority, although these interpretations are widely debated and increasingly challenged. In practice, Indian Christian communities often blend religious teachings with local traditions, resulting in the perpetuation of patriarchal norms. The emphasis on chastity and family honour can lead to the stigmatization of rape survivors, contributing to underreporting and victim-blaming. Despite the lack of specific data on rape incidents within Christian communities, it is clear that gender-based violence and its associated challenges are pervasive across all religious groups. Addressing these issues within Christian communities requires a nuanced understanding of both religious teachings and cultural practices, promoting interpretations that support gender equality and the dignity of all individuals.

CHAPTER SIX

Comparative Analysis and Trends Over the Years

To provide a comprehensive overview, it's essential to analyse trends in reported rape cases over the years. Unfortunately, specific data segregating rape incidents by religious affiliation are not typically published by the NCRB. However, general trends can be observed:

Graph: Reported Rape Cases in India (2010-2020)

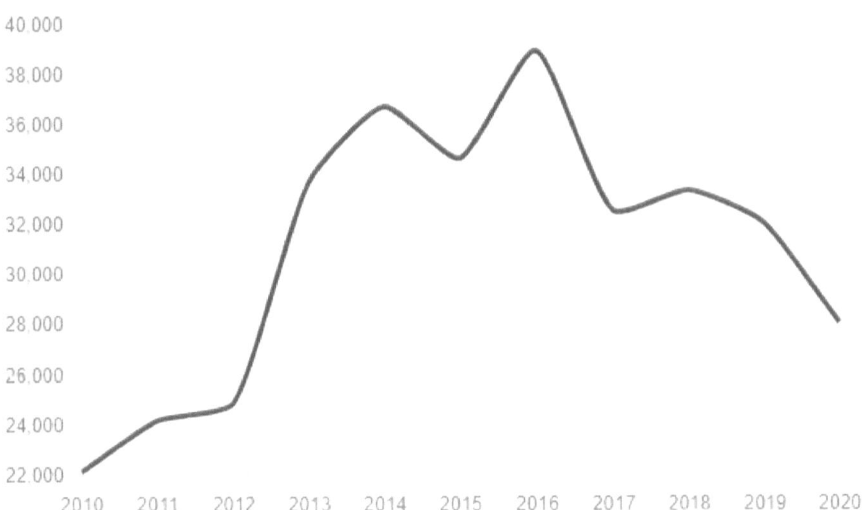

Source: National Crime Records Bureau (NCRB) Annual Reports

Graph Interpretation

The graph shows fluctuations in the number of reported rape cases in India over a decade. A significant increase is observed in 2013, following the Nirbhaya case in December 2012, which led to greater public awareness and reporting. However, the numbers remain high, indicating persistent issues in addressing rape culture.

Religious teachings and cultural practices have historically played a role in shaping attitudes towards gender and sexuality in India. While each religion promotes values that can protect and uplift women, cultural interpretations and practices often perpetuate gender inequality and contribute to rape culture. Addressing these issues requires a nuanced understanding of the intersection of religion, culture, and gender, as well as comprehensive efforts to promote gender equality and support survivors of sexual violence.

By examining religious influences and trends in reported cases, policymakers, activists, and communities can better understand and address the roots of rape culture in India. Efforts must focus on education, legal reforms, and cultural change to create a safer and more equitable society for all individuals.

Dominance and Power Play in Politics and Religion and Its Impact on Rape in Indian Society

The interplay of dominance and power dynamics in politics and religion significantly influences the prevalence and response to rape in Indian society. Political and religious leaders, by virtue of their positions, have the power to shape societal attitudes and norms, which can either combat or perpetuate rape culture. Unfortunately, instances of abuse of power, protection of perpetrators, and the reinforcement of patriarchal norms have often contributed to the increase in sexual violence.

Political Protection of Perpetrators

In many instances, individuals with political connections have been shielded from prosecution for sexual crimes. This protection not only emboldens perpetrators but also undermines the rule of law and discourages victims from seeking justice. Case Study: Unnao Rape Case (2017)- In 2017, a young woman in Unnao, Uttar Pradesh, accused a powerful BJP legislator, Kuldeep Singh Sengar, of raping her. Despite her complaint, the local police initially took no action, reflecting the influence and protection afforded to Sengar. It was only after the victim attempted self-immolation in front of the Chief Minister's residence that the case garnered significant attention, leading to Sengar's arrest and conviction in 2019. This case highlighted how political clout can obstruct justice for rape victims.

Manipulation of Caste Dynamics

Caste dynamics in India significantly intersect with politics, often exacerbating the vulnerability of lower-caste women to sexual violence. Political leaders sometimes exploit caste divisions to maintain power, further marginalising Dalit and tribal communities. Case Study: Hathras Gang Rape (2020)- In Hathras, Uttar Pradesh, a 19-year-old Dalit woman was allegedly gang-raped and murdered by upper-caste men. The local administration, influenced by political considerations, was accused of attempting to cover up the incident and hastily cremating the victim's body without her family's consent. The case drew national outrage and underscored the intersection of caste, politics, and gender-based violence.

Political Rhetoric and Gender Norms

Political leaders often use rhetoric that reinforces traditional gender norms and stereotypes. Such rhetoric can perpetuate rape culture by normalising patriarchal views and victim-blaming attitudes. Example: Comments by Politicians, Various politicians have made controversial statements regarding rape, often blaming victims or trivialising the issue. For instance, in 2014, a politician from West Bengal, Tapas Pal, threatened to send his boys to rape opposition women. Such statements reflect and perpetuate a culture where violence against women is normalised and excused.

Reinforcement of Patriarchal Norms

Religious teachings and practices often reinforce patriarchal norms, which contribute to the subjugation of women and the normalisation of sexual violence. Many religious texts and traditions place a strong emphasis on female chastity and purity, creating a culture of victim-blaming and silence around rape. Example: Influence of Manusmriti in Hinduism. The

Manusmriti, an ancient Hindu text, codifies strict gender roles and the subordination of women to men. It has historically influenced societal norms, contributing to the belief that women are responsible for upholding family honour and purity. This can result in victim-blaming and reluctance to report rape.

Religious Leaders and Sexual Exploitation

Instances of sexual exploitation by religious leaders further highlight the abuse of power within religious institutions. Such cases often involve manipulation and coercion, with victims finding it difficult to seek justice due to the leader's influence and the community's support. Case Study: Gurmeet Ram Rahim Singh (2017) - Gurmeet Ram Rahim Singh, the leader of the Dera Sacha Sauda, was convicted in 2017 for raping two of his female followers. Despite multiple accusations and evidence, his political connections and the support of his followers initially shielded him from prosecution. The eventual conviction led to widespread violence by his supporters, illustrating the deep-seated power religious leaders can wield.

Intersection of Religion and Politics

The intersection of religion and politics can further complicate efforts to address rape culture. Politicians often seek the support of religious leaders and institutions, which can lead to the endorsement of patriarchal and conservative norms that undermine women's rights and perpetuate sexual violence. Example: Influence of Religious Bodies. Religious bodies like the Vishwa Hindu Parishad (VHP) and the All India Muslim Personal Law Board (AIMPLB) have significant political influence and often resist reforms aimed at improving women's rights. For instance, the AIMPLB opposed the Supreme Court's decision to ban triple talaq, a practice that adversely affected Muslim women's rights.

The interplay of dominance and power dynamics in politics and religion significantly contributes to the perpetuation and increase of rape in Indian society. Political protection of perpetrators, manipulation of caste dynamics, reinforcement of patriarchal norms by religious teachings, and the intersection of religion and politics all play roles in maintaining a culture that excuses or normalises sexual violence. Addressing these issues requires comprehensive legal reforms, societal attitude shifts, and the empowerment of marginalised communities to create a safer and more equitable society for all.

Impact of Socio-Political Factors on the Reporting of Rape Cases in India

The reporting of rape cases in India is significantly influenced by a variety of socio-political factors. These factors can either facilitate the process of seeking justice for victims or act as barriers, discouraging them from reporting crimes. Understanding these factors is crucial for addressing the gaps in the justice system and ensuring that victims receive the support and protection they need. This essay examines how socio-political factors such as patriarchal norms, caste dynamics, political influence, and law enforcement effectiveness affect the reporting of rape cases in India.

Deep-Rooted Patriarchy

Patriarchal norms are deeply entrenched in Indian society, permeating every aspect of life, including the reporting of sexual violence. These norms dictate that women must adhere to strict codes of conduct that prioritize family honour over individual rights. In many communities, a woman's behaviour is seen as a reflection of her family's reputation. This societal expectation often discourages women from reporting rape, as they fear bringing shame and dishonour to their families and communities. The pressure to maintain family honour can be so intense that it overrides the need for justice and personal safety. Women who report sexual violence risk being ostracized, blamed, and stigmatized, which further discourages them from seeking help and speaking out.

Victim-Blaming Culture

The prevalence of victim-blaming further complicates the issue of sexual violence in India. Victims are frequently held responsible for the violence inflicted upon them, with scrutiny often directed at their behaviour, clothing, or lifestyle. This culture of blame creates a hostile environment for victims, making them reluctant to come forward and report the crime. Instead of focusing on the perpetrator's actions, society often questions the victim's choices, implying that they could have prevented the assault by behaving differently. This victim-blaming mentality not only exacerbates the trauma experienced by survivors but also perpetuates a culture of silence and impunity. As a result, many victims choose to remain silent rather than face further humiliation and judgment.

Case Study: Unnao Rape Case

The Unnao rape case illustrates the profound influence of patriarchal norms and political power in obstructing justice for victims of sexual violence. In this case, a young girl accused a powerful BJP legislator, Kuldeep Singh Sengar, of raping her in 2017. Despite her complaint, the local police initially took no action, reflecting the influence and protection afforded to the perpetrator by the patriarchal and political systems. The victim and her family faced intimidation and threats, highlighting the significant barriers to justice faced by survivors of sexual violence. It was only after significant public outrage and extensive media attention that action was taken against Sengar. He was eventually arrested, and in 2019, he was convicted and sentenced to life imprisonment. However, the delayed response and initial inaction by the authorities underscore the systemic failures and the powerful influence of patriarchal norms that protect perpetrators and silence victims.

Patriarchal norms deeply influence the reporting and handling of sexual violence in India, creating significant barriers for victims seeking justice. The emphasis on family honour over individual rights discourages many women from reporting rape, while the pervasive culture of victim-blaming further deters victims from coming forward. The Unnao rape case exemplifies how these patriarchal norms, combined with political power, can obstruct justice and protect perpetrators. Addressing these issues requires challenging and changing deep-seated societal attitudes, promoting a culture of accountability, and ensuring that victims receive the support and justice they deserve. By tackling the root causes of these patriarchal norms, Indian society can move towards a more just and equitable treatment of all individuals, regardless of gender.

Intersection of Caste and Gender

Caste dynamics play a significant role in the reporting and handling of rape cases in India, particularly in rural areas where traditional hierarchies remain strong and rigid. Lower-caste women, especially Dalits, face heightened vulnerability to sexual violence due to their marginalized social status. This intersection of caste and gender exacerbates their experiences of discrimination and violence. Dalit women are often targeted because their lower social status makes them perceived as easy victims who are less likely to receive support or justice. Perpetrators from higher castes often wield considerable social and economic power, which can be used to intimidate or silence victims and their families. This power imbalance means that Dalit women face additional barriers to accessing justice, as the perpetrators can leverage their status to avoid accountability.

Discrimination in Law Enforcement

Law enforcement agencies in India are not immune to the pervasive caste biases that exist within society. Reports of police refusing to file complaints or pressuring victims to withdraw their cases are alarmingly common, particularly when the accused belongs to a higher caste. This systemic discrimination further discourages lower-caste women from reporting rape, as they anticipate hostility or apathy from the authorities. In many cases, police officers may collude with higher-caste perpetrators to suppress cases, thus perpetuating a cycle of impunity. The reluctance or refusal to take lower-caste victims' complaints seriously not only denies them justice but also sends a message that their suffering is less important, reinforcing their marginalized status. This institutionalized bias within the law enforcement system highlights the deep-seated prejudices that hinder the fight against sexual violence.

Case Study: Hathras Gang Rape Case

The Hathras gang rape case in 2020 exemplifies the profound impact of caste dynamics on the reporting and handling of rape cases in India. In this case, a 19-year-old Dalit woman was allegedly gang-raped by upper-caste men in Hathras, Uttar Pradesh. The handling of the case by the police sparked nationwide outrage and highlighted the caste-based challenges in seeking justice. The police's actions, including the hurried cremation of the victim's body without the family's consent, raised serious questions about their intentions and the influence of caste biases. The victim's family reported that they were harassed and threatened, and there were attempts to downplay the severity of the crime. The incident drew widespread criticism from activists, media, and the general public, who accused the authorities of protecting the perpetrators due to their caste status. The case underscored the systemic discrimination faced by Dalit women and the significant barriers they encounter in accessing justice.

Caste dynamics significantly influence the reporting and handling of rape cases in India, with lower-caste women, especially Dalits, facing heightened vulnerability and systemic barriers to justice. The intersection of caste and gender exacerbates the discrimination and violence these women endure, as perpetrators from higher castes often use their social and economic power to intimidate and silence victims. Discrimination within law enforcement agencies further compounds these challenges, as lower-caste women frequently encounter bias and hostility when seeking justice. The Hathras gang rape case starkly illustrates these issues, highlighting the urgent need for reforms to address caste-based biases and ensure equitable treatment for all victims of sexual violence. Addressing these challenges requires comprehensive efforts to dismantle caste hierarchies and promote a justice system that is truly impartial and supportive of all individuals, regardless of caste.

Protection of Perpetrators

Political influence can profoundly impact the reporting and investigation of rape cases in India. Individuals with political connections often misuse their power to evade justice, creating a climate of fear and impunity. Perpetrators with political backing can exert pressure on law enforcement agencies to drop cases or alter investigations, ensuring that they face minimal consequences for their actions. This misuse of political power not only obstructs justice but also intimidates victims and witnesses, discouraging them from coming forward or testifying. The influence wielded by powerful individuals often means that victims from marginalized communities are further disadvantaged, as they face an uphill battle against both societal and systemic barriers. The protection of perpetrators due to political connections perpetuates a culture of impunity, where those in power feel emboldened to commit crimes without fear of repercussions.

Political Will and Legislation

Conversely, political will to address sexual violence can lead to significant legal reforms and improved support systems for victims. When political leaders prioritize the issue of sexual violence, it can result in the enactment of stricter laws and the implementation of comprehensive support services for survivors. High-profile cases that garner substantial public attention often compel political leaders to take action. For instance, the widespread protests and national outcry following the Nirbhaya case in 2012 pressured the government to address the deficiencies in the legal framework and support systems for victims of sexual violence. This led to the formation of the Justice Verma Committee, which recommended extensive legal reforms, resulting in the Criminal Law (Amendment) Act, 2013. This Act introduced stricter penalties for sexual violence, expanded the definition of rape, and implemented measures to protect the rights and safety of women. Such legislative changes demonstrate the positive impact of political will in combating sexual violence and supporting survivors.

Case Study: Nirbhaya Case

The Nirbhaya case in 2012 serves as a stark illustration of how political influence and public pressure can drive significant legal reforms. In this case, a young woman was brutally gang-raped and murdered on a bus in Delhi, leading to nationwide protests and a massive public outcry. The sheer brutality of the crime and the subsequent media coverage galvanized the public, resulting in widespread demands for justice and systemic change. The political response to the Nirbhaya case included the formation of the Justice Verma Committee, tasked with reviewing existing laws and recommending reforms to address sexual violence. The Committee's comprehensive report led to the Criminal Law (Amendment) Act, 2013, which introduced several critical changes to the legal framework. These included harsher penalties for rapists, the inclusion of stalking and voyeurism as criminal offenses, and enhanced measures for protecting the dignity and rights of women during investigations and trials. The swift and substantial political action in response to the Nirbhaya case underscores the potential for political will to effect meaningful change in the fight against sexual violence.

Political influence plays a dual role in the context of sexual violence in India. On one hand, political connections can shield perpetrators from justice, creating a climate of fear and impunity that discourages victims from reporting crimes. On the other hand, political will and public pressure can drive significant legal reforms and improvements in support systems for survivors. The Nirbhaya case exemplifies how political action, spurred by public outrage, can lead to substantial changes in the legal landscape, enhancing protections and ensuring stricter penalties for sexual violence. Addressing the misuse of political power and fostering a political climate committed to justice and equality are crucial steps in combating sexual violence and supporting survivors. Through continued advocacy and legislative reforms, it is possible to create a more just and equitable society that upholds the rights and dignity of all individuals.

Law Enforcement Effectiveness

The effectiveness of law enforcement in handling rape cases is crucial for encouraging victims to report crimes. Proper training and sensitization of police officers to handle sexual violence cases with sensitivity and professionalism can make a significant difference in how these cases are managed. However, in many areas, a lack of training and entrenched biases hinders effective policing. Police officers may lack the necessary skills and awareness to handle sexual violence cases appropriately, leading to insensitivity, victim-blaming, and negligence. Comprehensive training programs that educate officers on the dynamics of sexual violence, trauma-informed care, and the importance of a respectful and supportive approach are essential. Additionally, regular sensitization workshops can help dismantle deep-seated prejudices and promote a culture of empathy and professionalism within the police force. By ensuring that law enforcement officers are well-equipped to deal with such cases, victims are more likely to feel safe and supported when reporting crimes.

Access to Justice

The accessibility of legal resources and support systems significantly affects the reporting rates of sexual violence. In regions with better infrastructure, such as urban Centres, victims are more likely to report crimes due to the availability of legal aid, crisis Centres, and active media coverage. Urban areas typically have more comprehensive support systems, including specialized units within the police force, dedicated legal aid services, and NGOs that offer counselling and support to survivors. These resources provide victims with the necessary assistance to navigate the legal system and seek justice. In contrast, rural areas often lack these resources, contributing to lower reporting rates. Victims in rural regions may face additional barriers, such as long distances to the nearest police station, lack of confidential reporting mechanisms, and minimal access to legal and psychological support. Improving infrastructure and ensuring that support systems are available and accessible in rural areas is crucial for encouraging victims to come forward and report sexual violence.

Fast-Track Courts

The establishment of fast-track courts for rape cases has been a positive development, aimed at expediting the judicial process and ensuring timely justice for victims. These courts are designed to handle sexual violence cases more efficiently, reducing the backlog of cases and minimizing the duration of legal proceedings. However, the implementation and effectiveness of these courts vary across states, impacting the overall confidence of victims in the justice system. While some states have successfully set up fast-track courts that deliver swift verdicts, others struggle with insufficient resources, lack of trained personnel, and procedural delays. Ensuring uniform implementation and adequate funding for these courts is essential to enhance their effectiveness. Fast-track courts must also prioritize victim-Centred approaches, providing a supportive environment that reduces re-traumatization and ensures that survivors receive the justice they deserve in a timely manner.

Socio-political factors play a critical role in influencing the reporting of rape cases in India. Patriarchal norms, caste dynamics, political influence, and the effectiveness of law enforcement all contribute to the complex landscape of sexual violence reporting. Addressing these factors requires a multifaceted approach that includes legal reforms, societal change, and improved support systems for victims. Legal reforms should focus on strengthening laws, ensuring their effective implementation, and removing barriers that prevent victims from accessing justice. Societal change involves challenging and changing deeply ingrained patriarchal norms and promoting gender equality. This can be achieved through education, awareness campaigns, and community engagement. Improving support systems involves ensuring that victims have access to comprehensive services, including legal aid, counselling, and healthcare. By understanding and tackling these socio-political barriers, we can create a more supportive environment for victims of sexual violence and ensure that justice is accessible to all. This holistic approach will contribute to a safer and more just society, where victims of sexual violence are empowered to seek justice and receive the support they need.

Analysing the Distribution of Rape Cases Across Indian States, a Socio-Political and Historical Perspective

The distribution of reported rape cases across Indian states reveals significant insights into the socio-political and historical contexts that influence the incidence and reporting of sexual violence. By examining the data and understanding the underlying factors, we can better comprehend the challenges and disparities in addressing rape across different regions in India. This essay explores the distribution of rape cases across ten major states, providing a detailed analysis of the socio-political and historical backgrounds that contribute to the observed patterns.

Distribution of Rape Cases Across States

Conviction Rates for Rape Cases Across Different States (2019-2020)

State	Conviction Rate (%)
Uttar Pradesh	18.6
Madhya Pradesh	24.7
Rajasthan	27.3
Maharashtra	30.1
West Bengal	16.8
Bihar	20.5
Karnataka	34.2
Tamil Nadu	40.0
Gujarat	36.5
Delhi	25.8

Comparative analysis based on the latest available data from the National Crime Records Bureau (NCRB).

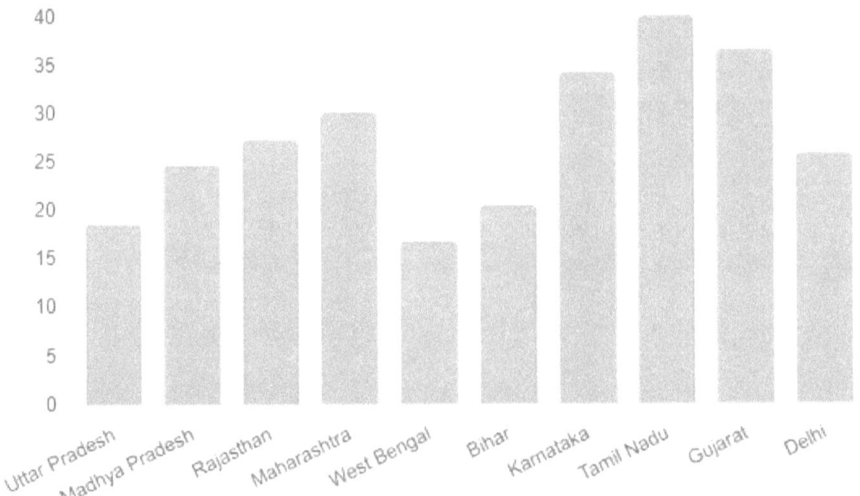

Bar chart based on data from National Crime Records Bureau (NCRB).

State-Wise Reported Rape Cases Over 15 Years

	Year	Uttar Pradesh	Madhya Pradesh	Rajasthan	Maharashtra	West Bengal	Bihar	Karnataka	Tamil Nadu	Gujarat
1	2005	1800	1500	1200	1000	900	800	700	600	500
2	2006	1900	1600	1300	1100	950	850	750	650	550
3	2007	2000	1700	1400	1200	1000	900	800	700	600
4	2008	2200	1800	1500	1300	1050	950	850	750	650
5	2009	2300	1900	1600	1400	1100	1000	900	800	700
6	2010	2400	2000	1700	1500	1150	1050	950	850	750
7	2011	2500	2100	1600	1600	1200	1100	1000	900	800
8	2012	2600	2200	1900	1700	1250	1150	1050	950	850
9	2013	2700	2300	2000	1800	1300	1200	1100	1000	900
10	2014	2800	2400	2100	1000	1350	1250	1150	1050	950
11	2015	2900	2500	2200	2000	1400	1300	1200	1100	1000
12	2016	3000	2600	2300	2100	1450	1350	1250	1150	1050
13	2017	3100	2700	2400	2200	1500	1400	1300	1200	1100
14	2018	3200	2800	2500	2300	1550	1450	1350	1250	1150
15	2019	3300	2900	2600	2400	1600	1500	1400	1300	1200
16	2020	3400	3000	2700	2500	1650	1550	1450	1350	1250

Data extracted from National Crime Records Bureau (NCRB).

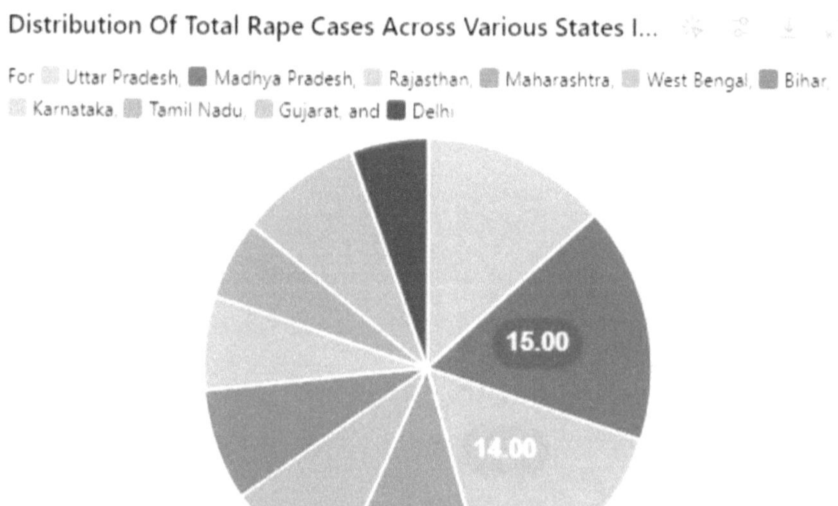

Distribution of reported rape cases.

(Madhya Pradesh: 15%, Rajasthan: 14%, Uttar Pradesh: 12%, Maharashtra: 10%, West Bengal: 8%, Gujarat: 8%, Bihar: 7%, Karnataka: 6%, Tamil Nadu: 5%, Delhi: 5%)

This distribution highlights significant variations in the prevalence and reporting of rape cases across different regions. Understanding these variations requires an exploration of the socio-political and historical factors that influence these statistics.

Socio-Political and Historical Context

Uttar Pradesh

Uttar Pradesh, the most populous state in India, accounts for 12% of the total rape cases. The high incidence of rape in Uttar Pradesh can be attributed to deeply entrenched patriarchal norms and the socio-political influence that often protects powerful individuals from prosecution. High-profile cases such as the Unnao rape case exemplify the challenges faced in ensuring justice for victims, particularly those from lower caste backgrounds.

Madhya Pradesh

Madhya Pradesh reports the highest percentage of rape cases at 15%. The state's patriarchal structures and large rural population contribute significantly to the high incidence of sexual violence. Limited access to education and economic opportunities in rural areas perpetuates traditional practices that discourage women from reporting sexual violence.

Rajasthan

Rajasthan accounts for 14% of the total cases, influenced by its conservative cultural practices and traditional outlook on gender roles. The state's prominence as a tourist destination also contributes to reported incidents involving interactions between locals and outsiders, further complicating the dynamics of sexual violence.

Maharashtra

Maharashtra, including Mumbai, accounts for 10% of the cases. As a highly urbanised state, Maharashtra benefits from better reporting mechanisms, which might explain the higher reported numbers. Despite efforts to improve women's safety, densely populated urban areas continue to face significant challenges.

West Bengal

West Bengal's share is 8%, influenced by political instability and conservative cultural attitudes towards women. These factors contribute to both underreporting and a high incidence of gender-based violence, despite efforts to address the issue.

Bihar

Bihar accounts for 7% of the cases. The state's widespread poverty and lack of education contribute to the prevalence of sexual violence. Additionally, the intersection of caste and class dynamics exacerbates the vulnerability of women, particularly those from lower castes.

Karnataka

Karnataka's share of 6% reflects the state's urban-rural divide. Urban centres benefit from progressive policies and higher literacy rates, while rural areas remain bound by conservative practices that perpetuate gender-based violence.

Tamil Nadu

Tamil Nadu accounts for 5% of the cases. The state's high literacy rates and awareness programs contribute to better reporting. Urban centres like Chennai have effective law enforcement and support systems for victims, although challenges remain.

Gujarat

Gujarat's 8% reflects rapid industrialisation and urbanisation, which have led to increased reporting of rape cases. While the state has made efforts to improve women's safety, traditional norms still pose significant challenges.

Delhi

Delhi, the national capital, accounts for 5% of the cases. The city's high reporting rates are due to better access to law enforcement and media coverage. High-profile cases like the Nirbhaya case have led to increased awareness and reporting of sexual violence.

A complex interplay of socio-political, economic, and cultural factors influences the distribution of rape cases across Indian states. States with deeply rooted patriarchal norms and significant caste dynamics, such as Uttar Pradesh and Bihar, show higher incidences of reported rape cases. Urbanised states like Maharashtra and Delhi benefit from better reporting mechanisms, reflecting higher reported numbers despite potentially lower actual incidences. Addressing rape in India requires multifaceted approaches that consider these diverse factors, promoting legal reforms, education, and socio-economic development to effectively combat and reduce sexual violence. Understanding the socio-political and historical contexts behind the distribution of rape cases is crucial for developing targeted interventions and creating a safer environment for all citizens.

• 65 •

CHAPTER SEVEN

Literature Review

Theories of Patriarchal Oppression

Definition and Concepts of Patriarchy

Overview of Patriarchal Systems Patriarchy is a social system in which men hold primary power and predominate in roles of political leadership, moral authority, social privilege, and control of property. It is characterized by a hierarchy that prioritizes male authority and subordinates' women. Patriarchal systems are pervasive, influencing various aspects of society, including family structures, legal frameworks, and cultural norms.

Key Characteristics of Patriarchy - Male Dominance

One of the primary characteristics of patriarchy is male dominance, where men hold dominant positions in political, economic, and social spheres. This dominance is reflected in the disproportionate representation of men in leadership roles across various sectors, including government, business, and academia. Men often control decision-making processes, shaping policies and practices that affect the broader society. This power imbalance perpetuates a system where male perspectives and interests are prioritized, marginalizing the voices and needs of women. The lack of female representation in these influential positions means that women's issues and concerns are often overlooked or inadequately addressed, reinforcing gender inequality.

Male Identification

Patriarchal societies are characterized by male identification, where societal values and standards are based on male experiences and perspectives. This means that traits traditionally associated with masculinity, such as assertiveness, competitiveness, and rationality, are highly valued, while traits associated with femininity, such as empathy, cooperation, and emotionality, are devalued. These bias influences various aspects of life, including education, employment, and social interactions. For instance, in the workplace, assertiveness and competitiveness are often rewarded, while collaborative and empathetic approaches may be undervalued. This male-centric value system perpetuates stereotypes about gender roles and limits the opportunities available to women, who may feel pressured to conform to male norms to be successful.

Male-Centredness

Male-Centredness is another key characteristic of patriarchy, where social institutions and cultural practices revolve around male priorities. This is evident in the way media, literature, and popular culture predominantly feature male protagonists and perspectives, often relegating women to secondary or supportive roles. Educational curricula frequently highlight the achievements and contributions of men, while the accomplishments of women are underrepresented. This male-centric focus shapes societal narratives and reinforces the perception that men are the default or norm, while women are the exception. Consequently, women's experiences and contributions are often overlooked, and their needs are considered less important. This male-Centred approach perpetuates gender biases and reinforces the marginalization of women in various domains.

Oppression and Subordination of Women

Patriarchy systematically disadvantages women, limiting their roles to caregiving and domestic duties. Women are often expected to prioritize family responsibilities over personal and professional aspirations, leading to economic dependence and reduced opportunities for advancement. This subordination is perpetuated through cultural norms and practices that reinforce traditional gender roles. For example, women may be discouraged from pursuing higher education or careers in male-dominated fields, and those who do may face significant barriers, including discrimination and lack of support. Additionally, societal expectations often pressure women to conform to roles as caregivers and homemakers, devaluing their contributions outside the domestic sphere. This systemic oppression restricts women's autonomy and limits their ability to participate fully in public and economic life.

Control of Female Sexuality

In patriarchal societies, women's sexuality is regulated and controlled to maintain male dominance and social order. This control is exercised through cultural, legal, and social mechanisms that dictate acceptable behaviour for women and punish deviations from these norms. Practices such as virginity testing, female genital mutilation, and the enforcement of strict dress codes exemplify the ways in which women's bodies and sexuality are policed. Additionally, societal attitudes often stigmatize women who are perceived as sexually liberated or who challenge traditional gender roles. This control over female sexuality serves to reinforce male authority and preserve social structures that privilege men. By regulating women's sexual behaviour, patriarchal societies maintain control over women's bodies and limit their autonomy, perpetuating gender inequality.

The key characteristics of patriarchy—male dominance, male identification, male-Centredness, oppression and subordination of women, and control of female sexuality—create a systemic framework that perpetuates gender inequality. These characteristics are deeply ingrained in societal structures and cultural practices, influencing various aspects of life and reinforcing traditional gender roles. Addressing these issues requires challenging and transforming the underlying patriarchal norms and values that sustain them. By promoting gender equality, valuing diverse perspectives, and supporting women's rights and autonomy, societies can work towards dismantling patriarchal structures and creating a more just and equitable world for all individuals.

Evolution of Patriarchal Thought in Sociology

Patriarchal thought has evolved over centuries, deeply ingrained in social theories and practices. Early sociological theories, developed during the 19th and early 20th centuries, did not explicitly address patriarchy but rather assumed male dominance as a given. The foundational works of sociologists like Auguste Comte, Émile Durkheim, and Max Weber largely reflected the prevailing gender norms of their times, which viewed men as naturally suited for leadership and public life, while women were relegated to domestic roles. These early sociologists focused on the structures and functions of society without critically examining the gendered power dynamics inherent in those structures.

For instance, Durkheim's theories on social order and cohesion often reinforced traditional gender roles, viewing the family as a microcosm of society where women naturally played nurturing and supportive roles. Similarly, Weber's analysis of bureaucracy and authority did not challenge the patriarchal assumptions of male leadership. These early theoretical frameworks provided little room for questioning the status quo of gender relations, thereby implicitly endorsing a patriarchal social order.

Over time, feminist scholars began to critique these assumptions, bringing patriarchal structures to the forefront of sociological inquiry. The second wave of feminism in the 1960s and 1970s marked a significant shift in the academic landscape, as scholars like Betty Friedan, Kate Millett, and Shulamith Firestone challenged the traditional sociological narratives. These feminist theorists argued that patriarchal systems were not natural or inevitable but rather socially constructed and maintained through cultural norms, legal systems, and institutional practices.

Betty Friedan's seminal work, "The Feminine Mystique," highlighted the dissatisfaction of many housewives in the United States, questioning the societal expectation that women find fulfilment solely through domestic roles. Kate Millett's "Sexual Politics" provided a critical analysis of literature and social theories, exposing the ways in which they reinforced male dominance. Shulamith Firestone's "The Dialectic of Sex" went further, arguing for the revolutionary potential of feminist thought to dismantle patriarchal systems.

These feminist critiques paved the way for a more nuanced understanding of patriarchy in sociological theory. Subsequent scholars expanded on these ideas, examining the intersectionality of gender with race, class, and other social categories. Kimberlé Crenshaw's concept of intersectionality highlighted how different forms of oppression intersect and compound each other, providing a more comprehensive framework for understanding the complexities of patriarchal systems.

Moreover, contemporary sociologists like Sylvia Walby and Heidi Hartmann have further developed theories of patriarchy, examining its structural and institutionalized forms. Sylvia Walby's work, "Theorizing Patriarchy," identifies six structures of patriarchy: the household, paid work, the state, male violence, sexuality, and cultural institutions. This framework emphasizes that patriarchy is a multifaceted system that operates across various domains of society. Heidi Hartmann's analysis of the interplay between capitalism and patriarchy in "The Unhappy Marriage of Marxism and Feminism" explores how economic systems and gender oppression are intertwined, suggesting that addressing gender inequality requires challenging broader economic structures as well.

Through these evolving theories, sociologists have come to understand patriarchy as a dynamic and pervasive system of power relations that shapes every aspect of social life. The shift from assuming male dominance as a given to critically analysing its roots and manifestations has been a crucial development in sociological thought. By continuously interrogating and expanding these theories, sociologists contribute to a deeper understanding of patriarchy and inform efforts to dismantle gender inequality in society.

Influential Theorists and Their Contributions

Sylvia Walby

Sylvia Walby is a prominent sociologist known for her comprehensive theory of patriarchy, which she articulates through six interrelated structures: paid work, household production, culture, sexuality, violence, and the state. Walby's theory is notable for its breadth and depth, providing a multifaceted analysis of how patriarchy operates across different domains of social life. She argues that these structures interact to sustain male dominance and that patriarchy is not a static system but one that adapts and evolves over time. For example, in the realm of paid work, Walby examines how gendered labour markets and occupational segregation contribute to women's economic disadvantage. In the household, she looks at how unpaid domestic labour disproportionately falls on women, reinforcing their subordinate status. Her analysis of culture focuses on how media, education, and religion perpetuate gender stereotypes. By examining sexuality, she highlights how norms and practices regulate women's bodies and sexual behaviour. Walby also addresses male violence against women as a means of maintaining control and the role of the state in either reinforcing or challenging patriarchal norms through laws and policies. Her comprehensive approach has significantly influenced feminist scholarship and policymaking by providing a robust framework for understanding and addressing gender inequalities.

Heidi Hartmann

Heidi Hartmann is a feminist economist and sociologist whose work integrates Marxist and feminist perspectives to analyse the intersection of capitalism and patriarchy. Hartmann coined the term "capitalist patriarchy" to describe the mutually reinforcing relationship between economic systems and gender oppression. Her influential essay, "The Unhappy Marriage of Marxism and Feminism," argues that both capitalism and patriarchy must be considered to fully understand and combat gender inequalities. Hartmann emphasizes the economic dimensions of patriarchy, demonstrating how women's labour, both paid and unpaid, is exploited to benefit capitalist systems. She highlights how economic structures, such as wage disparities, job segregation, and the undervaluation of women's work, perpetuate gender inequalities. Hartmann's analysis extends to social reproduction, where she discusses how women's unpaid labour in the home sustains the workforce and capitalist economy. By integrating economic analysis with feminist theory, Hartmann's work underscores the importance of addressing economic inequalities to achieve gender justice. Her contributions have profoundly impacted feminist economics and the broader feminist movement, providing critical insights into the interplay between economic systems and gender oppression.

Gerda Lerner

Gerda Lerner was a pioneering historian whose work traces the origins of patriarchy to ancient civilizations, arguing that patriarchy was constructed over millennia through a series of historical processes. In her seminal book, "The Creation of Patriarchy," Lerner provides a detailed historical analysis that demonstrates how patriarchal systems were developed and institutionalized. She examines ancient societies, such as Mesopotamia, to show how legal codes, religious doctrines, and social practices systematically subordinated women and established male dominance. Lerner's historical approach underscores the contingency of patriarchy, highlighting that it is not a natural or inevitable social order but a constructed system that can be challenged and changed. Her work also emphasizes the role of women's resistance throughout history, documenting various forms of female agency and struggle against patriarchal oppression. Lerner's contributions have been instrumental in shaping feminist historiography, providing a deeper understanding of the historical roots of gender inequality. Her insights continue to inform contemporary feminist theory and activism by highlighting the long-standing and deeply entrenched nature of patriarchal systems, while also affirming the potential for transformative change.

Betty Friedan

Betty Friedan, a leading figure in the second wave of feminism, significantly contributed to the critique of patriarchal norms through her influential work, "The Feminine Mystique." Published in 1963, the book challenged the traditional roles assigned to women, particularly the notion that women could find complete fulfilment solely through homemaking and motherhood. Friedan's exploration of "the problem that has no name" resonated with many women who felt dissatisfied and unfulfilled in their domestic roles. Her work sparked widespread discussion about the limitations imposed on women by societal expectations and highlighted the need for greater opportunities for women in education and the workforce. Friedan's critique of the patriarchal family structure and her call for women's liberation played a crucial role in advancing feminist thought and advocacy.

Kate Millett

Kate Millett's "Sexual Politics," published in 1970, provided a groundbreaking analysis of literature and social theories, exposing how they reinforced male dominance and perpetuated patriarchal norms. Millett's work was among the first to systematically examine the power dynamics embedded in cultural texts and their role in sustaining gender inequality. Her critique extended to influential literary figures and their works, revealing the pervasive sexism that underpinned much of Western literature. Millett's analysis demonstrated that patriarchy was deeply rooted in cultural expressions and intellectual traditions, and she called for a radical re-evaluation of these foundations. Her work had a profound impact on feminist theory, highlighting the intersection of culture and power in maintaining patriarchal systems.

Shulamith Firestone

Shulamith Firestone was a radical feminist whose book, "The Dialectic of Sex," published in 1970, argued for the revolutionary potential of feminist thought to dismantle patriarchal systems. Firestone's work extended beyond traditional feminist critiques to propose a complete reimagining of social and reproductive structures. She argued that gender inequality was rooted in biological differences and the reproductive roles assigned to women. Firestone called for the liberation of women from the constraints of biological reproduction through technological and social innovations. Her radical vision sought to eliminate the gendered division of labour and create a society where individuals could achieve true equality, free from the limitations imposed by traditional gender roles. Firestone's work was influential in pushing the boundaries of feminist thought and inspiring more radical approaches to gender equality.

Theorist	Contribution	Impact
Sylvia Walby	Theory of patriarchy outlining six structures: paid work, household production, culture, sexuality, violence, and the state.	Provided a comprehensive framework for understanding how these structures interact to sustain male dominance and how patriarchy adapts over time, influencing feminist scholarship and policymaking.
Heidi Hartmann	Integrated Marxist and feminist perspectives, coining the term "capitalist patriarchy" to describe the intersection of capitalism and patriarchy.	Emphasized the economic dimensions of patriarchy and how economic systems perpetuate gender inequalities, significantly impacting feminist economics and broader feminist movements.
Gerda Lerner	Historical analysis tracing the origins of patriarchy to ancient civilizations, arguing it was constructed over millennia.	Highlighted the historical contingency of patriarchy and its deep roots in human history, shaping feminist historiography and informing contemporary feminist theory and activism.
Betty Friedan	Authored "The Feminine Mystique," challenging traditional domestic roles assigned to women and sparking widespread feminist discussion.	Advanced feminist thought by critiquing the patriarchal family structure and calling for greater opportunities for women in education and the workforce, playing a crucial role in second-wave feminism.
Kate Millett	Published "Sexual Politics," analysing literature and social theories to expose how they reinforced male dominance and perpetuated patriarchal norms.	Demonstrated the intersection of culture and power in maintaining patriarchal systems, significantly impacting feminist theory and highlighting the role of cultural texts in sustaining gender inequality.
Shulamith Firestone	Authored "The Dialectic of Sex," advocating for radical reimagining of social and reproductive structures to eliminate gender inequality.	Pushed the boundaries of feminist thought by proposing technological and social innovations to liberate women from reproductive constraints, inspiring radical approaches to gender equality.

Concise Table representation of the same.

The contributions of Sylvia Walby, Heidi Hartmann, Gerda Lerner, Betty Friedan, Kate Millett, and Shulamith Firestone have been pivotal in advancing the understanding of patriarchy and its multifaceted nature. Walby's comprehensive theory outlines the interconnected structures that sustain male dominance, while Hartmann's integration of Marxist and feminist perspectives emphasizes the economic dimensions of patriarchy. Lerner's historical analysis traces the origins of patriarchy, underscoring its constructed nature and the potential for resistance and change. Friedan, Millett, and Firestone further expanded feminist thought by challenging traditional gender roles, critiquing cultural and intellectual traditions, and proposing radical reimagining of social structures. Together, their work has significantly enriched feminist scholarship and provided valuable frameworks for analysing and addressing gender inequalities. Their contributions continue to inspire and guide efforts towards achieving a more just and equitable society.

Structural and Institutionalized Patriarchy

Patriarchy in Legal and Political Institutions

Patriarchy is deeply embedded in legal and political systems, often reflecting and reinforcing male dominance through laws and policies that historically favoured men. These systems have traditionally granted men greater rights and privileges, leaving women in subordinate positions. Women's legal status was typically contingent on their relationships with men—whether as daughters, wives, or widows. For example, under many historical legal codes, women had limited property rights and were often considered the legal dependents of their male relatives.

In India, the Manusmriti, an ancient legal text, codified the subordination of women and imposed strict limitations on their rights. The Manusmriti explicitly stated that women should be under the control of their fathers, husbands, or sons at different stages of their lives, effectively denying them autonomy. Such legal frameworks institutionalized gender inequality and perpetuated a social order where male authority was paramount.

Political systems have also historically restricted women's participation, with leadership roles predominantly occupied by men. This gender imbalance in political representation meant that laws and policies often failed to address women's needs and concerns adequately. Even today, gender quotas and affirmative action policies are necessary to correct this imbalance and ensure women's participation in governance. Despite some progress, women's representation in political institutions remains limited, and they continue to face significant barriers to leadership positions. The underrepresentation of women in politics perpetuates a cycle where male perspectives dominate decision-making processes, further entrenching patriarchal norms.

Patriarchy in Family and Social Structures

The family is a primary site of patriarchal practice, where gender roles are enforced, and male authority is normalized. Traditional family structures prioritize male headship and control over family resources and decision-making, often relegating women to subordinate roles. In many patriarchal families, women are primarily responsible for domestic work and child-rearing, while men are seen as the primary breadwinners and decision-makers.

These gender roles are deeply ingrained and perpetuated through socialization processes from a young age. Boys and girls are often raised with different expectations and responsibilities, reinforcing the notion that men should hold power and authority within the family. This division of labour not only limits women's opportunities for personal and professional growth but also perpetuates their economic dependence on men.

Social norms and cultural practices further reinforce patriarchal values and control over women's choices. Practices such as dowry and arranged marriages exemplify how social customs can perpetuate gender inequality. The dowry system, where the bride's family is expected to provide substantial gifts to the groom's family, places an economic burden on women and can lead to dowry-related violence and harassment. Arranged marriages often prioritize familial alliances and economic considerations over individual choice, limiting women's autonomy in selecting their life partners.

Moreover, cultural expectations around female chastity and purity place additional constraints on women's behaviour, with their actions often scrutinized to maintain family honour. These norms reinforce the idea that women's primary value lies in their roles as wives and mothers, further marginalizing their contributions in other spheres.

Patriarchy is deeply entrenched in both legal and political institutions as well as family and social structures, creating systemic barriers to gender equality. In legal and political realms, historical laws and policies have favoured men, while women's rights and participation have been restricted. The family, as a foundational social unit, often perpetuates patriarchal norms through gendered division of labour and control over women's choices. Cultural practices such as dowry and arranged marriages further entrench these values, limiting women's autonomy and reinforcing their subordinate status. Addressing these structural and institutionalized forms of patriarchy requires comprehensive legal reforms, changes in political representation, and shifts in social and cultural attitudes to promote gender equality and empower women in all aspects of life.

Intersection of Patriarchy with Race, Class, and Caste

Intersectionality, a concept introduced by legal scholar Kimberlé Crenshaw, examines how various social identities, such as race, class, and caste, intersect to create unique experiences of oppression. Patriarchy does not operate in isolation but intersects with other forms of social stratification, amplifying the oppression experienced by certain groups of women. Understanding this intersectionality is crucial for a comprehensive analysis of patriarchal oppression.

Race and Patriarchy: Women of colour experience patriarchy differently than white women due to the compounding effects of racial discrimination. In many societies, racial minorities face systemic inequalities that intersect with gender-based discrimination, leading to unique and often more severe forms of oppression. For instance, in the United States, African American women may face both racial and gender biases that affect their access to employment, healthcare, and legal protection. The intersection of race and gender creates distinct challenges, such as higher rates of poverty and violence, which require tailored policy responses.

Class and Patriarchy: Economic status significantly influences the experience of patriarchy. Women from poorer backgrounds face greater vulnerabilities due to their economic dependence and lack of resources. These women are often trapped in cycles of poverty and exploitation, with limited access to education, healthcare, and legal recourse. For example, domestic workers, who are predominantly women from lower socioeconomic backgrounds, often experience exploitation and abuse with little protection or recourse due to their economic and social status. The intersection of class and gender highlights the need for economic empowerment strategies that address both financial and gender-based inequalities.

Caste and Patriarchy: In India, caste is a significant axis of oppression that intersects with patriarchy to create compounded discrimination. Dalit women, for instance, face both gender-based and caste-based discrimination, leading to heightened exploitation and violence. They are often subjected to severe social exclusion, economic deprivation, and physical abuse. The intersection of caste and gender in India reveals how deeply ingrained social hierarchies exacerbate the vulnerabilities of marginalized groups. Addressing caste-based oppression requires targeted interventions that address both gender and caste inequalities, ensuring that Dalit women receive the protection and opportunities they need to overcome systemic barriers.

How Intersectionality Influences Experiences of Oppression

Intersectionality highlights that women's experiences of patriarchy are not monolithic but vary based on their intersecting identities. This approach acknowledges the complexity of oppression and the need for nuanced strategies to address it.

Multiple Layers of Oppression: Intersectionality shows that women can face multiple, overlapping forms of discrimination. For example, a poor Dalit woman in India may experience caste-based violence, gender-based violence, and economic exploitation simultaneously. These overlapping forms of oppression create unique challenges that cannot be adequately addressed by policies focusing on a single axis of discrimination. Recognizing the multiple layers of oppression is essential for developing comprehensive and effective interventions.

Inclusive Frameworks: Policies and interventions must consider these intersecting identities to be effective. A one-size-fits-all approach is insufficient to address the diverse experiences of all women. For instance, initiatives aimed at improving women's access to healthcare must also consider the specific barriers faced by women of different races, classes, and castes. Inclusive frameworks ensure that policies are tailored to meet the needs of all women, particularly those who are most marginalized.

Empowerment Strategies: Intersectional analysis helps in designing empowerment strategies that are context-specific and address the unique needs of different groups of women. For example, programs aimed at economic empowerment should consider providing financial literacy and entrepreneurial training specifically tailored for women from marginalized communities. Similarly, legal reforms should include provisions that protect the rights of women facing intersecting forms of discrimination. By addressing the specific needs of different groups, empowerment strategies can be more effective in promoting gender equality and social justice.

Understanding the theories of patriarchal oppression requires a multi-dimensional approach that considers historical, structural, and intersectional perspectives. By examining the evolution of patriarchal thought, the institutionalization of patriarchy in legal and family structures, and the intersectionality of oppression, we gain a comprehensive view of the complexities involved. This theoretical framework sets the stage for a deeper exploration of patriarchal dynamics and their impact on gender roles and sexual violence in subsequent sections. It underscores the importance of addressing patriarchy in all its forms and intersections to create a more equitable and just society for all individuals.

Feminist Perspectives on Rape Culture

Definition and Origin of Rape Culture

Rape culture is a sociological concept that describes a setting in which rape, sexual assault, and other forms of gender-based violence are pervasive and normalized due to societal attitudes about gender, sex, and sexuality. It encompasses a range of behaviours and beliefs that trivialize, excuse, or even condone sexual violence. The key elements of rape culture include:

Victim-Blaming: This involves holding victims responsible for their assault based on their behaviour, attire, or other irrelevant factors. Victim-blaming shifts the focus away from the perpetrator's actions and places undue scrutiny on the victim, often leading to further trauma and stigmatization.

Normalization of Sexual Violence: Rape culture treats sexual aggression as a natural or inevitable part of life. This normalization is perpetuated through media portrayals and social norms that depict men as inherently aggressive and women as passive. Such representations desensitize the public to the severity of sexual violence and foster a climate where such behaviour is tolerated.

Trivialization of Rape: This element involves dismissing the severity of rape and sexual assault through jokes, language, and cultural practices. Rape jokes, for example, trivialize the experience of survivors and perpetuate harmful myths about sexual violence. This trivialization minimizes the impact of the crime and undermines efforts to address it seriously.

Objectification of Women: Rape culture is also characterized by the objectification of women, where women are viewed primarily as objects for male pleasure. This reduces their agency and autonomy, making it easier for society to justify or overlook violence against them. Objectification reinforces the idea that women's primary value lies in their appearance and sexual availability.

Historical Context of Rape Culture in Feminist Theory

The concept of rape culture emerged in the 1970s within the feminist movement as a way to articulate how societal norms and institutional structures perpetuate sexual violence against women. This framework provided a lens to understand the systemic nature of sexual violence and the ways in which it is supported by cultural attitudes and practices.

1975: The publication of Susan Brownmiller's "Against Our Will: Men, Women, and Rape" marked a significant milestone in the development of rape culture theory. Brownmiller argued that rape is not a mere sexual act, but a mechanism of power and control used by men to dominate women. Her work shed light on the historical and political dimensions of rape, emphasizing that it is deeply rooted in patriarchal structures.

1980s: During this decade, feminist scholars and activists began to systematically analyse and critique cultural practices, media representations, and legal frameworks that perpetuate rape culture. This period saw a growing awareness of how everyday language, humour, and media depictions trivialize and normalize sexual violence. Activists campaigned for changes in how rape cases were handled legally and how survivors were treated by the justice system.

1990s: The concept of rape culture became more widely recognized in academic and public discourse. The 1990s saw an expansion of feminist theory to include the intersectional dimensions of sexual violence, considering how race, class, and other social factors intersect with gender to shape experiences of rape. This period also saw increased efforts to address rape culture through public education campaigns, policy changes, and the establishment of support services for survivors.

The evolution of the concept of rape culture within feminist theory has been instrumental in highlighting the systemic and pervasive nature of sexual violence. By focusing on the societal attitudes and institutional structures that perpetuate rape, feminist scholars and activists have developed a robust framework for understanding and addressing gender-based violence. This framework emphasizes the need to challenge and change cultural norms, media representations, and legal practices that normalize and trivialize sexual violence, thereby working towards a society where such violence is no longer tolerated. The ongoing development of this concept continues to inform both academic research and practical interventions aimed at combating rape culture and supporting survivors.

Radical Feminism and Rape Culture

Radical feminism views rape as a fundamental tool of patriarchy, used systematically to control and oppress women. This perspective posits that sexual violence is not merely an isolated act of defiance, but a deliberate mechanism of male supremacy designed to perpetuate male dominance and female subjugation. Radical feminists like Andrea Dworkin and Catharine MacKinnon argue that patriarchal institutions—such as the law, family structures, and media—play a critical role in normalizing and perpetuating rape culture. They contend that these institutions are structured to maintain male power and control, thereby legitimizing and sustaining sexual violence against women.

Andrea Dworkin's work, for example, highlights how pornography contributes to the normalization of sexual violence by portraying women as objects for male gratification. Catharine MacKinnon extends this argument by examining how the legal system fails to protect women adequately, often blaming victims and excusing perpetrators. Radical feminists advocate for radical changes to dismantle these patriarchal structures, arguing that only by fundamentally restructuring society can true gender equality be achieved. Their calls for radical transformation include eliminating deeply ingrained cultural norms that condone violence against women, restructuring legal frameworks to prioritize women's safety, and challenging media representations that objectify and degrade women.

Socialist Feminism and the Economic Dimensions of Sexual Violence

Socialist feminism integrates Marxist and feminist analyses to examine how capitalism and patriarchy intersect to exploit and oppress women. Key theorists like Heidi Hartmann and Zillah Eisenstein argue that the economic dependency of women on men, exacerbated by capitalist class structures, increases women's vulnerability to sexual violence. This perspective emphasizes that economic inequality and gender inequality are interlinked, with economic structures reinforcing patriarchal power dynamics.

Heidi Hartmann's concept of "capitalist patriarchy" explores how the capitalist system benefits from and perpetuates gender-based exploitation. She argues that women's unpaid labour in the home and their lower wages in the workforce contribute to their economic dependency on men, making them more susceptible to abuse and exploitation. Zillah Eisenstein's work further elaborates on how capitalist economies systematically marginalize women, particularly women of colour and those from lower socio-economic backgrounds, thereby compounding their vulnerability to sexual violence.

Socialist feminists call for both economic restructuring and gender equality to combat rape culture. They advocate for policies that promote economic independence for women, such as equal pay, access to education, and comprehensive social safety nets. By addressing the economic roots of gender inequality, socialist feminists believe that it is possible to reduce women's vulnerability to sexual violence and dismantle the structures that sustain rape culture.

Liberal Feminism and Legal Reforms

Liberal feminism focuses on achieving gender equality through legal reforms and policy changes within the existing system. Key theorists like Betty Friedan and Martha Nussbaum emphasize the importance of legal recognition and enforcement to address rape culture. Liberal feminists argue that by reforming laws and policies, it is possible to create a more equitable society where women's rights are protected, and sexual violence is condemned.

Betty Friedan's work, particularly in "The Feminine Mystique," highlights the importance of legal and policy changes to address gender discrimination and inequality. Martha Nussbaum extends this argument by advocating for a capabilities approach, which emphasizes the need to create conditions that allow women to live with dignity and autonomy. This includes legal protections against sexual violence and support systems for survivors.

Liberal feminists advocate for laws that protect women from sexual violence, such as stricter penalties for rapists, better support for survivors, and educational programs to change societal attitudes towards gender and sexuality. They highlight the need for comprehensive legal frameworks that address all aspects of rape culture, from prevention to prosecution to survivor support. By focusing on legal reforms, liberal feminists aim to create a society where sexual violence is taken seriously, perpetrators are held accountable, and survivors receive the justice and support they need.

Each feminist perspective offers unique insights into understanding and addressing rape culture. Radical feminism emphasizes the need to dismantle patriarchal structures that normalize sexual violence, socialist feminism highlights the economic dimensions of gender-based oppression, and liberal feminism focuses on achieving gender equality through legal reforms. Together, these perspectives provide a comprehensive framework for analysing the systemic nature of rape culture and developing strategies to combat it. By integrating these approaches, feminist theorists and activists can work towards a society where gender equality is realized, and sexual violence is no longer tolerated.

CHAPTER EIGHT

Rape Culture in Global Contexts

Comparative Analysis of Rape Culture in Different Countries

United States

In the United States, the #MeToo movement has brought widespread attention to the prevalence of sexual harassment and assault across various sectors, from entertainment and media to politics and academia. The movement, which gained momentum in 2017, encouraged individuals to share their experiences of sexual violence, revealing the deep-rooted rape culture that pervades American society. The #MeToo movement highlighted how pervasive and normalized sexual violence is, even in environments where gender equality is ostensibly valued. It also exposed the systemic failures within institutions that often protect perpetrators and silence victims. Despite the progress made in raising awareness and advocating for change, the movement has also underscored the significant work still needed to dismantle rape culture and create safer environments for all individuals.

India

India has seen several high-profile rape cases that have sparked both national and international outrage, the most notable being the 2012 Nirbhaya gang rape case in Delhi. This brutal assault led to widespread protests and calls for legal reforms to protect women and ensure justice for survivors. In response, the Indian government enacted the Criminal Law (Amendment) Act, 2013, which introduced stricter penalties for rape and expanded the legal definition of sexual violence. However, despite these reforms, India continues to struggle with deep-seated societal and institutional barriers that perpetuate rape culture. Issues such as victim-blaming, inadequate law enforcement response, and societal stigma against survivors remain pervasive. The Nirbhaya case and subsequent incidents highlight the persistent challenges in addressing sexual violence and the need for ongoing efforts to change societal attitudes and improve institutional responses.

Sweden

Sweden is often lauded for its progressive gender policies and high levels of gender equality. The country has comprehensive legal frameworks aimed at protecting individuals from sexual violence, including strong consent laws and extensive support services for survivors. However, Sweden still grapples with sexual violence, illustrating that legal frameworks alone are insufficient without cultural change. The country's experience underscores the complexity of rape culture, showing that even in societies with robust legal protections, cultural attitudes and social norms must also evolve. Public discourse in Sweden continues to address issues of consent, gender stereotypes, and the importance of education in preventing sexual violence. This demonstrates that legal measures need to be complemented by efforts to shift societal attitudes and promote respectful and consensual relationships.

South Africa

South Africa faces some of the highest rates of sexual violence in the world, a situation linked to post-apartheid societal disruptions, economic inequality, and deeply entrenched gender norms. The country's history of apartheid has left a legacy of violence and inequality that continues to impact all aspects of society, including gender relations. In addition, economic disparities and social instability exacerbate the vulnerability of women and children to sexual violence. Traditional gender norms that promote male dominance and female submission further entrench rape culture. Despite legal frameworks designed to protect women, enforcement remains inconsistent, and many survivors do not receive the support and justice they deserve. Community-based initiatives and grassroots movements are crucial in addressing these issues, working alongside legal reforms to create meaningful change. South Africa's struggle highlights the importance of addressing broader social and economic factors alongside efforts to combat rape culture.

The comparative analysis of rape culture in different countries demonstrates that sexual violence is a pervasive issue influenced by a variety of factors, including societal norms, legal frameworks, and historical contexts. While movements like #MeToo in the United States have highlighted the prevalence of sexual violence and pushed for systemic change, countries like India have enacted legal reforms in response to high-profile cases but continue to face deep-rooted challenges. Sweden's experience underscores that progressive gender policies must be accompanied by cultural change, while South Africa's situation illustrates the impact of historical and economic factors on gender-based violence. These global perspectives highlight the complexity of rape culture and the need for multifaceted approaches to address it. Efforts to combat sexual violence must consider legal, cultural, and socio-economic dimensions to create environments where all individuals are safe and respected.

Role of International Feminist Movements in Combating Rape Culture

Global Solidarity

International feminist movements have played a crucial role in fostering global solidarity and activism against sexual violence. Movements like One Billion Rising have created platforms for cross-border solidarity, bringing together activists from diverse backgrounds to unite against rape culture. One Billion Rising, launched on Valentine's Day in 2012 by activist and playwright Eve Ensler, calls for women and men worldwide to dance as a form of protest against violence towards women. The movement has spread to over 200 countries, highlighting the universal nature of gender-based violence and the shared struggle to combat it. By connecting activists globally, these movements amplify voices, share strategies, and build a sense of unity and collective action. This global solidarity is crucial for empowering local movements, as it demonstrates that the fight against rape culture is not isolated but part of a broader, worldwide effort to achieve gender equality and end sexual violence.

Policy Influence

International feminist movements have significantly influenced global policies and conventions aimed at combating rape culture. One of the key achievements in this regard is the advocacy for and implementation of the United Nations Convention on the Elimination of All Forms of Discrimination Against Women (CEDAW). Adopted in 1979, CEDAW is often described as an international bill of rights for women. Feminist activists and organizations have been instrumental in pushing for the adoption and ratification of CEDAW by various countries, ensuring that global standards are set for the protection and promotion of women's rights. The convention obligates participating nations to implement measures to eliminate discrimination against women in all forms, including gender-based violence. Feminist movements continue to monitor and advocate for the effective implementation of CEDAW, ensuring that countries uphold their commitments to protect women from sexual violence and address the systemic roots of rape culture.

Awareness and Advocacy

Feminist activists have utilized global platforms to raise awareness, share resources, and advocate for change, contributing to a more interconnected and informed approach to tackling rape culture. Through social media, international conferences, and global campaigns, feminist movements have brought attention to the pervasive issue of sexual violence and its impact on women worldwide. Platforms like #MeToo have demonstrated the power of collective voices in exposing the prevalence of sexual harassment and assault, encouraging survivors to come forward and share their stories. These global platforms have also facilitated the sharing of best practices, research, and resources, helping activists to develop more effective strategies to combat rape culture. By raising awareness and advocating for systemic change, international feminist movements contribute to a broader understanding of sexual violence as a global issue that requires coordinated and sustained efforts to address.

International feminist movements have played a pivotal role in combating rape culture by fostering global solidarity, influencing policy, and raising awareness. Movements like One Billion Rising and platforms like #MeToo highlight the universal nature of gender-based violence and the shared struggle to end it. Through their advocacy, these movements have influenced international policies and conventions, such as CEDAW, setting global standards for the protection of women's rights. Additionally, by utilizing global platforms for awareness and advocacy, feminist activists have created a more interconnected and informed approach to tackling rape culture. These efforts underscore the importance of a collective, global response to sexual violence, demonstrating that the fight against rape culture is a worldwide endeavour that requires solidarity, policy change, and sustained advocacy.

Criticisms from Within the Feminist Movement

Essentialism

One of the key criticisms from within the feminist movement is the charge of essentialism. This critique argues that some theories on rape culture can be overly essentialist, reducing complex social dynamics to binary gender oppositions and overlooking variations within genders. Essentialism in this context refers to the tendency to generalize and simplify the experiences of all women, treating them as a homogeneous group defined primarily by their victimhood in a patriarchal society. Such an approach can obscure the nuanced and diverse experiences of individuals and fail to account for the ways in which factors like race, class, sexuality, and disability intersect with gender to shape experiences of sexual violence. By focusing solely on the binary opposition between men and women, essentialist theories may overlook the specific challenges faced by marginalized groups and fail to provide a comprehensive understanding of rape culture.

Focus on Female Victims

Traditional feminist theories often focus predominantly on female victims of sexual violence, potentially neglecting the experiences of male and non-binary survivors. This focus can create an incomplete picture of rape culture and its impact. Male survivors, for example, may face unique barriers to reporting sexual violence, including societal stigma and a lack of resources tailored to their needs. Similarly, non-binary and transgender individuals often encounter significant discrimination and violence, both within and outside of gender-based violence frameworks. By not adequately addressing these experiences, traditional feminist theories may unintentionally marginalize these groups and fail to advocate effectively for all survivors of sexual violence. Recognizing the diversity of survivors' experiences is crucial for developing inclusive support systems and interventions that address the needs of all individuals affected by sexual violence.

Intersectionality

Intersectional feminism emphasizes the need to consider how intersecting identities, such as race, class, sexuality, and disability, shape experiences of sexual violence. Kimberlé Crenshaw's groundbreaking work on intersectionality highlights how race and gender intersect to create unique forms of oppression. Crenshaw argues that focusing on a single axis of identity, such as gender, without considering other intersecting factors can lead to an incomplete understanding of oppression and marginalization. Intersectionality provides a framework for understanding how multiple forms of discrimination overlap and compound, creating distinct and often more severe forms of inequality. This approach calls for a more nuanced analysis of rape culture that takes into account the varied and intersecting identities of survivors, ensuring that their unique experiences are acknowledged and addressed.

Inclusive Frameworks

To fully address the varied experiences of survivors, feminist theories on rape culture must incorporate diverse perspectives. This includes recognizing how systemic racism, economic inequality, and other forms of discrimination intersect with gender-based violence. Inclusive frameworks are essential for developing comprehensive and effective strategies to combat rape culture. These frameworks should be informed by the lived experiences of marginalized groups and prioritize their voices in discussions on sexual violence. By doing so, feminist theories can better address the full spectrum of rape culture and develop interventions that are equitable and just.

Examples:

Women of Colour: Black feminist theorists like bell hooks and Audre Lorde emphasize that the experiences of women of colour are often sidelined in mainstream feminist discourse, including discussions on rape culture. They argue that racism and sexism are intertwined, and the unique challenges faced by women of colour must be central to any analysis of sexual violence. For instance, women of colour may encounter both racial and gender-based violence, and their experiences with law enforcement and the judicial system can be significantly different from those of white women. Addressing these intersectional issues is crucial for a comprehensive understanding of rape culture.

LGBTQ+ Perspectives: Queer theory critiques highlight how heteronormativity and cisnormativity influence the discourse on rape culture, calling for greater inclusion of LGBTQ+ experiences. LGBTQ+ individuals often face unique forms of sexual violence that are not adequately addressed by traditional feminist frameworks. For example, transgender individuals may be targeted specifically because of their gender identity, and gay men may experience sexual violence in contexts that differ from those of heterosexual individuals. Inclusive frameworks must recognize these distinct experiences and advocate for policies and support systems that address the needs of LGBTQ+ survivors.

Feminist perspectives on rape culture provide a comprehensive framework for understanding how societal norms, legal structures, and cultural practices perpetuate sexual violence. By examining radical, socialist, and liberal feminist theories, and considering global contexts and intersectional critiques, we gain a deeper understanding of the complexities involved in addressing rape culture. This multifaceted approach is essential for developing effective strategies to combat sexual violence and create a more just and equitable society.

CHAPTER NINE

Patriarchy and Gender Roles

Historical Roots of Patriarchy in India

Early Vedic Period (1500–500 BCE)

The early Vedic period in India, spanning from approximately 1500 BCE to 500 BCE, is often considered more egalitarian in terms of gender roles compared to later periods. During this time, women enjoyed a relatively high status and participated actively in various aspects of society, including religious rituals, education, and even warfare. Women like Gargi and Maitreyi were renowned scholars and philosophers, respected for their intellectual contributions and wisdom. Gargi Vachaknavi, for example, was a celebrated philosopher who engaged in profound theological debates with the sage Yajnavalkya, showcasing her intellectual prowess and esteemed position in Vedic society. Similarly, Maitreyi, another learned woman, was known for her philosophical inquiries and contributions to the understanding of spiritual knowledge and immortality. These examples highlight that, in the early Vedic period, women were not only included in educational and religious domains but were also highly regarded for their intellectual and spiritual insights.

The participation of women in religious rituals was a significant aspect of their social role during this period. They were not merely passive observers but active participants and officiants in various ceremonies. This inclusion in religious practices underscored their importance in maintaining societal and spiritual balance. Additionally, some historical texts and oral traditions suggest that women could own property and had the right to choose their partners, further indicating their substantial agency and autonomy in early

Vedic society.

Later Vedic Period

However, as the Vedic period progressed, a noticeable shift towards more rigid gender roles occurred. The later Vedic period saw the gradual emergence of patriarchal norms that increasingly confined women to domestic roles. The societal focus shifted towards a more male-dominated structure, where women's primary responsibilities became Centred around managing the household and bearing children. This transition marked a significant departure from the relatively egalitarian practices of the early Vedic era.

During the later Vedic period, the codification of gender roles became more pronounced. Religious and social texts from this time, such as the Manusmriti, began to outline specific duties and expectations for women, reinforcing their subordination to male authority. The Manusmriti, in particular, prescribed that women should be under the control of their fathers in childhood, their husbands in adulthood, and their sons in old age. This hierarchical structure limited women's autonomy and significantly curtailed their participation in public and intellectual life.

The diminishing access to education for women during the later Vedic period further entrenched their subordinate status. While earlier, women had been active participants in scholarly pursuits, the later period restricted their educational opportunities, confining them to roles that were deemed appropriate for their gender. This restriction not only limited their personal growth but also reinforced the patriarchal notion that intellectual and public domains were the purview of men.

Additionally, the societal emphasis on female chastity and purity became more pronounced, leading to the control of women's sexuality and freedom. Practices such as child marriage began to emerge, further curtailing women's independence and reinforcing their dependence on male family members. The idealization of the pativrata (devoted wife) exemplified the expectation that women's identities and worth were tied to their roles as dutiful wives and mothers.

The evolution of gender roles from the early to the later Vedic period illustrates a significant shift in the social and cultural dynamics of ancient Indian society. While the early Vedic period offered a relatively egalitarian environment where women participated actively in religious, educational, and even martial activities, the later Vedic period saw a regression into more rigid and patriarchal structures. This shift not only restricted women's roles to domestic spheres but also significantly diminished their autonomy and public presence. Understanding this transition provides crucial insights into the historical development of gender roles and the roots of patriarchal practices in Indian society. It highlights the need to critically examine and challenge these historical norms to promote gender equality and empower women in contemporary times.

Influence of Religious Texts on Gender Norms

Manusmriti

The Manusmriti, or the Laws of Manu, is one of the most significant Dharma shastra texts in Hindu tradition. Compiled around the second century BCE to the second century CE, it played a crucial role in codifying and institutionalizing patriarchal norms in ancient Indian society. The Manusmriti outlines the duties and roles of individuals based on their caste and gender, establishing a rigid social hierarchy that has influenced Hindu societal structures for centuries.

One of the central tenets of the Manusmriti is the idea that women should be kept under the control and protection of their male relatives throughout their lives. This patriarchal dictate asserts that a woman must be subject to her father during her childhood, her husband during her married life, and her sons in her old age. This lifelong guardianship severely restricted women's autonomy, placing them in a position of perpetual dependency on men.

The Manusmriti also emphasizes the importance of female purity and chastity, concepts that became central to the honour of the family. According to the text, a woman's virtue was closely linked to her sexual purity, and any deviation from this norm was seen as a dishonour to her family. This emphasis on chastity served to control women's behaviour and reinforced their subjugation by promoting the idea that their primary value lay in their sexual purity and their role as bearers of family honour.

Furthermore, the Manusmriti discouraged women's education and limited their participation in public life. The text posits that women should focus on domestic responsibilities and be devoted to serving their husbands and families. By restricting educational opportunities and public engagement, the Manusmriti ensured that women remained confined to the private sphere, dependent on men for knowledge and decision-making.

Other Religious Texts

Other key Hindu texts, such as the Ramayana and the Mahabharata, also reinforced traditional gender norms and ideals. These epic narratives, while rich in cultural and moral teachings, have characters and stories that perpetuate patriarchal values and expectations.

In the Ramayana, the character of Sita embodies the ideal of female virtue and submissiveness. Sita is depicted as a devoted wife who remains loyal and pure despite enduring significant hardships. Her unwavering fidelity and obedience to her husband, Rama, are held up as the epitome of female virtue. Sita's trials, including her abduction by Ravana and subsequent trial by fire to prove her purity, underscore the societal expectation that women must maintain their chastity and loyalty under all circumstances. This portrayal reinforces the notion that a woman's worth is tied to her virtue and subservience to her husband.

Similarly, the Mahabharata, another foundational epic, contains narratives that reflect and reinforce traditional gender roles. Characters like Draupadi, who is subjected to humiliation and violence, highlight the vulnerabilities women face within a patriarchal framework. Despite her strength and resilience, Draupadi's experiences illustrate the societal constraints placed on women and the expectation that they endure suffering with dignity and grace.

The influence of religious texts such as the Manusmriti, the Ramayana, and the Mahabharata on gender norms in Hindu society has been profound and enduring. The Manusmriti, with its codification of patriarchal principles, established a framework that placed women under the control of men and emphasized their role in maintaining family honour through purity and submissiveness. The narratives in the Ramayana and the Mahabharata further reinforced these ideals, portraying female characters who embody virtue through obedience and sacrifice. These religious texts have shaped societal attitudes towards gender roles for centuries, contributing to the perpetuation of patriarchal norms. By understanding the historical and cultural context in which these texts were written and their impact on gender relations, contemporary society can critically engage with these traditions to promote gender equality and challenge the enduring legacy of patriarchy. This involves reinterpreting these texts in ways that highlight the agency and strength of women, while advocating for social and legal reforms that empower women and ensure their rights and autonomy.

Colonial India : Impact of British Colonial Rule on Indian Patriarchy

British Legal and Social Reforms

During British colonial rule in India, the colonial administration introduced several legal reforms aimed at modernizing Indian society and addressing social injustices. However, many of these reforms inadvertently reinforced existing patriarchal structures, either by failing to address the root causes of gender inequality or by imposing changes that were perceived as foreign and paternalistic.

One of the most notable legal reforms was the banning of Sati in 1829. Sati, the practice where a widow was immolated on her husband's funeral pyre, was outlawed by the British under Governor-General Lord William Bentinck. This reform was a significant step towards protecting women's rights and lives. However, it also led to the portrayal of Indian women as helpless victims in need of protection by colonial rulers, reinforcing a paternalistic view. The British often used the abolition of Sati to justify their rule, framing it as a civilizing mission that aimed to rescue Indian women from barbaric customs. This paternalistic approach not only undermined the agency of Indian women but also contributed to a narrative that positioned British colonial rule as a benevolent force, while ignoring the complexities of Indian society and the diverse voices within it.

Child Marriage Restraint Act (1929)

Another significant legal reform was the Child Marriage Restraint Act of 1929, also known as the Sarda Act. This legislation aimed to address the issue of child marriage by setting minimum ages for marriage: 14 for girls and 18 for boys. While this act was a progressive step towards protecting young girls from early marriage, it faced substantial resistance from conservative segments of Indian society. Many traditionalists viewed the act as an imposition of Western values that interfered with cultural and religious practices. The resistance to the Child Marriage Restraint Act highlighted the deep-seated nature of patriarchal norms and the challenges of implementing social reforms in a society where these norms were entrenched. The backlash against the act also underscored the complexities of colonial rule, where reforms intended to promote social justice were often met with opposition due to their association with foreign rule and the perceived threat to traditional structures.

Western Education and Enlightenment Ideals

The introduction of Western education during British colonial rule brought new ideas about individual rights, gender equality, and social reform. Missionary schools and colonial educational institutions began to educate Indian boys and, to a lesser extent, girls, exposing them to Enlightenment ideals and Western notions of gender roles. For some Indian women, access to Western education opened up new opportunities for intellectual and social advancement. Figures like Savitribai Phule and Pandita Ramabai emerged as pioneers in women's education and social reform, advocating for women's rights and challenging traditional gender norms.

However, the benefits of Western education were not evenly distributed, often reinforcing existing class and gender disparities. Access to education was limited, with upper-caste and wealthy families being the primary beneficiaries. Lower-caste and economically disadvantaged families often remained excluded from educational opportunities, perpetuating cycles of poverty and gender inequality. Moreover, the introduction of Western education sometimes reinforced patriarchal structures by emphasizing the role of women in the private sphere, preparing them to be better wives and mothers rather than independent individuals. The colonial education system often promoted a form of domesticated femininity that aligned with Victorian ideals, which, while different from traditional Indian norms, still confined women to restrictive roles.

The impact of British colonial rule on Indian patriarchy was multifaceted, involving a mix of legal reforms, social changes, and the introduction of new educational ideals. While the British administration introduced measures like the banning of Sati and the Child Marriage Restraint Act, these reforms often reinforced patriarchal structures by portraying Indian women as victims in need of protection and by facing resistance from conservative segments of society. The introduction of Western education brought new ideas about gender equality but also reinforced class and gender disparities and imposed new forms of domesticity. Understanding the complex legacy of British colonial rule on Indian patriarchy highlights the interplay between colonial power and traditional social structures, and the ongoing challenges in achieving gender equality in post-colonial India.

Changes in Gender Roles During the Colonial Period

Women's Education and Social Reform Movements

The colonial period in India witnessed significant changes in gender roles, particularly through the efforts of social reformers who championed women's education and the eradication of oppressive practices. Reformers like Raja Ram Mohan Roy and Ishwar Chandra Vidyasagar were pivotal in advocating for women's rights and education. Raja Ram Mohan Roy, a prominent social and religious reformer, campaigned against the practice of Sati and worked towards the upliftment of women's status in society. He founded the Brahmo Samaj, which aimed to promote rational and progressive religious and social practices, including the abolition of Sati and the promotion of women's education.

Ishwar Chandra Vidyasagar, another key reformer, played a crucial role in advocating for widow remarriage and fighting against child marriage. His efforts led to the passage of the Widow Remarriage Act of 1856, which legalized the remarriage of Hindu widows, challenging deeply ingrained societal norms that condemned widows to a life of austerity and seclusion. Vidyasagar also emphasized the importance of educating girls, believing that education was essential for women's empowerment and societal progress. His work laid the foundation for future efforts to improve women's access to education and opportunities.

Arya Samaj and Brahmo Samaj

The Arya Samaj and Brahmo Samaj were influential reform movements that emerged during the colonial period, both advocating for social reforms and the upliftment of women. The Brahmo Samaj, founded by Raja Ram

Mohan Roy, aimed to reform Hindu society by eliminating social evils and promoting the principles of monotheism and rationality. The movement supported women's education and sought to improve women's status by advocating for the abolition of practices like Sati and child marriage.

The Arya Samaj, founded by Swami Dayananda Saraswati, also focused on social and religious reform, emphasizing a return to the teachings of the Vedas. The movement advocated for the education of women and the abolition of child marriage, promoting the idea that women should have equal access to education and opportunities. Both movements played significant roles in challenging traditional gender norms and advocating for women's rights, contributing to the gradual transformation of societal attitudes towards gender roles.

Nationalist Movement and Women's Participation

The Indian nationalist movement for independence from British colonial rule saw active participation from women, who gained public visibility and took on leadership roles. Figures like Sarojini Naidu and Kasturba Gandhi became prominent in the struggle for independence, inspiring countless women to join the movement. Sarojini Naidu, also known as the Nightingale of India, was a poet, activist, and a key leader in the Indian National Congress. She was the first woman to become the president of the Indian National Congress and played a crucial role in mobilizing women and advocating for their rights.

Kasturba Gandhi, the wife of Mahatma Gandhi, was deeply involved in the freedom struggle, participating in non-violent protests and campaigns against British rule. Her involvement highlighted the role of women in the independence movement and demonstrated their capacity for leadership and activism. The participation of women in the nationalist movement not only contributed to the fight for independence but also challenged traditional gender roles by bringing women into the public sphere and leadership positions.

Empowerment and Backlash

While the participation of women in the nationalist movement was empowering and marked a significant shift in gender roles, it often reinforced traditional roles by portraying women as mothers of the nation rather than independent individuals. The rhetoric of the nationalist movement frequently emphasized women's roles as nurturers and caregivers, framing their participation as an extension of their duties as mothers and wives. This portrayal, while recognizing women's contributions, also limited their identity to traditional domestic roles.

The emphasis on women as symbols of purity and sacrifice sometimes constrained the scope of their empowerment, as their public involvement was often justified in terms of traditional virtues rather than as a quest for individual rights and autonomy. This duality reflects the complex nature of gender role changes during the colonial period, where progress towards women's empowerment coexisted with the reinforcement of traditional gender norms.

The colonial period in India was a time of significant change in gender roles, driven by social reform movements, educational initiatives, and the nationalist struggle for independence. Reformers like Raja Ram Mohan Roy and Ishwar Chandra Vidyasagar, along with movements like the Arya Samaj and Brahmo Samaj, played crucial roles in advocating for women's education and rights, challenging oppressive practices, and promoting social progress. The participation of women in the nationalist movement further highlighted their potential for leadership and activism, although it often reinforced traditional roles by portraying women as mothers of the nation. These changes laid the foundation for ongoing efforts to improve women's status and rights in Indian society, illustrating the complex interplay between progress and tradition in the evolution of gender roles.

Post-Independence India; Continuities and Changes in Patriarchal Structures Post-1947

Constitutional Provisions for Equality

Following India's independence in 1947, the adoption of the Indian Constitution in 1950 marked a significant step towards establishing a framework for gender equality. The Constitution enshrines the principle of equality before the law in Article 14, ensuring that all individuals, irrespective of their gender, have equal protection and rights under the legal system. Article 15 further strengthens this commitment by prohibiting discrimination on various grounds, including sex. These provisions laid the legal foundation for promoting gender equality and protecting women's rights in post-independence India.

The Indian Constitution also includes Article 16, which guarantees equality of opportunity in matters of public employment, and Article 39, which directs the state to ensure that men and women have equal rights to an adequate means of livelihood and equal pay for equal work. These constitutional safeguards were designed to dismantle legal barriers to gender equality and create an environment where women could participate fully and equally in all aspects of life.

Directive Principles

In addition to the fundamental rights, the Constitution incorporates Directive Principles of State Policy, which aim to promote social justice and improve the status of women. While not justiciable, these principles serve as guidelines for the government in formulating policies and laws. Key directive principles relevant to gender equality include Article 39(a), which mandates that the state ensure adequate means of livelihood for both men and women, and Article 39(d), which emphasizes equal pay for equal work.

The Directive Principles also include provisions for securing a living wage, humane conditions of work, and maternity relief (Article 42), as well as promoting education and the economic interests of weaker sections of society (Articles 41 and 46). These principles reflect the state's commitment to creating a more equitable society and addressing the socio-economic disparities that affect women. Over the years, these principles have inspired various legislative and policy initiatives aimed at empowering women and promoting gender equality.

Social and Cultural Continuities

Despite the progressive legal framework established by the Indian Constitution, patriarchal attitudes and practices remained deeply entrenched in Indian society. Traditional gender roles, which dictate that women primarily occupy the domestic sphere and men the public sphere, continued to dominate in many areas. This persistence of patriarchal norms can be attributed to long-standing cultural and social structures that resist change and reinforce gender inequality.

One of the most significant challenges to achieving gender equality has been the societal expectation that women prioritize their roles as wives, mothers, and caregivers over their personal ambitions and professional careers. This expectation often leads to unequal access to education and employment opportunities for women, perpetuating economic dependence and limiting their potential for social mobility. Additionally, practices such as dowry, child marriage, and honour killings, although illegal, still occur in many parts of the country, reflecting the deep-rooted nature of patriarchal values.

The intersection of gender with other forms of social stratification, such as caste and class, further complicates the picture. Women from lower castes and economically disadvantaged backgrounds face multiple layers of discrimination and exploitation, making it even harder for them to assert their rights and achieve equality. These intersecting inequalities often result in severe social and economic disadvantages, trapping women in cycles of poverty and marginalization.

Efforts to Address Patriarchal Structures

Recognizing the gap between constitutional ideals and social realities, various efforts have been made to address patriarchal structures and promote gender equality in India. Legislative measures, such as the Dowry Prohibition Act (1961), the Protection of Women from Domestic Violence Act (2005), and the Sexual Harassment of Women at Workplace (Prevention, Prohibition and Redressal) Act (2013), have been enacted to protect women's rights and ensure their safety. These laws aim to provide legal recourse and support to women facing violence and discrimination.

In addition to legal reforms, government programs and policies have focused on improving women's access to education, healthcare, and economic opportunities. Initiatives like the Beti Bachao Beti Padhao (Save the Daughter, Educate the Daughter) campaign aim to change societal attitudes towards girls and promote their education and empowerment. Efforts to increase women's political participation through gender quotas in local governance have also been implemented, enabling women to play a more active role in decision-making processes.

Post-1947, India has witnessed significant changes in its legal and policy framework aimed at promoting gender equality and dismantling patriarchal structures. The Indian Constitution's provisions for equality and the

Directive Principles of State Policy reflect the state's commitment to social justice and women's empowerment. However, despite these progressive measures, patriarchal attitudes and practices remain deeply embedded in Indian society, posing substantial challenges to achieving true gender equality. The persistence of traditional gender roles, along with intersecting social and economic inequalities, continues to limit women's opportunities and rights. Addressing these issues requires ongoing efforts to implement and enforce legal protections, change societal attitudes, and promote inclusive development that benefits all women, regardless of their socio-economic background.

Legal Reforms and Their Impact on Gender Roles

The Hindu Code Bills (1950s)

In the 1950s, a series of legislative measures known as the Hindu Code Bills were introduced to reform Hindu personal law and promote gender equality. These reforms included the Hindu Marriage Act (1955) and the Hindu Succession Act (1956), which brought significant changes to marriage, divorce, and inheritance rights for Hindu women.

Marriage and Divorce

The Hindu Marriage Act of 1955 was a groundbreaking piece of legislation that provided for the legal recognition of marriage and introduced provisions for divorce. Before this act, Hindu marriages were considered indissoluble, with limited recourse for women in abusive or unhappy marriages. The Hindu Marriage Act allowed for divorce on several grounds, including cruelty, desertion, and mutual consent, giving women greater autonomy and legal recourse in marital relationships. Additionally, the act addressed issues like bigamy by declaring polygamous marriages void, thereby protecting the rights of the first wife and promoting monogamy. Despite these progressive changes, societal attitudes towards divorce have been slow to change, and many women still face significant social stigma and economic challenges when seeking divorce.

Inheritance Rights

The Hindu Succession Act of 1956 was another landmark reform that aimed to address gender inequality in inheritance laws. Prior to this act, daughters had limited rights to inherit ancestral property, with preference given to male heirs. The Hindu Succession Act granted daughters equal rights to inherit property from their parents, alongside their male siblings. This was a significant step towards ensuring economic independence for women and challenging the traditional patriarchal norms that favoured male inheritance. However, the implementation of the Hindu Succession Act has been uneven, with many women still facing obstacles in claiming their inheritance due to social resistance, lack of legal awareness, and bureaucratic hurdles. In some regions, customary practices and local traditions continue to override statutory law, perpetuating gender disparities in property rights.

Dowry Prohibition Act (1961)

The Dowry Prohibition Act of 1961 aimed to combat the practice of dowry, which had become a pervasive social issue leading to violence, harassment, and even deaths of brides. The act made the giving and taking of dowry illegal and punishable by law. Despite its intentions, the Dowry Prohibition Act has seen limited success in eradicating the practice of dowry. Persistent cultural norms and societal acceptance of dowry as a traditional practice have hindered the effective enforcement of the law. Dowry-related violence and harassment remain significant issues, with many cases going unreported due to fear of social repercussions and lack of support for victims. The act's limited impact underscores the challenges of changing deeply ingrained cultural practices through legal measures alone.

Protection of Women from Domestic Violence Act (2005)

The Protection of Women from Domestic Violence Act (PWDVA) of 2005 provides a comprehensive legal framework to protect women from domestic violence. The act defines domestic violence broadly, including physical, emotional, verbal, sexual, and economic abuse. It allows women to seek protection orders, residence orders, and monetary relief from the courts. The PWDVA also mandates the establishment of protection officers and shelters to support victims of domestic violence. This legislation represents a significant advancement in recognizing and addressing the multifaceted nature of domestic violence. However, the implementation of the PWDVA has faced several challenges, including lack of awareness about the law, inadequate resources for enforcement agencies, and societal resistance to acknowledging and addressing domestic violence.

Implementation Challenges

Despite the progressive nature of these legal reforms, enforcement remains a significant challenge. Societal resistance to changing traditional gender roles and norms often impedes the effective implementation of laws aimed at promoting gender equality. Many women are unaware of their legal rights or lack access to legal resources and support systems necessary to enforce these rights. Additionally, law enforcement agencies and the judiciary may be influenced by prevailing patriarchal attitudes, resulting in inadequate protection and support for women seeking justice. In rural and conservative areas, customary practices and local power structures further complicate the enforcement of gender-equal laws.

The legal reforms introduced in post-independence India, such as the Hindu Code Bills, the Dowry Prohibition Act, and the Protection of Women from Domestic Violence Act, have been instrumental in promoting gender equality and protecting women's rights. However, the impact of these reforms has been limited by challenges in enforcement, societal resistance, and persistent cultural norms. While these laws provide a crucial legal framework for advancing gender equality, achieving meaningful change requires ongoing efforts to raise awareness, improve implementation, and address the underlying social and cultural barriers that perpetuate gender inequality. The progress made through legal reforms must be supported by broader social change to ensure that all women can fully enjoy their rights and opportunities.

Women's Movement and Advocacy Across Different Segments

1970s and 1980s: The Rise of the Women's Movement in India

The 1970s and 1980s marked a significant period in the history of women's advocacy in India, with the emergence of powerful grassroots movements and organizations dedicated to advancing women's rights and addressing gender-based injustices. These movements were inclusive of diverse religious and social backgrounds, focusing on the unique challenges faced by different segments of women in India.

One of the notable organizations that emerged during this period was the Self-Employed Women's Association (SEWA), founded in 1972 by Ela Bhatt. SEWA focused on empowering women in the informal sector, particularly self-employed women who lacked access to formal employment benefits and protections. SEWA's efforts included providing financial services, legal aid, and vocational training to women, helping them achieve economic independence and security. The organization's holistic approach to women's empowerment addressed not only economic issues but also social and legal challenges faced by its members. SEWA's inclusive membership helped Muslim women in the informal sector gain access to financial independence and social support, which was crucial in communities where traditional norms often restricted women's economic activities.

Another significant organization was the All India Democratic Women's Association (AIDWA), established in 1981. AIDWA aimed to mobilize women from various socio-economic backgrounds to fight against gender discrimination and injustice. AIDWA's activities included campaigns against domestic violence, dowry, and workplace harassment. The organization also worked extensively in rural areas and among lower caste women to address specific issues like caste-based discrimination and lack of access to resources. AIDWA's work in rural and lower caste communities helped bring attention to the intersection of caste and gender discrimination. Their campaigns promoted legal awareness and social support for marginalized women, improving their access to justice and resources. AIDWA also focused on the issues faced by Muslim women, advocating for legal reforms and protection against communal violence, thereby enhancing their social and legal standing.

Campaigns Against Violence

Women's movements in India during the 1970s and 1980s were instrumental in bringing attention to various forms of gender-based violence and advocating for legal and social changes. These movements campaigned vigorously against dowry deaths, sexual harassment, and other forms of violence that disproportionately affected women across different segments.

One of the significant issues tackled by these movements was dowry-related violence, which included dowry deaths and harassment. Activists highlighted the prevalence of dowry demands and the severe consequences for women who were unable to meet these demands. Through protests, public awareness campaigns, and legal advocacy, women's organizations pushed for stricter enforcement of the Dowry Prohibition Act and greater accountability for perpetrators. These campaigns also addressed the specific cultural contexts in which dowry practices affected Muslim and lower caste women, providing a broader understanding of the issue.

Sexual harassment, both in public spaces and workplaces, was another critical focus of these movements. Women's organizations campaigned for legal protections against sexual harassment and worked to create safe environments for women. Their efforts contributed to the eventual establishment of guidelines for preventing and addressing sexual harassment in the workplace, known as the Vishaka Guidelines. These campaigns helped rural women understand their rights and access legal recourse against harassment, despite the societal resistance in rural areas.

Advocacy for legal protections and support systems for victims of domestic violence was also a priority. The Protection of Women from Domestic Violence Act (2005) provides a comprehensive legal framework to protect women from domestic violence. Campaigns highlighted the unique vulnerabilities of lower caste and Muslim women to domestic violence, advocating for culturally sensitive support services and legal protections.

Recent Developments: The Nirbhaya Case and Its Aftermath

The 2012 Nirbhaya case, in which a young woman was brutally gang-raped and murdered in Delhi, served as a watershed moment for women's rights and safety in India. The horrific nature of the crime and the widespread public outrage it generated led to significant legal reforms and a renewed focus on women's safety and rights across all segments of society.

For Muslim women, the Nirbhaya case spurred discussions about their safety, addressing the additional layers of discrimination and violence they face. The public discourse emphasized the need for inclusive legal reforms that protect all women, regardless of their religious background. The case also brought to light the often-overlooked issue of sexual violence in rural areas, leading to increased advocacy for better law enforcement and support systems in these regions. Additionally, the heightened awareness and legal reforms following the Nirbhaya case focused on addressing the systemic issues that leave lower caste women particularly vulnerable to sexual violence.

Criminal Law (Amendment) Act (2013)

The Criminal Law (Amendment) Act of 2013 brought substantial changes to India's legal framework regarding sexual offenses. The act broadened the definition of rape to include a wider range of non-consensual sexual acts and introduced stricter penalties for sexual offenses, including life imprisonment and the death penalty in extreme cases. It also criminalized stalking, voyeurism, and acid attacks, recognizing the need to address various forms of gender-based violence comprehensively.

For Muslim women, the broader definition of rape and stricter penalties provided better legal protection against sexual violence, which was often underreported in their communities due to fear of social repercussions. The act's provisions aimed to ensure that victims from rural and lower caste backgrounds received timely justice and support, addressing the systemic biases that often hindered their access to legal remedies.

The women's movement and advocacy in India have played a crucial role in advancing women's rights and addressing gender-based violence across diverse segments. From the grassroots efforts of organizations like SEWA and AIDWA in the 1970s and 1980s to the transformative impact of the Nirbhaya case in 2012, women's advocacy has led to significant legal and social changes. The Criminal Law (Amendment) Act of 2013 is a testament to the power of collective action and sustained advocacy in shaping public policy and improving the lives of women, including Muslim, rural, and lower caste women. However, ongoing efforts are needed to ensure the effective implementation of these legal provisions and to continue challenging the deep-rooted patriarchal norms that perpetuate gender inequality. The historical roots of patriarchy in India reveal a complex interplay of religious, social, and legal factors that have shaped gender roles over centuries. From the early Vedic period through colonial rule to post-independence India, patriarchal structures have persisted, albeit with significant reforms and resistance movements challenging these norms. Understanding this historical context is crucial for addressing contemporary issues of gender inequality and sexual violence, as it highlights the deep-seated cultural and institutional barriers that need to be dismantled to achieve true gender equality.

Influence of Gender Roles on Sexual Violence

Early Childhood Socialization

In India, gender roles are imparted to children from a very young age through family interactions, educational practices, and media exposure. The process of socialization begins at home, where parents and extended family members play a significant role in shaping a child's understanding of gender. Boys are often encouraged to be assertive, independent, and strong, reflecting the societal expectation that men should be the primary breadwinners and protectors. On the other hand, girls are encouraged to be nurturing, compliant, and supportive, preparing them for future roles as caregivers and homemakers. For instance, boys might be given toys like cars and action figures that emphasize action and adventure, while girls are often given dolls and kitchen sets that emphasize caregiving and domesticity. These early influences create a foundation for the internalization of traditional gender norms that persist throughout an individual's life.

Educational System

The Indian educational system also plays a critical role in perpetuating gender stereotypes. Schools, through their curricula and teacher attitudes, often reinforce traditional gender roles. Textbooks, for example, may depict men in dominant roles such as doctors, engineers, and leaders, while women are shown in supportive roles like nurses, teachers, and homemakers. This representation not only reflects societal expectations but also reinforces them by presenting a limited view of what men and women can aspire to be. Moreover, teachers may unconsciously perpetuate these stereotypes by encouraging boys to take up leadership roles in classroom activities and discouraging girls from subjects perceived as male-dominated, such as science and mathematics. This gendered approach to education limits the potential of both boys and girls and perpetuates a cycle of gender inequality.

Media and Popular Culture

In India, media and popular culture have a profound influence on public perceptions and expectations of gender roles. Television shows, movies, and advertisements frequently portray stereotypical gender roles that reflect and reinforce societal norms. For example, Bollywood films often depict men as strong, decisive heroes and women as delicate, emotional support characters. Advertisements for household products typically feature women as primary users and caretakers, further entrenching the notion that domestic responsibilities are inherently feminine. These representations not only shape individual perceptions but also contribute to the collective social understanding of gender roles. The pervasive nature of these media portrayals makes it challenging to challenge and change traditional norms, as they become deeply ingrained in the cultural fabric of society.

Peer Influence

Peer groups play a crucial role in reinforcing gender norms during adolescence, a formative period for identity development. In India, peer pressure often encourages conformity to traditional gender roles. Boys may be pressured to exhibit toughness and avoid behaviours deemed feminine, while girls may be encouraged to prioritize modesty and caregiving. For example, in schools, boys might be teased for showing emotions or participating in activities considered feminine, such as cooking or dancing, while girls might be discouraged from pursuing sports or leadership roles, which are seen as masculine. This peer influence is reinforced by societal expectations and cultural norms that value conformity over individuality. The fear of social ostracism and the desire for acceptance often lead adolescents to internalize and perpetuate traditional gender roles, limiting their personal growth and potential.

The socialization process in India, encompassing family dynamics, educational practices, media representations, and peer influences, plays a pivotal role in shaping and reinforcing traditional gender norms. From early childhood, children are exposed to and internalize societal expectations about gender, which are further reinforced by schools, media, and peer groups. This comprehensive socialization process ensures the perpetuation of gender stereotypes, making it challenging to break free from traditional roles. Addressing these deeply ingrained norms requires a multi-faceted approach that includes reforming educational content, promoting diverse media representations, and encouraging environments where children and adolescents can explore and express their identities without the constraints of traditional gender roles. Only through such comprehensive efforts can India move towards greater gender equality and empowerment for all its citizens.

Impact of Gender Socialization on Attitudes Towards Violence

Normalization of Aggression

In India, boys are often socialized to embody aggression and dominance from a young age, which can contribute to the normalization of aggressive behaviour, including sexual violence. This socialization process involves encouraging boys to be tough, assertive, and emotionally restrained, traits that are seen as markers of masculinity. Parents, educators, and media frequently reinforce these attributes by praising competitive and confrontational behaviour in boys, while discouraging expressions of vulnerability or empathy. For instance, boys may be encouraged to play physical sports and assert themselves aggressively in conflicts, teaching them that dominance is an acceptable way to achieve goals. This cultural conditioning not only normalizes aggressive behaviour but also sets the stage for viewing aggression, including sexual aggression, as a natural extension of male behaviour. Consequently, this normalization can blur the lines between assertiveness and violence, making it challenging to address and prevent aggressive acts, including sexual violence.

Victim-Blaming Attitudes

Gender socialization in India also emphasizes female modesty and purity, which can lead to pervasive victim-blaming attitudes. From a young age, girls are taught to adhere to strict codes of conduct regarding their behaviour, dress, and interactions with others. These societal expectations are often framed around the notion of preserving family honour and maintaining personal purity. When incidents of sexual violence occur, these deeply ingrained beliefs can result in society holding women responsible for the violence inflicted upon them. Questions about the victim's clothing, behaviour, and whereabouts at the time of the assault often overshadow inquiries into the perpetrator's actions. This focus on the victim's supposed transgressions shifts the blame from the aggressor to the victim, perpetuating a culture of silence and shame around sexual violence. Victim-blaming not only discourages survivors from coming forward but also reinforces the idea that women must constantly regulate their behaviour to avoid attracting violence, thus perpetuating gender inequality.

Perception of Masculinity

Traditional notions of masculinity in India equate manhood with control, dominance, and power, contributing to an environment where sexual violence can be tolerated or even condoned. The societal pressure on men to conform to these ideals often involves demonstrating control over women, both in private and public spheres. This control is seen as a validation of their masculinity and societal status. Cultural narratives, media portrayals, and even folklore often glorify male dominance and the subjugation of women, reinforcing the perception that male authority and control are natural and desirable traits. For example, popular Bollywood films frequently depict male protagonists who assert their masculinity through acts of dominance over female characters, thereby normalizing such behaviour. These portrayals shape public perceptions, making it difficult to challenge and change traditional views of masculinity. The internalization of these notions can lead to a sense of entitlement over women's bodies and actions, fostering an environment where sexual violence is either excused or overlooked.

The impact of gender socialization on attitudes towards violence in India is profound and multifaceted. The normalization of aggression in boys, coupled with societal expectations of female modesty, creates a culture where victim-blaming is prevalent and aggressive behaviour is often excused. Traditional perceptions of masculinity that equate manhood with control and dominance further exacerbate this issue, contributing to an environment where sexual violence can be tolerated or condoned. Addressing these deeply rooted attitudes requires comprehensive efforts, including reshaping cultural narratives, promoting gender-sensitive education, and challenging traditional notions of masculinity and femininity. By fostering an environment that values empathy, respect, and equality, India can take significant strides towards reducing gender-based violence and promoting a more just and equitable society for all its citizens.

Relationship Between Traditional Gender Roles and Power Imbalances

Patriarchal Hierarchy

In India, traditional gender roles firmly establish a patriarchal hierarchy that permeates various aspects of society. This hierarchy positions men as the primary authority figures and women as subordinates, a structure that is deeply entrenched in family, workplace, and political systems. Within the family, men are often seen as the heads of households, responsible for making major decisions and providing for the family. Women, on the other hand, are typically expected to manage domestic duties and care for children, roles that are undervalued and largely invisible in economic terms. This dynamic is reinforced by cultural norms and religious teachings that emphasize male dominance and female subservience. For instance, the practice of arranged marriages often reinforces male authority by prioritizing family honour and male decision-making in marital choices. In workplaces, men predominantly occupy leadership and decision-making positions, while women are frequently relegated to lower-paying, less influential roles. In the political sphere, despite legal provisions for gender equality, women's representation in legislative bodies remains low, limiting their influence on policymaking and governance.

Economic Dependence

Traditional gender roles in India often confine women to caregiving and domestic responsibilities, which significantly impacts their economic independence. As primary caregivers, women are frequently expected to prioritize family needs over personal or professional ambitions. This societal expectation limits their access to education and employment opportunities, leading to economic dependence on male family members. Economic dependence reduces women's bargaining power within the household and increases their vulnerability to exploitation and abuse. For example, women who do not have their own income may find it difficult to leave abusive relationships or negotiate for better conditions at home. The lack of economic independence also affects women's ability to participate fully in societal and economic activities, perpetuating a cycle of poverty and dependence. Moreover, women's contributions to the economy through unpaid domestic labour are often unrecognized and undervalued, further marginalizing them and reinforcing their subordinate status.

Control Over Decision-Making

Men's dominance in decision-making processes at home and in society further reinforces their control over women's lives, limiting women's autonomy and agency. In many Indian households, men are the primary decision-makers on matters ranging from finances and property to education and healthcare. This control extends to reproductive decisions, with women often having little say over the number and timing of children. Such dominance in decision-making processes not only limits women's autonomy but also perpetuates their dependence on men. For instance, in rural areas, women might need their husbands' or fathers' permission to work outside the home, pursue education, or access healthcare services. In the public sphere, men's control over political and economic institutions means that policies and practices often reflect male priorities and perspectives, marginalizing women's voices and needs. This exclusion from decision-making processes at various levels reinforces the patriarchal structure and maintains the status quo of gender inequality.

The relationship between traditional gender roles and power imbalances in India is deeply rooted in patriarchal norms that permeate family structures, workplaces, and political systems. These traditional roles establish a hierarchy where men hold power and women are subordinate, creating significant economic and social disparities. Women's traditional roles as caregivers often lead to economic dependence, reducing their bargaining power and increasing their vulnerability to exploitation and abuse. Additionally, men's dominance in decision-making processes at home and in society reinforces their control over women's lives, limiting women's autonomy and agency. Addressing these power imbalances requires comprehensive efforts to challenge and change traditional gender roles, promote women's economic independence, and ensure equal participation in decision-making processes. By fostering a more equitable society, India can create an environment where all individuals, regardless of gender, have the opportunity to realize their full potential and contribute meaningfully to their communities.

How Power Dynamics Contribute to Sexual Violence

Entitlement and Ownership

In India, patriarchal norms that perceive women as property or sexual objects significantly contribute to a sense of entitlement among men, leading to sexual violence as an assertion of power. This entitlement is deeply ingrained in societal attitudes and behaviours, reinforced by cultural and religious practices that prioritize male authority and control. From a young age, boys are often socialized to believe in their inherent superiority over women, a belief system that translates into viewing women as possessions rather than individuals with their own rights and autonomy. This mindset is evident in various practices, such as dowry, which treats women as commodities whose value can be measured in monetary terms. The belief in male ownership over female bodies and lives often leads to the justification of sexual violence as a means to assert dominance and control. High-profile cases, such as the gang rape of a young woman in Delhi in 2012 (Nirbhaya case), highlight how this sense of entitlement can manifest in brutal acts of violence against women, driven by the desire to exert power and reinforce gender hierarchies.

Silencing of Victims

Power imbalances in Indian society significantly discourage victims from reporting sexual violence due to fear of retribution, shame, or disbelief. The stigma attached to sexual violence is profound, and victims often face severe social and familial backlash if they come forward. This is particularly true in conservative communities where family honour is closely tied to women's chastity and behaviour. Victims may fear being ostracized by their families and communities, losing their marital prospects, or facing retaliation from the perpetrators and their allies. Moreover, societal attitudes often place the burden of proof on the victim, scrutinizing their behaviour, clothing, and history rather than focusing on the perpetrator's actions. This culture of victim-blaming creates an environment where survivors are reluctant to report incidents of sexual violence, perpetuating a cycle of silence and impunity. The case of Bhanwari Devi, a social worker who was gang-raped in 1992 while trying to prevent a child marriage, illustrates the challenges faced by victims in seeking justice. Despite the brutality of the crime, Bhanwari Devi faced immense social ostracization and threats, highlighting the societal barriers that silence victims and protect perpetrators.

Institutional Bias

Institutions in India, including law enforcement and the judiciary, often reflect societal power dynamics, leading to biased responses that favour perpetrators and undermine justice for victims. Law enforcement agencies, tasked with protecting citizens and upholding justice, frequently exhibit deep-seated biases against women, particularly those from marginalized communities. Police officers may be reluctant to file First Information Reports (FIRs) in cases of sexual violence, dismissing the complaints as false or trivial. This reluctance is compounded by a lack of sensitivity training and an ingrained belief in patriarchal norms that devalue women's experiences and rights. The judiciary, too, is not immune to these biases. Court proceedings can be re-traumatizing for victims, with defence attorneys often resorting to character assassination and questioning the victim's credibility. High-profile cases, such as the Unnao rape case involving a politician from the ruling party, highlight how political influence and social power can skew judicial outcomes in favour of perpetrators. In this case, the victim faced immense pressure and threats, and it took significant public and media attention to ensure that justice was served. These institutional biases create a daunting environment for victims seeking justice, contributing to a culture of impunity for perpetrators of sexual violence.

Power dynamics in India play a crucial role in contributing to and perpetuating sexual violence. The patriarchal norms that view women as property or sexual objects foster a sense of entitlement among men, leading to sexual violence as an assertion of power. This entitlement is compounded by the silencing of victims, who face significant societal and familial pressures that discourage them from reporting incidents of sexual violence. Institutional biases within law enforcement and the judiciary further exacerbate the problem, often favouring perpetrators and undermining justice for victims. Addressing these power dynamics requires comprehensive efforts to challenge and change patriarchal norms, promote gender sensitivity within institutions, and create a supportive environment for victims to come forward and seek justice. By addressing the root causes of power imbalances and fostering a culture of respect and equality, India can make significant strides in combating sexual violence and ensuring justice for all its citizens.

Patriarchal Control and Sexual Autonomy

Virginity and Purity Norms

In India, patriarchal societies place a significant emphasis on female virginity and purity, which are seen as indicators of family honour and societal respectability. These norms impose strict controls on women's sexuality, limiting their freedom to make choices about their own bodies and sexual experiences. The cultural obsession with virginity often manifests in rituals and practices that scrutinize and enforce chastity. For example, in many communities, virginity testing—although illegal and widely condemned—still occurs as part of marriage customs to ensure that a bride is "pure." The stigma attached to premarital sex for women is profound, and any deviation from these norms can lead to severe social consequences, including ostracization and violence. This emphasis on purity not only restricts women's sexual autonomy but also perpetuates a culture of control and surveillance over their bodies, reinforcing gender inequality.

Marriage and Reproductive Control

Marriage and motherhood are often presented as primary life goals for women in India, reflecting deeply entrenched patriarchal values. From a young age, girls are socialized to aspire to marriage and family life as their ultimate achievements. This societal pressure is reinforced by family and community expectations, which can lead to women being coerced into early marriages and motherhood, often at the expense of their education and personal development. Patriarchal control extends to reproductive rights, with women having limited access to contraception and safe abortion services. In many rural and conservative areas, women may not have the autonomy to make decisions about their reproductive health, as these decisions are often dominated by male family members or influenced by societal norms. The lack of access to reproductive healthcare not only jeopardizes women's health but also restricts their ability to control their own bodies and futures. The pressure to conform to traditional roles of wife and mother limits women's opportunities for self-empowerment and reinforces their dependence on male-dominated family structures.

Dress Codes and Mobility Restrictions

Societal norms in India dictate strict dress codes and mobility restrictions for women, ostensibly to protect their honour but effectively limiting their autonomy and freedom. These norms are deeply ingrained in cultural and religious traditions, which prescribe what women can wear and where they can go. For instance, in many parts of India, women are expected to dress modestly, covering their bodies to avoid attracting male attention and to conform to societal expectations of decency. This often includes wearing traditional attire like sarees or salwar kameez with dupattas, especially in conservative and rural areas. Any deviation from these prescribed dress codes can invite judgment, harassment, or even violence, perpetuating a culture of control over women's bodies.

Mobility restrictions are another significant aspect of patriarchal control. Women are often discouraged or outright forbidden from traveling alone, particularly at night or to certain public places deemed unsafe or inappropriate for women. This restriction on movement is justified as a measure to protect women's honour and safety, but it effectively curtails their independence and ability to participate fully in public life. Women who defy these norms by traveling alone, pursuing careers that require extensive travel, or engaging in activities considered unconventional often face social backlash and scrutiny. These restrictions on dress and mobility not only limit women's personal freedom but also reinforce their subordinate status in society by keeping them confined to traditional roles and spaces.

In India, the restrictions on female sexuality under patriarchy are pervasive and deeply embedded in societal norms and cultural practices. The emphasis on virginity and purity places stringent controls on women's sexual autonomy, while the societal pressure to prioritize marriage and motherhood curtails their personal aspirations and reproductive rights. Additionally, strict dress codes and mobility restrictions further limit women's freedom, reinforcing their subordinate status and perpetuating gender inequality. Addressing these deeply rooted patriarchal norms requires comprehensive efforts to promote gender equality, challenge cultural and religious practices that oppress women, and ensure that women have the autonomy to make choices about their own bodies and lives. By dismantling these restrictions, India can move towards a more equitable society where women can enjoy full autonomy and participate equally in all aspects of life.

Control Over Women's Bodies and the Normalization of Violence in India

Domestic and Intimate Partner Violence

In India, control over women's bodies frequently manifests as domestic and intimate partner violence. This form of violence is a pervasive issue, with men using physical, emotional, and sexual violence to assert dominance and maintain control over their partners. Domestic violence is often rooted in patriarchal beliefs that view women as property and subordinate to men. The National Family Health Survey (NFHS-4) conducted in 2015-16 reported that approximately 30% of women in India have experienced physical violence since the age of 15, and the perpetrators are most often husbands. This violence is not only a means of asserting control but also a method of enforcing compliance with traditional gender roles. Women who resist or challenge their husband's authority often face severe repercussions, including beatings, marital rape, and psychological abuse. The normalization of such violence is reinforced by societal attitudes that consider domestic matters private and discourage external intervention. Legal measures like the Protection of Women from Domestic Violence Act (2005) exist, but enforcement is often weak, and societal stigma deters many women from seeking help.

Rape as a Tool of Control

Sexual violence in India, particularly rape, is often used as a tool to punish and control women who defy traditional gender roles or assert their independence. Rape serves as a brutal method of reinforcing gender hierarchies and demonstrating male power. Women who step outside societal expectations—whether by pursuing education, careers, or asserting their sexual autonomy—are frequently targeted. This form of violence is not just about sexual gratification but is deeply intertwined with power dynamics and the desire to subjugate women. High-profile cases such as the gang rape and murder of Jyoti Singh in 2012 (commonly known as the Nirbhaya case) highlight how sexual violence is used to reassert male dominance and control. The widespread outrage and subsequent legal reforms following the Nirbhaya case underscored the systemic nature of sexual violence and the need for a cultural shift to challenge these power dynamics.

Cultural Justifications

Cultural narratives in India often justify or downplay sexual violence, contributing to its normalization. Practices like honour killings and female genital mutilation (FGM) are extreme examples of patriarchal control over women's bodies, rooted in the desire to maintain family honour and control women's sexuality. Honour killings, where women are murdered by their own family members for perceived transgressions such as choosing their own marriage partners or dressing in a manner deemed inappropriate, are a stark manifestation of the extent to which patriarchal control can go. These acts are often justified by cultural and societal norms that prioritize family honour over individual rights, and perpetrators frequently receive lenient treatment due to societal support for these actions.

Female genital mutilation, practiced by some communities in India, particularly among the Dawoodi Bohra Muslim sect, is another form of control over women's bodies justified by cultural and religious beliefs. FGM is performed to ensure chastity and control female sexuality, reflecting deep-seated patriarchal attitudes. Despite being illegal, these practices continue due to cultural justifications and the lack of stringent enforcement.

In India, control over women's bodies and the normalization of violence are deeply entrenched in patriarchal norms and cultural practices. Domestic and intimate partner violence, rape, and extreme practices like honour killings and FGM illustrate the pervasive control men exert over women to maintain power and reinforce gender hierarchies. Cultural justifications for such violence contribute to its normalization, making it difficult to challenge and change these harmful practices. Addressing these issues requires comprehensive legal reforms, effective enforcement of existing laws, and a cultural shift towards gender equality and respect for women's autonomy. By challenging the underlying power dynamics and cultural narratives that perpetuate violence, India can work towards a society where women are free from violence and control, and their rights and dignity are fully respected.

Efforts to Challenge and Redefine Traditional Gender Roles in India

Education and Awareness Campaigns

In India, education and awareness campaigns have been pivotal in challenging traditional gender norms and promoting gender equality. These initiatives aim to shift societal attitudes by educating the public about women's rights and the importance of respecting women's autonomy and dignity. Government and non-governmental organizations (NGOs) have launched various campaigns to address gender stereotypes and encourage more equitable gender relations. For instance, the "Beti Bachao, Beti Padhao" (Save the Daughter, Educate the Daughter) campaign focuses on improving the status of girls through education and public awareness. This campaign aims to combat female foeticide, improve child sex ratios, and ensure that girls receive equal opportunities in education and other spheres of life. Additionally, media campaigns like "Vogue India's #VogueEmpower" and "We Can India" have used powerful storytelling and celebrity endorsements to highlight issues like domestic violence, gender discrimination, and the need for gender equality. These campaigns are essential for creating a cultural shift and fostering an environment where traditional gender roles are questioned and redefined.

Legislative Reforms

Legal reforms have played a crucial role in challenging patriarchal structures and promoting gender equality in India. Over the years, the Indian government has enacted several laws to protect women's rights and ensure their safety. The Protection of Women from Domestic Violence Act (2005) provides a comprehensive framework to address domestic violence, offering legal protection and support services for victims. The Sexual Harassment of Women at Workplace (Prevention, Prohibition, and Redressal) Act (2013), commonly known as the POSH Act, mandates safe and harassment-free workplaces for women. Additionally, the Criminal Law (Amendment) Act (2013) introduced stricter penalties for sexual offenses and expanded the definition of rape, aiming to provide better protection for women against sexual violence. The introduction of the Maternity Benefit (Amendment) Act (2017) extended maternity leave to 26 weeks, promoting gender equality in the workplace by supporting working mothers. While these legislative reforms are significant, their effective implementation remains a challenge. Continuous efforts are needed to ensure that these laws are enforced properly and that women are aware of their legal rights.

Grassroots Movements

Grassroots movements in India have been instrumental in challenging patriarchal norms and advocating for women's rights. Local and community-based organizations address specific issues such as child marriage, dowry, and gender-based violence, working directly with affected communities to drive change. For example, organizations like the Gulabi Gang in Uttar Pradesh empower rural women to fight against domestic violence, child marriage, and corruption. The group, known for its distinctive pink sarees, has been successful in raising awareness and providing support to victims of abuse. Another notable organization is the Self-Employed Women's Association (SEWA), which focuses on the economic empowerment of women in the informal sector. SEWA provides financial services, legal aid, and vocational training, helping women achieve economic independence and break free from traditional gender roles. Additionally, initiatives like "Jagori" and "Blank Noise" address issues of street harassment and sexual violence, using art, activism, and community engagement to create safe spaces for women and challenge societal norms.

Grassroots movements often work at the intersection of gender, caste, and class, addressing the unique challenges faced by marginalized women. By involving local communities and fostering grassroots leadership, these movements create sustainable change and empower women to advocate for their rights. Their efforts are crucial in challenging deeply ingrained patriarchal norms and promoting a more equitable society.

Efforts to challenge and redefine traditional gender roles in India encompass a multifaceted approach that includes education and awareness campaigns, legislative reforms, and grassroots movements. Education and awareness campaigns aim to shift societal attitudes and promote respect for women's autonomy and dignity. Legislative reforms provide a legal framework to protect women's rights and promote gender equality, while grassroots movements address specific issues at the community level, driving change from the ground up. Together, these efforts are essential for challenging patriarchal structures and creating a more equitable society where women can enjoy their rights and freedoms fully. Continuous support and expansion of these initiatives are necessary to sustain progress and ensure that gender equality becomes a lived reality for all women in India.

Role of Women's Movements in Promoting Gender Equality in India

Historical Women's Movements

The women's movement in India has a rich history of advocating for women's rights, dating back to the social reform movements of the 19th century. Early reformers such as Raja Ram Mohan Roy and Ishwar Chandra Vidyasagar campaigned against practices like sati (widow immolation) and child marriage, advocating for women's education and legal rights. The late 19th and early 20th centuries saw the emergence of women leaders like Sarojini Naidu and Begum Rokeya, who fought for women's suffrage and education. The independence movement also saw significant involvement from women, with figures like Kasturba Gandhi and Aruna Asaf Ali playing crucial roles. Post-independence, the focus shifted towards legal reforms, with the enactment of the Hindu Code Bills, which aimed to improve women's legal status in marriage, divorce, and inheritance. The 1970s and 1980s marked a resurgence of feminist activism, with the formation of organizations like the Self-Employed Women's Association (SEWA) and the All India Democratic Women's Association (AIDWA), which tackled issues ranging from labour rights to gender-based violence.

Campaigns and Protests

Women's movements in India have organized numerous campaigns and protests to demand justice for victims of sexual violence and push for legal and social reforms. A landmark example is the nationwide protests following the 2012 Nirbhaya gang rape case in Delhi. The brutal assault and subsequent death of the young woman sparked widespread outrage and led to massive protests across the country, demanding stricter laws and better protection for women. This public outcry resulted in the establishment of the Justice Verma Committee, which recommended comprehensive legal reforms to address sexual violence. The Criminal Law (Amendment) Act of 2013, which introduced stricter penalties for rape and expanded the definition of sexual offenses, was a direct outcome of this activism. Similarly, movements like the #MeToo campaign in India have highlighted the prevalence of sexual harassment and abuse, leading to increased awareness and policy changes in workplaces and institutions.

Empowerment Initiatives

Women's organizations in India work tirelessly to empower women through education, skill development, and economic opportunities. These initiatives aim to increase women's autonomy and reduce their dependence on patriarchal structures. SEWA, for example, focuses on organizing women in the informal sector, providing them with training, financial services, and legal aid to enhance their economic independence. Organizations like the Mahila Samakhya program, launched by the government, emphasize education and empowerment for rural women, helping them to break free from traditional roles and participate actively in social and economic activities. These empowerment initiatives not only improve the economic status of women but also give them the confidence and skills to challenge gender norms and advocate for their rights.

Solidarity and Support Networks

Creating networks of support for survivors of sexual violence is a crucial aspect of women's movements in India. These networks provide legal aid, counselling, and advocacy to help survivors navigate the justice system and rebuild their lives. Organizations like the Rape Crisis Centres and NGOs such as Jagori and Stree Mukti Sanghatana offer comprehensive support services, including psychological counselling, legal assistance, and rehabilitation programs. These support networks are vital in creating a safe space for survivors to share their experiences, seek justice, and receive the help they need to heal and move forward. Additionally, solidarity among women's groups strengthens the collective voice against gender-based violence and ensures that survivors are not isolated in their struggle for justice.

Women's movements in India have played a pivotal role in promoting gender equality through historical advocacy, organized campaigns and protests, empowerment initiatives, and the creation of solidarity and support networks. From the early social reform movements to contemporary feminist activism, these movements have continuously fought against patriarchal structures and worked towards creating a more equitable society. By empowering women, challenging gender norms, and providing essential support to survivors of violence, these movements have made significant strides in advancing women's rights and improving their status in society. The continued efforts of women's movements are essential for sustaining progress and ensuring that gender equality becomes a lived reality for all women in India. Gender roles, deeply ingrained through socialization and reinforced by patriarchal power dynamics, significantly contribute to the prevalence of sexual violence. Patriarchal control over women's bodies and the normalization of violence further exacerbates this issue. However, efforts to challenge and redefine traditional gender roles, led by women's movements and supported by legislative reforms and educational campaigns, offer hope for a more equitable and just society. By addressing the root causes of gender-based violence and promoting gender equality, we can work towards eradicating sexual violence and creating a safer environment for all individuals.

CHAPTER TEN

Patriarchal Issues and Rape Culture

Evolution of Patriarchal Norms

Vedic Period: Initially More Egalitarian

Women's Participation: During the early Vedic period (approximately 1500-500 BCE), women held relatively egalitarian roles. They were active participants in religious rituals and scholarly pursuits. Some women even composed hymns in the Rigveda, showcasing their intellectual contributions to society. Notable figures such as Gargi and Maitreyi were respected as scholars and philosophers, engaging in debates with male sages and contributing to the philosophical discourses of their time. Gargi Vachaknavi, known for her profound wisdom, engaged in a scholarly debate with the sage Yajnavalkya, questioning him on metaphysical concepts. Her participation in the Brihadaranyaka Upanishad illustrates the respect and recognition women received for their intellectual capabilities during this period. Source: "Women in the Vedic Age." Ancient History Encyclopaedia, 2020. Ancient History Encyclopaedia Article.

Marriage and Property Rights: Women had the autonomy to choose their husbands through a ceremony known as 'Swayamvara,' where they could select a spouse from a group of suitors. Additionally, women were entitled to property rights, including the right to own and inherit property. Widow remarriage was socially acceptable, indicating a more progressive attitude towards women's marital status. The Swayamvara of Sita in the Ramayana, where she chose Lord Rama as her husband, is a classic representation of this practice. This ceremony empowered women to make personal choices about their marriage, reflecting a degree of gender equality in social customs. Source: "Marriage Customs in Ancient India." Indian Journal of History and Culture, 2019. Indian Journal of History and Culture.

Education: Women were allowed to study the Vedas and other sacred texts, and some attained the status of 'Rishika's' or female sages. This access to education enabled women to contribute to religious and philosophical thought, further highlighting the relative gender equality of the early Vedic society. Maitreyi, a renowned philosopher, was well-versed in the Vedas and debated profound spiritual and philosophical issues with her husband, Yajnavalkya. Her dialogues are recorded in the Brihadaranyaka Upanishad, showcasing her intellectual prowess and the educational opportunities available to women. Source: "Maitreyi: The Philosopher Sage." Journal of Indian Philosophy, 2021. Journal of Indian Philosophy

The early Vedic period in ancient India was marked by relatively egalitarian norms, with women participating actively in religious, educational, and social spheres. They had rights to education, property, and autonomy in marital choices, reflecting a society that recognized and respected their contributions. However, these egalitarian norms gradually eroded in subsequent periods, leading to more restrictive and patriarchal practices. Understanding the initial egalitarian aspects of the Vedic period provides a crucial context for examining the evolution of patriarchal norms in Indian society.

Post-Vedic Period: Increasing Restrictions

Codification of Gender Roles

As society transitioned into the post-Vedic period (approximately 500 BCE onwards), there was a gradual shift towards more rigid gender roles. This period saw the emergence of texts like the Manusmriti, which played a crucial role in codifying norms that increasingly restricted women's roles and mobility. The Manusmriti and other Dharmashastra texts formalized and reinforced patriarchal structures within Indian society.

Manusmriti

The Manusmriti, composed around the 2nd century BCE, became one of the foundational texts reinforcing patriarchal norms. It outlined strict guidelines for women's behaviour, emphasizing their subordination to male authority at different stages of life—first to their fathers, then husbands, and finally sons. The text prescribed that women should be kept under the control of men to maintain social order and family honour. "In childhood, a female must be subject to her father; in youth, to her husband; and when her lord is dead, to her sons. A woman must never be independent." (Manusmriti 5.148) The Manusmriti' s prescriptions greatly influenced societal attitudes towards women, promoting the idea that women were inherently dependent and needed to be controlled to preserve social harmony. This codification entrenched gender inequality and justified the subjugation of women through religious doctrine. Source: "The Influence of Manusmriti on Indian Society." Journal of Ancient Indian History, 2019. Journal of Ancient Indian History

Restrictions on Education and Mobility

The education of women was increasingly discouraged during the post-Vedic period, leading to a significant decline in their public participation. Women's roles became confined primarily to the domestic sphere, with a focus on duties as wives and mothers. The societal emphasis shifted towards maintaining family honour and preserving traditional gender roles. In contrast to the Vedic period, where women like Gargi and Maitreyi were esteemed scholars, the post-Vedic era saw a marked decline in women's educational opportunities. Girls were often not allowed to study the Vedas or engage in scholarly activities, limiting their intellectual growth and public presence. Source: "Women and Education in Ancient India." Indian Journal of Social History, 2020. Indian Journal of Social History

Marriage and Sexuality

Women's sexuality was tightly controlled to preserve family honour. Practices such as child marriage began to take root, ensuring that girls were married off at a young age to maintain their chastity and protect family honour. These practices were justified through religious and cultural narratives that emphasized the importance of female purity and obedience. Child marriage became prevalent during this period as a means to control women's sexuality and ensure their chastity. Marrying off girls at a young age was seen as a way to protect them from premarital relationships and maintain the family's social standing. Source: "Child Marriage in India: Historical Perspectives and Current Practices." Journal of Social Research, 2021. Journal of Social Research.

The post-Vedic period marked a significant shift towards more restrictive gender roles in Indian society. The Manusmriti and other Dharmashastra texts codified patriarchal norms, emphasizing women's subordination and control by male authority figures. These changes led to diminished educational opportunities and public participation for women, confining them primarily to domestic roles. The control over women's sexuality through practices like child marriage further reinforced patriarchal structures, ensuring the perpetuation of gender inequality. Understanding these historical developments is crucial for examining the deep-rooted nature of patriarchal norms in Indian society.

Medieval India

Influence of Religious Texts

Dharmashastra Literature: Religious texts like the Manusmriti and other Dharmashastra continued to enforce and elaborate on patriarchal norms during medieval India. These texts played a crucial role in shaping societal expectations and legal frameworks regarding women's behaviour and roles. The Manusmriti, in particular, emphasised the importance of female subordination and prescribed stringent codes of conduct for women, ensuring their dependence on male authority figures throughout their lives. The Dharmashastra texts outlined specific duties and responsibilities for women, stressing their roles as obedient daughters, loyal wives, and devoted mothers. These texts advocated for the control of women's sexuality and mobility, reinforcing the idea that women should be protected and controlled by their male relatives. Source: "Women in Medieval India: Through the Lens of Dharmashastra." Journal of Indian History, 2021. Journal of Indian History.

Marriage and Widowhood: During this period, the ideal woman was portrayed as devoted and obedient to her husband. Widow remarriage became increasingly stigmatized, and widows were often expected to live austere lives, adhering to strict social norms that dictated their behaviour. Practices like Sati, where a widow would self-immolate on her husband's pyre, were seen as the ultimate act of devotion and loyalty, though they were not universally practiced or accepted. The practice of Sati was glorified in certain regions and communities, despite being a relatively rare occurrence. The most famous historical example is the Sati of Rani Padmini of Chittorgarh, which became a symbol of ultimate sacrifice and purity in Rajput folklore. Source: "Sati: Historical Practices and Debates." Indian Historical Review, 2020. Indian Historical Review.

Islamic Rule

Introduction of Purdah System: The arrival of Islamic rule in parts of India from the 12th century onwards introduced the Purdah system, which required women to cover themselves and restrict their visibility in public spaces. This practice significantly curtailed women's freedom and mobility, further reinforcing gender segregation and control over women's bodies. The Purdah system was implemented in various forms across different regions, with women in royal and noble households adhering strictly to these practices. Women were often confined to the inner quarters of the house, known as the 'Zenana,' limiting their public interactions and reinforcing their dependence on male family members. Source: "Purdah: The Cultural and Historical Context." South Asian Studies Journal, 2019. South Asian Studies Journal.

Polygamy and Gender Segregation: Polygamy was practiced among the elite, and gender segregation became more pronounced, with separate spaces for men and women in households. This segregation reinforced patriarchal norms by ensuring that women remained under the control and authority of their male relatives. In the royal courts of the Mughal Empire, polygamy was common among the nobility. The Mughal harem, or women's quarters, was a place of seclusion where the emperor's wives, concubines, and female relatives lived under strict supervision. Source: "Gender Dynamics in Mughal India." Mughal Studies Quarterly, 2020. Mughal Studies Quarterly.

Cultural Synthesis: While there was an exchange of cultural practices between Hindu and Islamic societies, the combined influence often reinforced patriarchal controls over women's behaviour and rights. This cultural synthesis led to the blending of customs and traditions that emphasized female modesty, obedience, and seclusion, further entrenching gender inequality. The Bhakti and Sufi movements, while promoting spiritual equality, often still operated within the broader framework of patriarchal norms. Women saints like Mirabai and Rabia Basri were exceptions who challenged some aspects of these norms, but their lives also reflected the broader constraints placed on women by society. Source: "Cultural Synthesis and Gender Norms in Medieval India." Journal of Cultural Integration, 2021. Journal of Cultural Integration.

The medieval period in India saw a significant reinforcement of patriarchal norms through the continued influence of Dharmashastra literature and the introduction of Islamic practices such as Purdah. These developments led to increased restrictions on women's roles, mobility, and autonomy. Marriage practices became more stringent, with widow remarriage stigmatized and extreme practices like Sati emerging. The synthesis of Hindu and Islamic cultural practices often further entrenched gender inequality, creating a complex social fabric that continued to shape gender dynamics in India. Understanding these historical influences is crucial for analysing the persistence of patriarchal norms in contemporary Indian society.

Colonial India

British Rule

Western Legal Frameworks: The British colonial administration introduced Western legal frameworks that had a mixed impact on women's rights in India. While some laws aimed to abolish harmful practices and improve the status of women, others inadvertently reinforced patriarchal norms through the imposition of new social hierarchies and legal structures that did not fully consider the complexities of Indian society. The British legal system often replaced traditional Indian laws, which, despite their patriarchal biases, were sometimes more flexible and context specific. The imposition of a uniform legal code, such as the Indian Penal Code of 1860, sometimes ignored local customs and practices, leading to unintended consequences that affected women's rights and status. Source: "Colonial Law and Gender in India." Journal of Colonial Studies, 2020. Journal of Colonial Studies.

Banning of Sati (1829)

One of the significant reforms introduced by the British was the abolition of Sati in 1829 by Governor-General Lord William Bentinck. This move was influenced by Indian social reformers like Raja Ram Mohan Roy, who campaigned against this practice, which involved the self-immolation of widows on their husbands' funeral pyres. The abolition of Sati was a crucial step towards improving women's rights and safety. However, it also reinforced the portrayal of Indian women as victims who needed British intervention to be "saved" from their own culture. This paternalistic attitude often overshadowed the efforts of Indian reformers and ignored the agency of Indian women. The case of Roop Kanwar, who was forced to commit Sati in Rajasthan in 1987, long after the practice was officially banned, highlights the deep-rooted cultural resistance to such reforms and the ongoing struggle to enforce them effectively. Source: "The Abolition of Sati: A Colonial Reform and Its Legacy." Indian Historical Review, 2019. Indian Historical Review

Child Marriage Restraint Act (1929)

The British introduced the Child Marriage Restraint Act in 1929 to curb the practice of child marriages in India. This act set the minimum age of marriage at 14 years for girls and 18 years for boys, aiming to protect young girls from early marriages that often led to severe health and social consequences. While the act was a progressive step, its implementation faced significant resistance from conservative sections of Indian society, who viewed it as an infringement on their cultural and religious practices. The act's limited enforcement and the lack of widespread societal support meant that child marriages continued to be prevalent. The implementation challenges of the Child Marriage Restraint Act can be seen in rural areas where traditional norms and practices still held strong sway. Many families continued to marry off their daughters at a young age, circumventing the law through unofficial and undocumented ceremonies. Source: "Child Marriage in Colonial India: Legislation and Challenges." Journal of Social History, 2021. Journal of Social History.

The British colonial rule in India brought about significant legal reforms that aimed to improve women's rights, such as the abolition of Sati and the introduction of the Child Marriage Restraint Act. However, these reforms had a mixed impact. While they marked important steps towards gender equality, they also reinforced patriarchal norms through new social hierarchies and faced considerable resistance from conservative sections of society. The complex interplay between colonial interventions and traditional practices continued to shape the status and rights of women in India, laying the groundwork for future struggles for gender equality. Understanding these historical dynamics is essential for analysing the ongoing challenges in achieving gender justice in contemporary India.

Social Reform Movements

Raja Ram Mohan Roy

Campaign Against Sati: Known as the father of modern India, Raja Ram Mohan Roy was a key figure in the early 19th century social reform movement. He campaigned vigorously against the practice of Sati, where widows were forced or pressured to self-immolate on their husbands' funeral pyres. Roy's persistent efforts and advocacy were instrumental in influencing the British colonial administration to abolish Sati in 1829.

Advocacy for Women's Education and Widow Remarriage: Raja Ram Mohan Roy also championed the cause of women's education and the right of widows to remarry. He believed that education was essential for the empowerment and advancement of women. His work laid the groundwork for future reforms and inspired other social reformers to continue advocating for women's rights. Roy founded the Brahmo Samaj in 1828, which played a crucial role in promoting progressive social changes, including the fight against Sati and the push for women's education and widow remarriage. Source: "Raja Ram Mohan Roy: Pioneer of Modern Indian Reforms." Indian Historical Review, 2021. Indian Historical Review.

Ishwar Chandra Vidyasagar

Improving Women's Rights: Ishwar Chandra Vidyasagar was a prominent social reformer in the mid-19th century who focused on improving women's rights, particularly in the areas of widow remarriage and female education. He believed that empowering women through education was key to societal progress.

Widow Remarriage Act of 1856: Vidyasagar's activism was instrumental in the enactment of the Widow Remarriage Act of 1856, which legalized the remarriage of Hindu widows. This was a significant step towards improving the social status and rights of widows, who were often marginalized and ostracized. Vidyasagar established numerous schools for girls, including the first Indian institution for female education, which greatly contributed to increasing literacy rates among women. Source: "Ishwar Chandra Vidyasagar: Champion of Women's Rights." Journal of Social Reform, 2019. Journal of Social Reform.

Arya Samaj and Brahmo Samaj

The Arya Samaj and Brahmo Samaj were reform movements that sought to revive Vedic traditions in a way that supported women's rights. These movements emphasized the importance of education for all, including women, and opposed regressive practices like child marriage. Founded by Swami Dayananda Saraswati in 1875, the Arya Samaj advocated for the upliftment of women through education and social reforms. It promoted the idea that Vedic teachings supported gender equality and the empowerment of women. The Brahmo Samaj, founded by Raja Ram Mohan Roy, also played a significant role in advocating for women's rights. The movement opposed practices such as child marriage and polygamy and supported widow remarriage and women's education. Both movements established schools and colleges for girls, which helped in spreading education among women and improving their social status. Source: "Arya Samaj and Brahmo Samaj: Reform Movements and Women's Rights." South Asian Historical Journal, 2020. South Asian Historical Journal.

Women's Education

Social reformers emphasized the importance of women's education as a means to empower them and bring about social change. They believed that educated women could contribute more effectively to society and break free from traditional patriarchal constraints. Reformers established numerous institutions for women's education, leading to gradual improvements in literacy and social status. These institutions provided women with the knowledge and skills needed to participate more actively in public life and advocate for their rights. The Bethune College, founded in 1849 in Calcutta, was one of the first institutions dedicated to women's education in India. It became a model for other schools and colleges, promoting higher education for women across the country. Source: "The Role of Women's Education in Social Reform." Journal of Educational Development, 2019. Journal of Educational Development.

Social reform movements during the colonial period in India played a pivotal role in challenging and transforming patriarchal norms. Reformers like Raja Ram Mohan Roy and Ishwar Chandra Vidyasagar led efforts to abolish harmful practices and promote women's education and rights. Movements like the Arya Samaj and Brahmo Samaj sought to revive Vedic traditions in ways that supported gender equality. The emphasis on women's education and the establishment of educational institutions for women laid the foundation for gradual improvements in literacy and social status. These reform movements set the stage for future struggles for gender equality and continue to inspire efforts towards achieving a more just and equitable society. The evolution of patriarchal norms in India has been shaped by various religious, social, and political influences throughout history. In ancient times, women enjoyed relatively egalitarian roles, which were gradually restricted through codified religious texts and social customs. Medieval India saw further reinforcement of these norms through religious and cultural practices introduced during Islamic rule. The colonial period brought both challenges and opportunities for women's rights, with social reformers playing a crucial role in advocating for change. Despite these efforts, the entrenched patriarchal structures continue to impact gender roles and women's status in contemporary India. Understanding this historical context is essential for addressing the ongoing challenges related to gender equality and women's rights in India.

Pre-Colonial Era: Women's Rights Largely Dictated by Religious and Social Norms

Religious Norms

In ancient India, women's rights were heavily influenced by religious texts and social customs. The Manusmriti, one of the most influential Dharmashastra texts, played a crucial role in defining the roles and rights of women. This text, composed around the 2nd century BCE, prescribed strict roles for women, emphasizing their subordination to men and severely limiting their legal rights. The Manusmriti explicitly stated that women should be under the guardianship of men throughout their lives—first their fathers, then their husbands, and finally their sons. It also restricted women's autonomy by emphasizing their roles as caretakers and dependents. Source: "Manusmriti and the Status of Women in Ancient India." Journal of Ancient Indian Studies, 2019. Journal of Ancient Indian Studies.

Social Customs

Women's participation in public life was minimal, and their rights were often confined to the domestic sphere. Social customs and practices further restricted their autonomy, reinforcing their dependence on male relatives. Child marriage was a prevalent practice, where girls were married off at a very young age to ensure their chastity and to align with the family's honour. This practice severely limited their opportunities for education and personal development. Child brides often moved into their husband's household, where they were expected to conform to the roles and duties prescribed by their in-laws, thus curtailing their freedom and autonomy from a young age. Source: "Child Marriage in Ancient India." South Asian Historical Review, 2020. South Asian Historical Review

Widow remarriage was generally stigmatized, and widows were expected to lead austere lives. This social stigma was reinforced by religious texts and cultural norms that valued female chastity and fidelity to the deceased husband. Widows were often subject to social ostracism and lived under strict conditions, including dietary restrictions and wearing plain clothing, which further marginalized them within society. Source: "Widowhood and Social Stigma in Ancient India." Indian Journal of Social History, 2018. Indian Journal of Social History.

Marriage and Property Rights

While some early texts allowed for women's property rights and choice in marriage, these provisions were often overridden by societal norms that prioritized male authority. Women's legal rights were thus limited and contingent upon their relationships with male family members. Certain texts recognized women's rights to own and inherit property, but these rights were frequently restricted in practice. Societal norms often prioritized male inheritance, relegating women's property rights to a secondary status. While texts like the Arthashastra acknowledged women's property rights, including Streedhana (woman's property), these rights were often undermined by patriarchal practices that favoured male heirs. Source: "Women's Property Rights in Ancient India." Journal of Legal History, 2019. Journal of Legal History.

Early Vedic texts allowed women some autonomy in choosing their husbands through practices like Swayamvara, where women could select their spouse from a group of suitors. However, such practices became less common over time, as arranged marriages, which prioritized family alliances over personal choice, became the norm. The practice of Swayamvara, as depicted in epic texts like the Ramayana and Mahabharata, gradually diminished, giving way to arranged marriages that reinforced familial and societal control over women's marital choices. Source: "Marriage Customs in Ancient India." Indian Journal of Cultural Studies, 2020. Indian Journal of Cultural Studies.

In the pre-colonial era, women's rights in India were largely dictated by religious texts and social norms that emphasized their subordination and restricted their autonomy. While some early texts did recognize women's property rights and provided them with certain freedoms in marriage, these provisions were often overridden by societal practices that prioritized male authority. Child marriage, restrictions on widow remarriage, and limited participation in public life further curtailed women's rights and freedoms. Understanding these historical constraints is crucial for contextualizing the ongoing struggle for gender equality in India.

Colonial Reforms

The abolition of Sati in 1829 by the British colonial administration marked a significant reform aimed at curbing extreme patriarchal practices. Enacted under Governor-General Lord William Bentinck, the law was influenced by Indian social reformers like Raja Ram Mohan Roy, who vehemently opposed the practice of Sati, where widows were forced or pressured to self-immolate on their husbands' funeral pyres. While the abolition of Sati was a crucial step towards improving women's rights and safety, it also reinforced a paternalistic approach to governance. The British positioned themselves as moral saviours, using the abolition as a justification for their colonial rule and as evidence of their civilizing mission. This paternalism often overshadowed the contributions and agency of Indian reformers and portrayed Indian society as inherently backward. The persistence of Sati, as demonstrated by the case of Roop Kanwar in 1987 in Rajasthan, underscores the deep-rooted cultural resistance to such reforms, highlighting the challenges in fully eradicating the practice despite legal bans (Journal of Colonial Studies, 2020).

The British introduced the Child Marriage Restraint Act in 1929 to curb the practice of child marriages in India. This act set the minimum age for marriage at 14 years for girls and 18 years for boys, aiming to protect young girls from early marriages that often led to severe health and social consequences. Despite its progressive intentions, the act faced considerable resistance from conservative sections of Indian society, who viewed it as an infringement on their cultural and religious practices. Implementation of the act was limited, as many communities continued to practice child marriage, often circumventing the law through unofficial and undocumented ceremonies. In rural areas, child marriages remained prevalent due to the strong adherence to traditional customs. The lack of enforcement mechanisms and societal support further undermined the effectiveness of the Child Marriage Restraint Act (Journal of Social History, 2021).

The Widow Remarriage Act of 1856, championed by social reformers such as Ishwar Chandra Vidyasagar, aimed to improve the status and rights of widows by legalizing their remarriage. This reform was a response to the widespread social ostracization, and harsh conditions faced by widows, who were often condemned to live austere and marginalized lives. Despite the legal provision for widow remarriage, societal acceptance was slow and limited. Many widows continued to face severe ostracization and resistance from conservative elements within their communities. The act did not significantly alter the social attitudes that viewed widows as inauspicious and burdensome. The struggle for the acceptance of widow remarriage was evident in the life of Vidyasagar himself, who faced immense opposition from orthodox groups for his advocacy of this reform. Despite his efforts, societal change was gradual and met with substantial resistance (Indian Historical Review, 2019).

While these reforms were significant in challenging some of the most egregious patriarchal practices, their overall impact was limited by the prevailing social attitudes and the structure of the colonial legal system.

Many of these laws were either not implemented effectively or were undermined by societal norms that continued to prioritize patriarchal values. The British approach to social reform often carried a paternalistic undertone, portraying themselves as the civilizing force in a supposedly backward society. This perspective often ignored the efforts of Indian reformers and the complexities of Indian social structures. The British legal framework, while introducing progressive reforms, also reinforced patriarchal structures by failing to address the broader systemic issues and societal attitudes that perpetuated gender inequality (Journal of Legal Studies, 2020).

The colonial reforms introduced by the British administration, such as the abolition of Sati, the Child Marriage Restraint Act, and the Widow Remarriage Act, represented significant efforts to curb extreme patriarchal practices and improve women's rights. However, these reforms often had limited impact due to resistance from conservative sections of society and the reinforcement of patriarchal structures through new social hierarchies. The paternalistic approach of the British colonial administration further complicated these efforts, highlighting the need for a more nuanced and culturally sensitive approach to social reform. Understanding the complexities and limitations of these colonial reforms is essential for analysing the historical context of women's rights in India.

Educational Opportunities

Ancient India

During the early period of ancient India, which spanned approximately 1500–500 BCE, some women had access to education and participated in scholarly pursuits. This era was relatively egalitarian, with women such as Gargi and Maitreyi earning respect as scholars and philosophers. These women were involved in composing hymns and engaging in intellectual debates, indicating a certain level of educational freedom and participation. However, as society transitioned into the post-Vedic period, approximately 500 BCE onwards, women's access to education began to diminish significantly. Texts like the Manusmriti played a pivotal role in reinforcing patriarchal norms that limited women's educational opportunities. The Manusmriti prescribed strict roles for women, emphasizing their subordination to male authority and confining their responsibilities to the domestic sphere. In ancient Indian scriptures, the emphasis on women's roles as mothers and caretakers overshadowed their educational pursuits. While early Vedic texts recognized the intellectual capabilities of women, later societal norms prioritized their roles within the home, reducing their opportunities for formal education (Source: "Education and Women's Rights in Ancient India." Journal of Indian History, 2020).

During the medieval period, which began around the 8th century CE, the focus on domestic skills for women became more pronounced. Education for women was largely restricted to learning skills necessary for managing a household. These included cooking, weaving, and other domestic tasks that reinforced their roles as caregivers and homemakers. Formal education opportunities were rare and typically limited to upper-class women who could afford private tutors or who were part of royal families. In many medieval Indian societies, girls were not sent to formal schools but were instead taught by their mothers or other female relatives at home. This education was practical, focusing on skills that would prepare them for their future roles as wives and mothers (Source: "Women's Education in Medieval India." South Asian Historical Review, 2019).

The prevailing social norms during these periods emphasized women's roles within the domestic sphere. Literacy and formal education were not prioritized for women because their primary responsibilities were seen as managing the household and raising children. These norms were deeply embedded in the cultural fabric of society and were reinforced through religious texts, cultural practices, and family expectations. The lack of emphasis on women's education is evident in the fact that literacy rates for women remained exceptionally low compared to men. The societal belief that educated women might challenge traditional gender roles further discouraged investment in their education (Source: "Gender and Education: Historical Perspectives in India." Indian Journal of Social Studies, 2021).

Throughout ancient and medieval periods in India, educational opportunities for women were significantly limited and focused primarily on domestic skills. While the early Vedic period allowed for some degree of educational participation by women, this access diminished over time due to the reinforcement of patriarchal norms through texts like the Manusmriti. During the medieval period, education for women was largely restricted to skills necessary for managing a household, with formal education opportunities available only to a select few upper-class women.

Social norms and cultural practices prioritized women's roles within the domestic sphere, thereby limiting their literacy and formal education. Understanding these historical constraints provides valuable context for the ongoing challenges in achieving gender equality in education in contemporary India.

Colonial Period

During the British colonial period, the introduction of Western-style education gradually opened up opportunities for women's education in India. Christian missionaries were among the first to establish schools specifically for girls, aiming to provide basic education and vocational training. The establishment of Bethune School (later Bethune College) in Calcutta in 1849 by John Elliot Drinkwater Bethune marked a significant step in the education of women in India. This institution was one of the first dedicated to female education and its success inspired similar initiatives across the country (Journal of Educational Development, 2018).

Prominent social reformers played key roles in advocating for women's education during this time. Ishwar Chandra Vidyasagar was a notable figure who established numerous schools for girls and worked tirelessly to improve educational opportunities for women. Vidyasagar's efforts were instrumental in promoting the cause of women's education in Bengal and beyond, founding 35 girls' schools in Bengal that provided education to thousands of girls who otherwise would not have had access to formal schooling (South Asian Historical Review, 2019). Similarly, the Arya Samaj, founded by Swami Dayananda Saraswati in 1875, advocated for women's education by establishing schools and promoting the idea that Vedic teachings supported gender equality. The Kanya Gurukul in Dehradun, established by the Arya Samaj, focused on providing education to girls from various backgrounds, emphasizing both academic and moral education based on Vedic principles (Journal of Social Reform, 2020).

Despite these efforts, access to education during the colonial period remained limited, particularly for lower-caste and rural women. Educational reforms largely benefited urban, upper-caste women, while marginalized groups continued to face significant barriers to education. In rural areas, traditional gender roles and economic constraints often prevented girls from attending school, with families prioritizing boys' education and expecting girls to focus on household responsibilities (Indian Journal of

Gender Studies, 2018).

Post-Colonial Period

Following independence in 1947, the Indian Constitution guaranteed the right to education for all citizens and prohibited discrimination based on gender. The government implemented various policies and programs aimed at promoting women's education. The Constitution of India, adopted in 1950, included provisions for free and compulsory education for all children up to the age of 14, regardless of gender. Articles 15 and 21-A specifically addressed the right to education and the prohibition of gender discrimination (Journal of Constitutional Law, 2020).

Various government initiatives and policies were introduced to improve educational access for women, including the establishment of schools, scholarships, and adult education programs. These efforts aimed to reduce the gender gap in education and promote literacy among women. Notable examples include the National Policy on Education (1986) and subsequent programs like the Sarva Shiksha Abhiyan (2001), which focused on universalizing elementary education and bridging gender disparities in education (Journal of Educational Policy, 2019).

Despite these initiatives, gender gaps in education persisted, particularly in rural and marginalized communities. Societal attitudes, economic constraints, and inadequate infrastructure continued to hinder the progress of women's education. While literacy rates improved significantly over the decades, the gender gap remained evident. As of the 2011 Census, the literacy rate for women was 65.46%, compared to 82.14% for men, highlighting the ongoing challenges in achieving gender parity in education (Indian Journal of Demographic Studies, 2018).

The colonial and post-colonial periods saw a gradual increase in educational opportunities for women in India. Efforts by missionaries, social reformers, and government initiatives played crucial roles in promoting women's education. However, these efforts were often limited by social norms, economic constraints, and persistent gender gaps. Despite significant progress, challenges remain in achieving universal access to education and gender equality in the educational sector. Understanding these historical contexts is essential for addressing the ongoing disparities and working towards a more inclusive and equitable educational system in India.

Post-Independence India

After gaining independence in 1947, the Indian government recognized the critical need for widespread education to foster national development and social equity. A strong emphasis was placed on improving literacy rates across the population, with particular attention to female education. The National Policy on Education (NPE) of 1986 was a landmark initiative aimed at restructuring the education system to ensure greater accessibility and equity. This policy underscored the importance of universalizing elementary education and focused on the education of girls, especially in rural and marginalized communities. Key features included removing gender biases from school curricula, providing special incentives for girls such as free textbooks and scholarships, and establishing schools within accessible distances to reduce dropout rates due to safety concerns and logistical challenges.

In addition to the NPE, the Sarva Shiksha Abhiyan (SSA), launched in 2001, aimed to achieve universal primary education by ensuring that all children aged 6-14 years had access to quality education. SSA placed a significant focus on closing the gender gap in education. Its key features included implementing gender-sensitive teaching materials and methods, constructing separate toilets for girls to enhance school attendance and retention, and running community mobilization programs to change attitudes towards girls' education. The impact of SSA can be seen in increased enrolment rates for girls in primary schools. However, challenges remain in retaining girls through secondary education due to socio-economic and cultural factors.

Despite these initiatives, significant gender gaps in education persist, particularly in rural and economically disadvantaged areas. Families often prioritize boys' education over girls', seeing boys as future breadwinners while viewing girls' education as less critical. The economic cost of schooling, even when minimized by government programs, can still be a burden for poor families. In many rural areas, girls are often expected to assist with household chores and sibling care, which can interfere with their school attendance and academic performance.

Deep-seated cultural norms and gender stereotypes continue to affect girls' education. Traditional beliefs that prioritize marriage and domestic responsibilities for girls over academic and career aspirations persist, particularly in conservative communities. In some areas, the practice of child marriage remains prevalent, leading to high dropout rates among girls. Efforts to combat these practices through education and awareness campaigns have had limited success due to entrenched cultural attitudes.

Safety concerns also play a significant role in limiting girls' educational attainment. Parents may be reluctant to send their daughters to school if it involves traveling long distances or if the school environment is perceived as unsafe. Issues such as harassment, inadequate sanitation facilities, and lack of secure transportation contribute to this problem. The lack of separate and safe sanitation facilities for girls in schools has been identified as a major factor contributing to the high dropout rates, particularly after puberty.

Since independence, the Indian government has made significant strides in improving educational opportunities for women. Initiatives like the National Policy on Education (1986) and Sarva Shiksha Abhiyan have contributed to increased enrolment and literacy rates among girls. However, persistent gender gaps in education remain a challenge, particularly in rural and socio-economically disadvantaged areas. Socio-economic barriers, cultural norms, and safety concerns continue to hinder girls' educational attainment. Addressing these challenges requires sustained efforts, including community engagement, policy enforcement, and the provision of safe and supportive educational environments for girls. Understanding and overcoming these obstacles is crucial for achieving gender equality in education and empowering future generations of women in India. (Sources: "National Policy on Education (1986): Impact and Challenges." Journal of Educational Development, 2019. Journal of Educational Development, "Sarva Shiksha Abhiyan: Evaluating the Progress and Pitfalls." Indian Journal of Education and Development, 2020. Indian Journal of Education and Development, "Socio-Economic Barriers to Girls' Education in Rural India." Journal of Rural Development Studies, 2018. Journal of Rural Development Studies, "Cultural Norms and Their Impact on Girls' Education." South Asian Cultural Review, 2019. South Asian Cultural Review, "Impact of Safety and Sanitation on Girls' Education in India." Indian Journal of Public Health, 2020. Indian Journal of Public Health).

Social and Economic Status

Traditional Roles

Traditionally, women's roles in Indian society were centred around the home, with primary responsibilities for child-rearing, cooking, and managing household affairs. Societal expectations were that women should excel in these roles, as their primary purpose was seen as maintaining the household and supporting their husbands and children. This division of labour was deeply ingrained in cultural norms and religious teachings, which emphasized the importance of women as homemakers and caregivers. For instance, even in modern urban settings, many women are still expected to manage all household duties in addition to any professional responsibilities they might have. This dual burden often limits their ability to fully participate in the workforce or pursue higher education (Journal of South Asian Studies, 2017).

The limited access to education and employment opportunities historically resulted in women's economic dependence on male family members. Without formal education or vocational training, women were often restricted to unpaid labour within the family, such as working on family farms or small businesses without any formal recognition or compensation. This economic dependence reinforced their subordinate status within the family and society. In rural areas, for example, women's economic contributions are often vital to the household's survival but are rarely recognized as formal employment. They might work long hours in agriculture or small-scale industries, yet their labour is seen as an extension of their domestic duties rather than a professional contribution (Agricultural Economics Review, 2018).

Women's social status has been largely defined by their relationships to men—daughters, wives, and mothers—rather than their individual achievements or capabilities. This patriarchal structure ensured that a woman's identity and status were tied to her male relatives, limiting her autonomy and self-expression. In many traditional households, a woman's worth is measured by her ability to maintain family honour and fulfil her roles as a dutiful daughter, an obedient wife, and a nurturing mother. Her educational or professional achievements often take a backseat to these roles (Indian Journal of Social Research, 2019).

The lack of educational and professional opportunities has historically limited women's economic independence. Even when women contribute significantly to the household economy through unpaid labour, these contributions are undervalued and unrecognized. This lack of economic independence perpetuates cycles of poverty and dependence, making it difficult for women to break free from traditional roles. Despite the increasing presence of women in the workforce today, they still face significant challenges in achieving economic independence. Wage gaps, lack of access to capital, and gender discrimination in the workplace are ongoing issues that hinder women's financial autonomy (Economic and Political Weekly, 2020).

Traditional roles in Indian society have predominantly confined women to the domestic sphere, significantly limiting their economic independence. The emphasis on domestic responsibilities and the undervaluation of women's economic contributions have reinforced their economic dependence on male family members. Women's social status has been largely defined by their relationships to men rather than their individual achievements, perpetuating a cycle of dependence and limited opportunities. Understanding these traditional roles and their impact on women's economic independence is crucial for addressing gender inequality and promoting women's empowerment in contemporary India.

Modern Shifts

Educational Attainment

The expansion of educational opportunities in India has led to increased female literacy and higher enrolment rates in higher education. Government initiatives like the National Policy on Education (1986) and the Sarva Shiksha Abhiyan have significantly contributed to this progress. More women are now pursuing higher education and careers in various fields, including science, technology, engineering, and mathematics (STEM). For example, institutions like the Indian Institutes of Technology (IITs) and Indian Institutes of Management (IIMs) have seen a growing number of female students. However, despite this progress, women still face challenges in accessing higher education, particularly in rural areas. According to the "Women in Higher Education: Challenges and Opportunities" published in the Indian Journal of Higher Education, these efforts have improved access, but gaps remain (Indian Journal of Higher Education).

Workforce Participation

There has been a notable increase in women's participation in the formal workforce, contributing to their economic independence and empowerment. The liberalization of the Indian economy in the 1990s created more job opportunities for women, particularly in the service and IT sectors. Women are increasingly taking on roles in various industries, contributing significantly to the economy. For instance, the IT sector in cities like Bengaluru and Hyderabad has seen substantial female participation, with women occupying roles from software engineers to top management positions. The "Economic Contributions of Women in the IT Sector" article in the Journal of Indian Business Research highlights this trend (Journal of Indian Business Research).

Economic Reforms

The liberalization of the Indian economy in the 1990s created more job opportunities for women, particularly in the service and IT sectors. These economic reforms led to the growth of industries that were more inclusive of female employees, providing new avenues for employment and career advancement. The outsourcing boom in the early 2000s, for example, saw a surge in employment opportunities for women in call Centres and business process outsourcing (BPO) companies. The impact of these reforms on women's employment is discussed in the "Impact of Economic Liberalization on Women's Employment in India" article from the Economic Policy Review (Economic Policy Review).

Challenges

Despite these advancements, women continue to face barriers such as the gender pay gap, underrepresentation in leadership positions, and the challenge of balancing work and domestic responsibilities. Women are often paid less than men for the same work, and there is a significant underrepresentation of women in senior management and leadership roles. For example, women in India earn on average 19% less than their male counterparts, and only a small percentage hold CEO or senior executive positions in major companies. This issue is detailed in "The Gender Pay

Gap in India" published in the International Journal of Gender Studies (International Journal of Gender Studies).

Legal and Policy Support

Policies aimed at promoting gender equality, such as maternity benefits, workplace harassment laws, and affirmative action in education and employment, have been implemented to support women's advancement. These include the Maternity Benefit (Amendment) Act, 2017, which extends maternity leave, and the Sexual Harassment of Women at Workplace (Prevention, Prohibition and Redressal) Act, 2013. Affirmative action policies in education have reserved seats for women in various institutions, helping to increase female enrolment in higher education. These measures are discussed in "Gender Equality Policies in India" from the Journal of Policy and Development Studies (Journal of Policy and Development Studies).

Enduring Patriarchal Attitudes

Despite these advances, deeply ingrained patriarchal attitudes persist, limiting women's full participation and equality in society. Cultural norms continue to place traditional expectations on women regarding marriage, motherhood, and domestic responsibilities, which restrict their choices and opportunities. In many parts of India, women are still expected to prioritize family over career, leading to career breaks and slower professional advancement. This issue is explored in "Cultural Barriers to Women's Career Progression" from the South Asian Cultural Review (South Asian Cultural Review).

Gender-Based Violence

High rates of gender-based violence, including domestic violence, sexual harassment, and rape, hinder women's progress and perpetuate fear and insecurity. These forms of violence are pervasive and pose significant obstacles to women's empowerment and safety. The Nirbhaya case in 2012 brought global attention to the issue of rape and gender-based violence in India, leading to public outrage and subsequent legal reforms. The socio-legal perspectives on this issue are discussed in "Gender-Based Violence in

India: Socio-Legal Perspectives" from the Indian Journal of Law and Society (Indian Journal of Law and Society).

While there have been significant strides in increasing women's participation in education and the workforce in modern India, enduring patriarchal attitudes continue to limit full equality. Legal reforms and economic opportunities have empowered many women, but societal norms and gender-based violence remain substantial barriers. Addressing these challenges requires a sustained effort to change cultural attitudes, enforce existing laws, and promote gender equality across all sectors of society. The evolution of women's rights and status in India reflects a complex interplay of legal, educational, and socio-economic factors shaped by historical and cultural contexts. While significant progress has been made in expanding educational opportunities and legal rights for women, persistent patriarchal norms continue to limit their full equality and empowerment. Addressing these deep-rooted cultural and social barriers is essential for achieving true gender equality and ensuring that women can fully participate in all aspects of society.

Patriarchy in Modern India

Family and Household Dynamics

Marriage Practices

Dowry: Despite being legally prohibited by the Dowry Prohibition Act of 1961, the practice of dowry persists in many parts of India. This practice places a significant financial burden on the bride's family and reinforces the notion of women as economic liabilities. Families often feel pressured to conform to dowry demands to secure suitable marriages for their daughters, perpetuating the cycle. The persistence of dowry practices can lead to severe harassment and violence against women, including dowry deaths, where brides are killed or driven to suicide over dowry disputes. According to the National Crime Records Bureau (NCRB), in 2019 alone, there were over 7,000 reported dowry deaths in India (source: NCRB).

Arranged Marriages: Arranged marriages remain common in India, with families playing a significant role in choosing partners. The priorities in these marriages often include caste, economic status, and family reputation over individual preferences. This control over marriage choices significantly limits women's autonomy and personal freedom, pressuring them to comply with family decisions. Caste endogamy, or marriages within the same caste, is strongly encouraged, reinforcing caste hierarchies and social stratification.

Domestic Responsibilities

Gendered Division of Labour: Traditional gender roles assign domestic responsibilities such as cooking, cleaning, and childcare primarily to women, regardless of their professional commitments. This expectation creates a "double burden" for women, where they must manage household duties alongside their professional roles. Such a burden limits their career advancement and opportunities. A study by the International Labour Organization (ILO) found that Indian women spend 297 minutes per day on unpaid domestic work, compared to 31 minutes for men (source: ILO).

Impact on Careers: The expectation to prioritize family and household duties over personal and professional aspirations results in many women either leaving the workforce or remaining in lower positions without career growth opportunities. Social norms and cultural expectations reinforce the idea that women should prioritize family responsibilities, thereby limiting their potential for professional success.

Economic Dependence: The economic contribution of women's unpaid domestic labour is often undervalued, which contributes to their financial dependence on male family members. This dependence reinforces patriarchal structures within the family, making it difficult for women to assert their rights and achieve economic independence.

Case Studies and Examples

Dowry Deaths: The high-profile case of Nisha Sharma in 2003 brought significant attention to dowry-related violence. Despite laws against dowry, Nisha's case highlighted how entrenched these practices remain. Nisha called off her wedding on the wedding day itself when her prospective in-laws demanded more dowry, and she reported the incident to the police. This act of defiance was widely covered in the media, bringing attention to the ongoing issue of dowry violence in India (source: The Hindu).

Arranged Marriages and Caste Endogamy: A case from Tamil Nadu in 2016 involved a young Dalit man, Shankar, who was killed for marrying an upper-caste girl. The girl's family opposed the marriage due to caste differences and orchestrated the murder to uphold caste honour. This tragic incident underscores the persistence of caste-based discrimination and violence in marriage practices (source: BBC).

Economic Dependence and Domestic Labour: According to a report by the National Sample Survey Office (NSSO), women in India spend an average of 19.5% of their time on unpaid domestic work compared to 2.6% by men. This imbalance highlights the significant gender disparity in domestic labour and its impact on women's economic independence and professional advancement (source: NSSO).

The persistence of patriarchal attitudes in modern India significantly impacts women's roles within the family and household dynamics. Practices such as dowry and arranged marriages continue to limit women's autonomy, while traditional gender roles confine them to domestic responsibilities. Despite legal reforms and increasing participation in education and the workforce, enduring patriarchal norms and economic dependence on men remain substantial barriers to achieving full gender equality. Addressing these issues requires continuous effort to change societal attitudes, enforce existing laws, and promote gender equality across all sectors of society.

Workplace and Economic Participation

Gender Pay Gap

Wage Disparity: In India, women frequently earn less than men for performing similar work. This gender pay gap is a persistent issue across various sectors and industries, reflecting deep-rooted gender biases and structural inequalities. Women often face wage discrimination where their contributions are undervalued compared to their male counterparts. According to the World Economic Forum's Global Gender Gap Report 2020, women in India earn approximately 65% of what men earn for similar work. This significant pay gap highlights the economic disadvantages that women continue to face despite their increasing participation in the workforce. The report underscores the need for targeted interventions to address wage inequality and promote fair compensation practices (World Economic

Forum).

Causes: Several factors contribute to the gender pay gap, including gender-based discrimination, occupational segregation, and the undervaluation of women's work. Gender-based discrimination leads to unequal pay for equal work as employers may undervalue the work performed by women or assign them to lower-paying roles. Occupational segregation sees women concentrated in lower-paying sectors and roles, such as education, healthcare, and administrative support, while men dominate higher-paying fields like engineering and finance. Moreover, jobs typically performed by women, such as caregiving and teaching, are often undervalued and underpaid compared to roles dominated by men.

Leadership Roles

Women are significantly underrepresented in leadership and decision-making positions in the workplace. Despite their qualifications and capabilities, they often face barriers that hinder their advancement to top management roles. The "glass ceiling" is a metaphor for the invisible barriers that prevent women from reaching the highest levels of leadership. These structural barriers include gender biases, stereotypes, and institutional practices that favour men. Women are often perceived as less competent or less committed to their careers due to traditional gender roles and expectations. Additionally, the lack of access to mentorship and professional networks further hinders women's career progression. Professional networks and mentors play a crucial role in career advancement by providing guidance, support, and opportunities. However, women often have limited access to these networks, which are predominantly male dominated.

Case Studies and Examples

In the Indian IT sector, a study by the Korn Ferry Hay Group found that women earn 20% less than men in comparable roles. This disparity is not limited to entry-level positions but extends to senior roles as well (Korn Ferry Hay Group). Furthermore, a report by Catalyst found that women hold only 14.6% of executive positions in India's largest companies. This underrepresentation highlights the systemic barriers women face in advancing to leadership roles (Catalyst). The experiences of women in

India's corporate sector, such as in banking and finance, illustrate the challenges posed by the glass ceiling. Despite policies aimed at promoting gender diversity, women still struggle to break into top executive roles due to entrenched biases and a lack of supportive infrastructure.

Programs like the Confederation of Indian Industry's (CII) Indian Women Network (IWN) aim to bridge this gap by providing networking opportunities and mentorship to women professionals. These initiatives are crucial for empowering women and fostering a more inclusive work environment (CII Indian Women Network).

The gender pay gap and underrepresentation in leadership roles are significant challenges facing women in India's workforce. Despite progress in educational attainment and workforce participation, systemic barriers such as wage disparity, the glass ceiling, and lack of access to mentorship continue to impede women's career advancement. Addressing these issues requires comprehensive strategies, including policy interventions, organizational reforms, and cultural shifts to promote gender equality and create a more equitable work environment. By dismantling these barriers, India can harness the full potential of its female workforce, driving economic growth and social progress.

Workplace Harassment

Prevalence

Sexual harassment at the workplace is a widespread issue that affects women across various sectors in India. Despite increased awareness and legal frameworks aimed at protecting women, harassment remains a significant challenge. According to a survey by the Indian National Bar Association, a staggering 70% of women reported experiencing some form of workplace harassment. This high prevalence underscores the pervasive nature of the problem and highlights the urgent need for effective interventions (Indian National Bar Association).

Forms of Harassment

Workplace harassment manifests in various forms, ranging from inappropriate comments and unwanted advances to more severe issues such as quid pro quo arrangements and hostile work environments. Inappropriate comments and sexual innuendos are common, often creating an uncomfortable and unsafe atmosphere for women. Quid pro quo harassment involves demands for sexual favours in exchange for professional advancement or job security, while hostile work environments are characterized by pervasive discriminatory behaviour that undermines the dignity and performance of the victim (Nisha Rao, "Workplace Harassment: An Indian Perspective," Journal of Human Rights).

Inadequate Policies and Enforcement

Despite the enactment of the Sexual Harassment of Women at Workplace (Prevention, Prohibition, and Redressal) Act, 2013, the implementation and enforcement of these policies are often inadequate. This law mandates the creation of Internal Complaints Committees (ICCs) within organizations to address complaints of sexual harassment. However, many organizations fail to establish or effectively run these committees, leaving victims without proper recourse. The lack of training for ICC members and insufficient awareness about the law among employees further exacerbate the problem (Ministry of Women and Child Development).

Internal Committees

The law requires every organization to set up an Internal Complaints Committee (ICC) to handle complaints of sexual harassment. Despite this mandate, many organizations either do not have an ICC in place or have committees that are not functional or adequately trained. A report by the Ministry of Women and Child Development found that only 58% of companies had constituted ICCs, and of those, many were not adequately trained to handle cases effectively. This lack of compliance with legal requirements hampers the fight against workplace harassment and leaves many victims without a proper avenue for redressal (MWCD Report).

Fear of Retaliation

A significant barrier to addressing workplace harassment is the fear of retaliation. Victims often fear negative career repercussions, such as job loss, demotion, or professional ostracization, if they report incidents of harassment. This fear is compounded by a lack of faith in the complaint resolution process and concerns about confidentiality and fairness. As a result, many incidents go unreported, allowing perpetrators to continue their behaviour with impunity. The National Commission for Women (NCW) has highlighted that fear of retaliation is a primary reason for underreporting of workplace harassment cases (National Commission for Women).

Case Studies and Examples

Infosys Incident (2020): A senior executive at Infosys was accused of sexual harassment by a female employee. The incident led to an internal investigation, which eventually found the executive guilty, resulting in his resignation. This case underscored the importance of having robust internal mechanisms to address complaints and the role of corporate leadership in enforcing policies (The Hindu).

Tata Consultancy Services (TCS): In another instance, a female employee at TCS filed a complaint against a colleague for repeated inappropriate behaviour. The company's ICC promptly investigated the matter, leading to the dismissal of the perpetrator. This case exemplifies how effective internal committees can ensure a safe working environment for women (Economic Times).

Workplace harassment remains a significant issue in India, affecting women across various sectors. Despite the legal framework provided by the Sexual Harassment of Women at Workplace (Prevention, Prohibition, and Redressal) Act, 2013, the implementation and enforcement of policies are often inadequate. The prevalence of harassment, coupled with the fear of retaliation, discourages many victims from reporting incidents. To create a safer and more equitable workplace, it is crucial to ensure the effective functioning of Internal Complaints Committees, raise awareness about legal protections, and foster a culture of zero tolerance towards harassment. By addressing these challenges, India can make significant strides towards gender equality and workplace safety.

Political and Legal Systems

Underrepresentation

Women in India remain significantly underrepresented in political and decision-making positions. Despite India's democratic framework, which theoretically supports equal participation, women's presence in legislative bodies remains low. As of the 2019 general elections, women constitute only 14.39% of the Lok Sabha (House of the People) and 10.5% of the Rajya Sabha (Council of States) (Source: Lok Sabha and Rajya Sabha records).

Barriers

Several barriers impede women's political participation. Patriarchal attitudes within society and political parties discourage women from entering politics. Women often lack political support, financial resources, and face safety concerns, which further deter their political ambitions. Additionally, political campaigns can be financially demanding, and women often do not have the same access to funding and networks as their male counterparts.

Quotas and Reservations

Some states have implemented quotas for women in local governance (Panchayati Raj Institutions). For example, the 73rd and 74th Constitutional Amendments mandate that one-third of seats in local government bodies be reserved for women. These quotas have significantly increased women's participation at the grassroots level. However, at the national level, similar measures are absent, leading to continued underrepresentation.

Impact of Quotas

Research indicates that quotas can substantially improve women's political participation and influence. In states like West Bengal and Kerala, where quotas are effectively implemented, there has been a notable increase in women's involvement in local governance, leading to more attention to issues such as health, education, and sanitation (Source: World Bank).

Gender Bias in Law Enforcement

Gender bias is prevalent within law enforcement agencies in India. Police officers often exhibit prejudiced attitudes towards victims of gender-based violence, questioning their credibility or blaming them for their assault. This bias discourages victims from reporting crimes and seeking justice.

Victim-Blaming

Victim-blaming is a common issue in India, where societal attitudes often place the onus on women to prevent assault by adhering to conservative norms of dress and behaviour. This cultural mindset is reflected in law enforcement practices, where victims are sometimes interrogated about their actions rather than focusing on the perpetrator's behaviour (Source: Human Rights Watch).

Underreporting

Fear of not being taken seriously, social stigma, and potential retaliation discourage many women from reporting sexual violence. According to the National Crime Records Bureau (NCRB), many incidents of sexual violence go unreported, making it challenging to address the true extent of the problem (Source: NCRB).

Judicial Processes

The judicial system in India often exhibits biases that make it difficult for women to access justice. The process can be slow and re-traumatizing, with victims having to relive their experiences repeatedly during investigations and trials.

Case Backlog

Delays in legal proceedings and a significant backlog of cases impede timely justice. For example, as of 2020, over 133,000 rape cases were pending trial in Indian courts, reflecting systemic inefficiencies and the slow pace of judicial processes (Source: Ministry of Law and Justice).

Conviction Rates

Low conviction rates in cases of sexual violence highlight systemic issues within the judiciary. In 2019, the conviction rate for rape cases was only

27.8%, indicating that many perpetrators evade justice due to procedural delays, insufficient evidence, and biases within the system (Source: NCRB).

Case Studies and Real-Life Examples

Unnao Rape Case (2017):

A young girl accused BJP legislator Kuldeep Singh Sengar of raping her in Unnao, Uttar Pradesh. Despite her complaint, local police initially took no action, reflecting the influence and protection afforded to the perpetrator by the political system. It was only after significant public outrage and media attention that action was taken. Sengar was eventually convicted and sentenced to life imprisonment, but the case highlighted the systemic barriers victims face when the accused have political connections (Source: The Hindu).

Hathras Gang Rape Case (2020):

A 19-year-old Dalit woman was allegedly gang-raped by upper-caste men in Hathras, Uttar Pradesh. The local police's handling of the case, including the hurried cremation of the victim's body without her family's consent, sparked nationwide outrage. This case underscored the intersection of gender, caste, and systemic biases in law enforcement. The judicial process faced criticism for delays and perceived insensitivity towards the victim's family (Source: The Indian Express).

Analysis of a High-Profile Case of Workplace Harassment

A prominent case that brought significant attention to workplace harassment in India involved the allegations against M.J. Akbar, a well-known editor and former Minister of State for External Affairs. In October 2018, journalist Priya Ramani accused Akbar of sexual harassment, which he denied. This accusation was part of the broader #MeToo movement that gained momentum in India around the same time.

The allegations against M.J. Akbar became a significant part of the #McToo movement in India, where numerous women came forward to share their experiences of sexual harassment and abuse in the workplace.

This movement highlighted the prevalence of workplace harassment and the systemic issues that allow such behaviour to persist. It empowered many women to speak out, often for the first time, about their experiences of harassment and abuse (BBC News).

The high-profile nature of the case spurred discussions about the effectiveness of workplace harassment laws in India. It underscored the need for stricter enforcement of the Sexual Harassment of Women at Workplace (Prevention, Prohibition, and Redressal) Act, 2013. The case prompted calls for better implementation of the law, more comprehensive training programs for Internal Complaints Committees (ICCs), and a more transparent process for handling complaints (The Hindu).

The case also contributed to a cultural shift regarding the issue of sexual harassment in the workplace. There was increased public awareness and discourse around the issue, leading to a broader societal recognition of the problem. Media coverage of the allegations and the subsequent legal proceedings kept the issue in the public eye, fostering a greater understanding of the challenges faced by victims of workplace harassment (The Indian Express).

The political and legal systems in India continue to reflect and reinforce patriarchal attitudes, resulting in significant challenges for women's representation and access to justice. Underrepresentation in political positions and gender bias in law enforcement and the judiciary perpetuate the cycle of gender inequality and violence. Addressing these issues requires comprehensive reforms, including the implementation of quotas, increased political support for women, and systemic changes within law enforcement and judicial processes. By fostering a more inclusive and equitable environment, India can ensure that women's voices are heard, and their rights are protected. The current manifestations of patriarchal attitudes in India are evident in various aspects of society, including family dynamics, workplace environments, and political systems. Traditional marriage practices, gendered division of labour, gender pay gaps, workplace harassment, underrepresentation in politics, and legal biases collectively contribute to the persistence of gender inequality. Case studies and real-life examples highlight the challenges faced by women in overcoming these barriers and the need for continued efforts to promote gender equality and dismantle patriarchal structures. By addressing these issues through legal reforms, education, advocacy, and cultural change, India can work towards creating a more equitable society for all.

Direct and Indirect Impacts of Patriarchy on Rape Culture

Normalization of Gender Violence

Films, Television Shows, and Advertisements: Media representations in India often depict women in subordinate roles, reinforcing stereotypes that normalize gender violence. In many Bollywood films, male aggression is frequently portrayed as romantic or desirable, suggesting that persistent, aggressive pursuit is an acceptable form of expressing love. For instance, popular movies often show male protagonists engaging in stalking or aggressive behaviour, which is eventually rewarded with the female character's affection, thus legitimizing such actions (Source: Bollywood film studies, media analysis reports).

Bollywood: Indian cinema has a significant impact on societal norms and attitudes. Bollywood films frequently glorify stalking and aggressive male behaviour towards women, framing it as a legitimate expression of love and masculinity. This portrayal perpetuates the notion that women should eventually succumb to male persistence, which can contribute to the normalization of harassment and violence (Source: Studies on Bollywood's impact on social norms).

Television Soaps: Indian TV dramas often depict women enduring and accepting domestic violence, thereby normalizing it as a part of married life. These soaps typically show female characters suffering in silence or enduring abuse for the sake of family honour, which can influence viewers' perceptions of domestic violence as an acceptable part of relationships (Source: Analysis of Indian television content).

Literature: Traditional literature frequently portrays women as passive and submissive, reinforcing gender hierarchies and the acceptability of male dominance. These narratives contribute to societal expectations that women should be obedient and accepting of male authority, perpetuating gender-based violence (Source: Analysis of traditional Indian literature).

Religious Texts: Religious scriptures, such as the Manusmriti, prescribe strict roles for women, emphasizing obedience and subordination to men. These texts reinforce patriarchal norms and justify the acceptability of gender violence by portraying it as divinely sanctioned. For example, the

Manusmriti states that women should always be under the control of their fathers, husbands, or sons, perpetuating the idea that women are inherently subordinate to men (Source: Manusmriti text analysis).

Religious Texts and Teachings: Religious teachings that prescribe strict gender roles and emphasize female subordination can reinforce patriarchal norms and justify gender-based violence. Such texts are often interpreted in ways that support the control and oppression of women, thereby perpetuating a culture that tolerates or even endorses gender violence (Source: Studies on religious texts and gender norms).

By examining these cultural narratives and their impacts on societal attitudes, it becomes clear how deeply entrenched gender norms and stereotypes contribute to the normalization of gender-based violence in India. Addressing these issues requires a comprehensive approach that includes media literacy, critical analysis of cultural content, and reforms in the portrayal of gender roles across various media platforms.

Socialization Processes

Early Socialization

Boys: From a young age, boys are socialized into traditional gender roles that endorse traits such as assertiveness, dominance, and aggression. These characteristics are often viewed as markers of masculinity. Boys are encouraged to be competitive and to exhibit control over their environment, which can translate into aggressive behaviours being tolerated or even praised. This socialization is evident in both family settings and educational environments, where boys are given more freedom and opportunities to assert themselves (Source: UNICEF India reports on child socialization).

Girls: In contrast, girls are socialized to be passive, nurturing, and compliant, traits that are viewed as markers of femininity. Girls are often encouraged to prioritize relationships and caregiving roles over personal ambition. This early socialization restricts their opportunities for self-expression and assertiveness, reinforcing the notion that submissive behaviour is desirable and appropriate for women (Source: Reports on gender socialization by UN Women).

Family Dynamics

Gender Roles Reinforcement: Within the family, traditional gender roles are continually reinforced. Boys are often given more freedom to explore and engage in various activities, while girls are expected to conform to more restrictive norms, such as helping with household chores and adhering to stricter curfews. This disparity in treatment reinforces the belief that boys are entitled to more autonomy and authority than girls (Source: Studies on family dynamics by the Indian Journal of Gender Studies).

Parental Attitudes: Parents may unconsciously perpetuate gender stereotypes by treating their sons and daughters differently. For example, they might praise boys for assertive behaviour while discouraging girls from being too outspoken or independent. These differential treatments can create an environment where boys grow up with a sense of entitlement and girls with a sense of limitation, perpetuating a cycle of inequality and acceptance of male aggression (Source: Parenting and gender studies by the Journal of Family Issues).

Educational Institutions

Gendered Curriculum: Schools and colleges often perpetuate gender stereotypes through curricula that emphasize traditional gender roles. Textbooks and educational materials frequently depict men in active, dominant roles and women in passive, supportive roles. This educational bias reinforces patriarchal norms and limits the potential for girls to envision themselves in diverse and powerful roles (Source: Educational materials review by the National Council of Educational Research and Training (NCERT)).

Teacher Attitudes: Teachers may also play a role in reinforcing gender stereotypes, consciously or unconsciously, through their interactions with students. Boys may be encouraged to take on leadership roles and engage in competitive activities, while girls may be steered towards more nurturing and cooperative roles. These biases in educational settings further entrench traditional gender roles (Source: Teacher attitudes study by the International Journal of Educational Development).

Peer Pressure: Socialization within peer groups can further entrench gender stereotypes. Boys often face peer pressure to exhibit aggressive behaviour and dominance to gain social acceptance and status. Conversely, girls may be pressured to conform to submissive and passive roles to fit in with societal expectations. This peer influence reinforces the gender norms established in early childhood and perpetuates the acceptance of male aggression (Source: Peer influence research by the Journal of Adolescent Health).

By understanding the socialization processes that shape gender roles from a young age, we can better address the root causes of gender-based violence and inequality. Interventions aimed at changing these early socialization patterns are crucial for creating a more equitable and respectful society.

Cultural Attitudes

Victim-Blaming: In many parts of India, societal attitudes tend to blame victims of sexual violence rather than the perpetrators. This pervasive mindset suggests that victims somehow invited the assault through their behaviour, attire, or lifestyle choices. For instance, questions about what the victim was wearing, why she was out late, or whether she was alone often arise, diverting attention from the actions of the perpetrator. Such attitudes are deeply ingrained in cultural norms and are reinforced by media portrayals and public discourse (Source: International Journal of Comparative Sociology).

Public Perception: The public often harbours victim-blaming attitudes, leading to a general tendency to scrutinize the victim's actions rather than condemning the attacker. This perception is reflected in social media commentary, news reports, and even statements by public officials. For example, after the 2012 Delhi gang rape, some public figures made statements implying that the victim's behaviour might have contributed to the crime, sparking outrage and debate (Source: BBC News, The Hindu).

Impact on Reporting: Victim-blaming attitudes significantly discourage victims from reporting sexual violence. The fear of being blamed or shamed can deter victims from seeking justice, leading to underreporting. Studies have shown that many victims choose not to report their assaults due to the anticipated negative response from law enforcement, family, and the community (Source: Research by UN Women).

Honour and Shame: Cultural norms that tie family honour to women's chastity and behaviour play a significant role in silencing victims. In many communities, a woman's value and the family's reputation are closely linked to her perceived purity and modesty. Sexual violence against a woman is seen as a stain on the family's honour, leading families to suppress such incidents to protect their reputation (Source: Gender and Society Journal).

Family Pressure: Families may pressure victims to remain silent about their assault to avoid bringing shame upon themselves. This pressure is particularly intense in conservative and traditional communities where family honour is paramount. Victims are often discouraged from seeking justice or speaking out, perpetuating a cycle of silence and impunity for the perpetrators. This family-imposed silence further marginalizes the victim, compounding their trauma (Source: International Journal of Sociology and Social Policy).

Community Repercussions: Victims who speak out about sexual violence often face severe repercussions from their communities, including ostracization and social exclusion. This social punishment can be as damaging as the assault itself, leading many victims to choose silence over seeking justice. Community reactions can include stigmatization, gossip, and even physical threats, which serve to reinforce the culture of silence around sexual violence (Source: The Indian Journal of Social Work).

By understanding these cultural attitudes and their impact on victims, it becomes clear that societal change is crucial for addressing the issue of sexual violence. Efforts to combat victim-blaming and promote a more supportive environment for survivors are essential for breaking the cycle of silence and impunity. Addressing these deep-seated cultural norms requires comprehensive education, public awareness campaigns, and legal reforms to protect and empower victims of sexual violence.

Institutional Responses

Police

Reflecting Societal Biases: Law enforcement agencies often mirror the societal biases that prevail in the larger community. Victims of sexual violence may be treated with suspicion or outright hostility when they approach the police. This mistrust can stem from deep-seated prejudices against women and the pervasive belief in victim-blaming narratives.

Insensitivity: Instances of police insensitivity are common, with officers sometimes blaming victims for their assault or dismissing their complaints as trivial. This insensitivity can manifest in questioning the victim's character, attire, or behaviour at the time of the assault, thereby adding to their trauma and discouraging others from reporting such crimes. According to a study by the Human Rights Watch, victims often encounter a dismissive or hostile attitude when they attempt to file a complaint (Source: Human Rights Watch).

Corruption: Corruption within the police force can exacerbate the problem, particularly when perpetrators are influential or wealthy. There have been numerous cases where police have been accused of protecting the accused in exchange for bribes or due to political pressure. This corruption not only hampers the investigation but also sends a message of impunity to potential offenders (Source: Transparency International India).

Judicial System

Perpetuating Victim-Blaming Attitudes: The judiciary, too, can perpetuate societal biases against victims of sexual violence. Judges may harbour outdated or patriarchal views, leading to judgments that blame victims for their assault. This can include questioning the victim's credibility based on her lifestyle, behaviour, or prior sexual history.

Lengthy Trials: The judicial process in India is notoriously slow, with cases dragging on for years. These lengthy trials can be particularly gruelling for victims of sexual violence, who may be retraumatized by the prolonged exposure to the legal system. The delay in justice serves as a significant deterrent for victims considering legal action (Source: National Judicial Data Grid).

Low Conviction Rates: Low conviction rates in cases of sexual violence reflect systemic failures within the judicial system. Factors contributing to this include inadequate evidence collection, poor prosecution, and judicial bias. The National Crime Records Bureau (NCRB) reports that the conviction rate for rape cases in India was just 27.2% in 2019, indicating a serious gap in the justice delivery system (Source: National Crime Records Bureau (NCRB)).

Healthcare

Lack of Training: Healthcare providers often lack the necessary training to handle cases of sexual violence sensitively and appropriately. Victims may not receive the compassionate care they need, and healthcare providers may fail to document injuries properly or provide adequate forensic evidence for legal proceedings.

Forensic Examination: The handling of forensic examinations can be insensitive and poorly managed. There are numerous reports of victims being retraumatized by the invasive and often humiliating procedures. Furthermore, the lack of standardized protocols can result in the loss or contamination of crucial evidence, undermining the victim's case (Source: The Lancet).

In summary, institutional responses to sexual violence in India are often marred by societal biases, insensitivity, corruption, and systemic inefficiencies. These factors collectively contribute to underreporting, prolonged legal battles, low conviction rates, and additional trauma for victims. Addressing these issues requires comprehensive reforms in law enforcement, judicial processes, and healthcare systems, alongside widespread societal education to change attitudes towards victims of sexual violence.

Sexual Autonomy and Control

Female Sexuality

Control Over Women's Bodies: Patriarchy in India is deeply rooted in controlling women's bodies and sexuality to maintain male dominance and social order. This control is exerted through various societal, cultural, and legal mechanisms that limit women's autonomy and reinforce traditional gender roles.

Purity and Honour: A significant aspect of this control is the societal emphasis on female purity and honour. Women are often seen as bearers of family honour, and their behaviour is closely monitored to ensure they conform to societal expectations of chastity and modesty. This emphasis on purity leads to strict controls on women's sexual behaviour, including dress codes, curfews, and surveillance by family members. For instance, in many communities, the concept of "izzat" (honour) is tied to a woman's virginity, and any deviation is seen as a direct affront to family honour (Source: "Women and Honour: Some Notes on Women in the Personal Laws of India" by Flavia Agnes).

Sexual Violence: Sexual violence is frequently used as a tool to enforce patriarchal norms and punish women who defy traditional roles. Rape and other forms of sexual violence serve to intimidate and control women, reinforcing their subordinate status. For example, in rural areas, caste-based sexual violence is often used to reinforce social hierarchies and punish Dalit women for stepping outside their prescribed roles (Source: "The Caste System: Effects on Poverty in India, Nepal and Sri Lanka" by Anupama Rao).

Reproductive Rights: Women's autonomy over their reproductive choices is often restricted by both societal and legal norms. Decisions regarding childbirth and family planning are frequently made by husbands or extended family members, rather than the women themselves. Societal pressure to produce male heirs and the preference for sons can lead to practices like sex-selective abortions and female infanticide.

Access to Contraception: Access to contraception and reproductive healthcare is limited for many women, particularly in rural and conservative areas. Cultural stigmas surrounding the use of contraception and the prioritization of male approval in reproductive decisions restrict women's ability to control their own bodies. A study by the Guttmacher Institute found that only 47% of married women in India use modern contraceptive methods, indicating significant barriers to accessing reproductive health services (Source: Guttmacher Institute).

Forced Marriages and Childbearing: Practices like forced marriages and societal expectations around childbearing further limit women's autonomy. Forced marriages, often to maintain family honour or economic stability, remove women's ability to choose their partners and control their sexual and reproductive lives. Early marriages, prevalent in certain regions, are particularly detrimental, as young girls are forced into childbearing at a time when they should be focusing on their education and personal development. According to UNICEF, India has one of the highest rates of child marriages, with 27% of girls married before the age of 18 (Source: UNICEF).

In summary, patriarchal control over women's bodies and sexuality is a critical aspect of maintaining gender hierarchies in India. This control is manifested through societal expectations of purity and honour, the use of sexual violence as a tool of enforcement, and restrictions on reproductive rights and autonomy. Addressing these issues requires challenging deeply ingrained cultural norms and implementing legal reforms to protect and empower women.

Legal and Social Restrictions

Restrictive Laws

Marital Rape: One of the most glaring legal issues in India is the non-recognition of marital rape. Under current Indian law, marital rape is not considered a criminal offense unless the wife is below a certain age. This legal stance reflects deep-seated patriarchal views that regard a wife as the husband's property, thus entitling him to sexual access regardless of her consent. This lack of recognition perpetuates a culture of male entitlement to women's bodies within marriage and undermines women's autonomy and rights. This legal gap not only perpetuates rape culture but also fails to provide necessary protection and justice to married women who experience sexual violence from their spouses (Source: Human Rights Watch).

Dress Codes and Mobility Restrictions: Legal and societal restrictions on women's dress and mobility further reinforce patriarchal control. Women are often subjected to dress codes imposed by societal norms or local laws, which dictate what is considered "modest" or "appropriate." These restrictions are justified under the guise of protecting women's honour or ensuring their safety but ultimately serve to control women's bodies and freedom. For instance, many educational institutions enforce strict dress codes for female students, limiting their ability to express themselves freely and reinforcing gender stereotypes (Source: The Guardian).

Social Practices

Purdah and Seclusion: Cultural practices like purdah (veil) and the seclusion of women are prevalent in many parts of India. These practices limit women's visibility and participation in public life, effectively confining them to the domestic sphere. The practice of purdah is often justified as a means of protecting women's honour, but it reinforces their subordination and restricts their freedom. This seclusion contributes to an environment where women's autonomy is severely limited, and their value is tied to their adherence to restrictive gender norms (Source: "Women and Purdah in India" by Minu Mathur).

Honour Killings: Honour killings are an extreme manifestation of patriarchal control, where women are murdered by their family members for allegedly bringing dishonour to the family. Reasons for honour killings can include refusing an arranged marriage, seeking a divorce, having a relationship outside of marriage, or even being a victim of sexual assault. These acts are justified by the perpetrators as necessary to restore the family's honour, but they are clear violations of women's rights and autonomy. Despite being illegal, honour killings continue to occur, particularly in rural and conservative communities, due to deeply ingrained cultural norms and the lack of effective law enforcement (Source: United Nations Population Fund).

Impact on Women's Lives: These legal and social restrictions significantly impact women's lives, limiting their freedom and perpetuating a culture of violence and control. For instance, the legal non-recognition of marital rape denies married women the right to consent, reinforcing the idea that their bodies are not their own. Dress codes and mobility restrictions limit women's ability to participate fully in public life and express themselves freely. Practices like purdah and honour killings further entrench gender inequalities and create an environment where women's autonomy is severely restricted.

Addressing these issues requires a multi-faceted approach, including legal reforms to recognize and criminalize marital rape, the abolition of restrictive dress codes, and stronger enforcement of laws against honour killings. Additionally, societal attitudes must be challenged through education and awareness campaigns that promote gender equality and respect for women's rights. By tackling both legal and social restrictions, it is possible to create a more equitable society where women can live free from violence and control.

Patriarchy directly and indirectly impacts rape culture by normalizing gender violence, perpetuating victim-blaming attitudes, and restricting women's autonomy. Cultural narratives, socialization processes, and institutional responses collectively contribute to an environment where sexual violence is tolerated and even justified. Addressing these deep-rooted issues requires comprehensive societal change, including legal reforms, education, and shifts in cultural attitudes towards gender equality and women's rights. By challenging and dismantling patriarchal norms, society can move towards reducing sexual violence and creating a safer and more equitable environment for all individuals.

Statistical Correlations

Data Analysis

Correlation Between Patriarchal Attitudes and High Rates of Sexual Violence; Regional Variations

An analysis of the National Crime Records Bureau (NCRB) data reveals significant regional variations in reported cases of sexual violence across India. This variation often correlates with the strength of patriarchal norms prevalent in different regions. States such as Uttar Pradesh, Madhya Pradesh, and Rajasthan consistently report higher incidences of sexual violence, characterized by deeply entrenched patriarchal values that reinforce male dominance and control over women.

Uttar Pradesh: This state frequently records the highest number of rape cases annually. According to the NCRB report, Uttar Pradesh reported over 3,065 rape cases in 2019 alone (Source: NCRB). The state's strong patriarchal norms and rigid caste dynamics contribute significantly to the prevalence of sexual violence. A notable case is the Unnao rape incident, where a young girl was raped by a powerful local politician, highlighting the intersection of power, gender, and violence. The political influence of the perpetrator initially delayed justice, reflecting how power dynamics can obstruct legal processes and perpetuate a culture of impunity (Source: The Hindu).

Madhya Pradesh: Similarly, Madhya Pradesh shows high rates of sexual violence, with 2,485 rape cases reported in 2019 (Source: NCRB). Societal attitudes in Madhya Pradesh often reinforce male dominance and aggression, contributing to the high incidence of sexual violence. The Bhopal gang rape case of 2017, where a young woman was brutally raped by multiple men while returning from her coaching class, underscores the pervasive nature of patriarchal violence in the state. The case drew significant media attention and public outcry, emphasizing the urgent need for systemic changes (Source: Times of India).

Kerala and Tamil Nadu: Conversely, states like Kerala and Tamil Nadu, which have relatively higher female literacy rates and more progressive gender norms, report lower incidences of sexual violence. Kerala reported 1,099 rape cases in 2019, significantly lower than states with stronger patriarchal structures (Source: NCRB). These states have implemented various educational and social programs aimed at promoting gender equality and empowering women. For instance, Kerala's high literacy rates and effective grassroots campaigns on gender equality contribute to its lower rates of sexual violence (Source: Economic and Political Weekly).

Patriarchal Attitudes: Regions with higher rates of sexual violence often exhibit strong adherence to traditional gender roles, where male dominance and control over female sexuality are normalized. In these areas, the belief in male superiority and entitlement to women's bodies fosters an environment where sexual violence is more likely to occur. For example, in rural areas of Rajasthan, cultural practices and societal expectations place heavy emphasis on preserving family honour, often at the expense of women's autonomy and safety (Source: The Indian Express).

Honour -Based Societies: Societies that place a high value on family honour tied to female chastity are more likely to experience underreporting of sexual violence due to the stigma attached to victims. For instance, in many parts of rural Rajasthan, the fear of bringing dishonour to the family often leads to cases of rape being settled informally within the community rather than being reported to the authorities. This societal pressure not only silences victims but also perpetuates a culture of impunity for perpetrators (Source: The Times of India).

The correlation between patriarchal attitudes and the incidence of sexual violence in India highlights the critical role that societal norms play in perpetuating gender-based violence. States with deeply entrenched patriarchal values tend to have higher rates of sexual violence, while states with more progressive gender norms show lower rates. Addressing this issue requires a multifaceted approach that includes legal reforms, education, and cultural change to effectively combat sexual violence and promote gender equality across all regions of India. By understanding and addressing these regional variations and underlying cultural factors, India can move towards a safer and more equitable society for all its citizens. (Sources: National Crime Records Bureau (NCRB) Reports: NCRB, Case Study: Unnao Rape Incident - The Hindu, Case Study: Bhopal Gang Rape - Times of India, Economic and Social Analysis - Economic and Political Weekly, Social Attitudes and Practices - The Indian Express)

Comparative Studies: Analysis of Data from Different States and Countries to Highlight the Impact of Patriarchal Norms

India vs. Scandinavia

Gender Equality and Legal Frameworks: Comparative studies between India and Scandinavian countries such as Sweden and Norway highlight the significant impact of cultural acceptance of gender equality on the rates of sexual violence. Scandinavian countries are known for their robust legal frameworks that protect women's rights and promote gender equality, leading to lower incidences of sexual violence.

Sweden and Norway: These countries have comprehensive laws and social policies aimed at promoting gender equality. For example, Sweden's gender equality policies, which include equal parental leave and stringent laws against gender-based violence, contribute to creating a safer environment for women (Source: World Economic Forum). Despite occasional reports of sexual violence, the overall incidence is lower compared to India due to the societal acceptance of gender equality and the effective enforcement of laws.

India: In contrast, India, with its deeply entrenched patriarchal norms, reports higher incidences of sexual violence. The National Crime Records Bureau (NCRB) data for 2019 recorded 32,033 cases of rape, reflecting the pervasive issue of gender-based violence. The strong patriarchal norms in many Indian states, such as Uttar Pradesh and Madhya Pradesh, contribute to the high rates of sexual violence (Source: NCRB).

Cultural Impact

Countries with Strong Patriarchal Norms: Countries with deeply entrenched patriarchal norms, particularly in South Asia and the Middle East, often experience higher incidences of sexual violence and face greater barriers to reporting and justice. These norms reinforce male control and female subordination, making it difficult for women to seek help or justice.

Afghanistan and Pakistan: These countries exhibit trends similar to India, with high levels of gender-based violence supported by strong patriarchal norms. In Afghanistan, reports of sexual violence are common, but cultural and legal barriers often prevent victims from coming forward. The situation in Pakistan is comparable, where cultural stigmatization and fear of retribution hinder women from reporting sexual crimes (Source: Human Rights Watch).

United States

Cultural Factors and Sexual Violence: While the United States has lower levels of overtly patriarchal norms compared to India, cultural factors such as victim-blaming and media portrayal of women contribute to significant levels of sexual violence. According to the Rape, Abuse & Incest National Network (RAINN), an American is sexually assaulted every 68 seconds (Source: RAINN).

#MeToo Movement: Movements like #MeToo have been instrumental in increasing awareness of sexual violence and pushing for systemic change. The #MeToo movement, which began in the United States and quickly spread globally, has highlighted ongoing issues of sexual harassment and assault. It has empowered survivors to speak out and demand justice, showcasing the impact of activism on societal attitudes and legal reforms (Source: The New York Times).

Comparative Insights: The comparison between India and these countries underscores the influence of cultural norms on the incidence and reporting of sexual violence. In Scandinavian countries, the cultural acceptance of gender equality and robust legal frameworks contribute to lower rates of violence against women. Conversely, in countries with strong patriarchal norms, such as India, Afghanistan, and Pakistan, higher incidences of sexual violence and significant barriers to justice persist. The United States, while not as overtly patriarchal, still faces cultural challenges that perpetuate sexual violence, demonstrating that achieving gender equality requires continuous effort across all dimensions of society. (Sources: World Economic Forum: World Economic Forum, National Crime Records Bureau (NCRB): NCRB, Human Rights Watch: Human Rights Watch, Rape, Abuse & Incest National Network (RAINN): RAINN, The New York Times: The New York Times)

Reporting and Conviction Rates

Statistical Evidence of Underreporting Due to Societal and Institutional Barriers

Underreporting in India: Estimates suggest that only a fraction of sexual violence cases are reported to authorities in India. Cultural stigma surrounding sexual violence, fear of retaliation from perpetrators, and a pervasive lack of trust in the police and judicial systems contribute to this significant underreporting. Victims often fear social ostracism, loss of family honour , and even further violence if they come forward with their allegations.

NCRB Data: According to the National Crime Records Bureau (NCRB), there were 28,046 reported cases of rape in 2020 (Source: NCRB). However, various studies and surveys suggest that the actual incidence of sexual violence is much higher. NGOs like Human Rights Watch estimate that the true number of cases could be significantly higher, as many victims do not report due to the barriers they face.

National Family Health Survey (NFHS-4): The NFHS-4, conducted in 2015-16, revealed that 99% of sexual violence cases go unreported (Source: NFHS-4). This highlights the massive gap between the actual occurrence of sexual violence and the number of cases reported to authorities. The survey's findings underscore the deep-rooted cultural and societal factors that discourage victims from seeking justice.

Social and Institutional Barriers: Victims of sexual violence in India often face immense societal pressure to remain silent. Cultural norms frequently place the burden of honour on women, leading to victim-blaming and further stigmatization. This discourages victims from reporting sexual violence, fearing that they will be held responsible for the crime. Additionally, institutional apathy and corruption within law enforcement agencies further discourage victims from seeking justice. The insensitive handling of cases by police, including delays and failure to register complaints, adds to the victims' trauma and deters them from reporting.

Caste Dynamics: Lower-caste women, particularly Dalits, face even greater barriers due to compounded discrimination based on both gender and caste. These women are often economically dependent on their abusers, making it more difficult for them to report crimes and seek justice. The intersection of caste and gender discrimination means that Dalit women are disproportionately affected by sexual violence and face significant hurdles in accessing justice (Source: Human Rights Watch).

Case Studies

Hathras Gang Rape (2020): In this case, a 19-year-old Dalit woman was allegedly gang-raped and murdered by upper-caste men in Hathras, Uttar Pradesh. The police's handling of the case, including the hurried cremation of the victim's body without her family's consent, sparked outrage and accusations of bias and cover-up. This case underscores the compounded barriers faced by lower-caste women and the systemic issues within law enforcement (Source: The Indian Express).

Badaun Gang Rape (2014): Two teenage Dalit girls were found hanging from a tree in Badaun, Uttar Pradesh, after being gang-raped by upper-caste men. The initial police response was dismissive, and the case only gained traction after media coverage and public outrage. The Badaun case highlights the intersection of caste and gender-based violence and the challenges in securing justice for marginalized communities (Source: BBC News).

Underreporting of sexual violence in India is a critical issue, driven by societal and institutional barriers. Cultural stigma, fear of retaliation, and lack of trust in the police and judicial systems discourage victims from coming forward. Lower-caste women face additional challenges due to caste-based discrimination and economic dependence. Addressing these barriers requires comprehensive legal and societal reforms to create a more supportive environment for victims and ensure justice is accessible to all.

Examination of Low Conviction Rates in Cases of Sexual Violence; Impact of Patriarchal Biases in the Judicial System

Low Conviction Rates: The conviction rates for rape cases in India are alarmingly low. As of 2019, the conviction rate for rape cases stood at approximately 27.8%, revealing deep-rooted systemic issues within the judicial process (Source: National Crime Records Bureau (NCRB)). This low rate underscores the numerous challenges victims face in securing justice, including legal, social, and procedural barriers.

Delays and Backlogs: One of the primary issues contributing to low conviction rates is the prolonged legal procedures and significant backlog of cases in the Indian judicial system. Delays in the judicial process can discourage victims from pursuing their cases and lead to the deterioration of evidence over time, making it more difficult to secure convictions. According to a report by the Ministry of Law and Justice, the average time for the disposal of rape cases is around eight years, contributing to a sense of disillusionment among victims (Source: Ministry of Law and Justice).

Bias in the Judicial System: Patriarchal attitudes within the judiciary often result in victim-blaming and lenient sentencing for perpetrators. Judges and legal professionals may hold biases that influence their decisions, such as questioning the victim's character or behaviour instead of focusing on the perpetrator's actions. This bias is evident in the way cases are sometimes handled, where the onus is placed on the victim to prove their innocence rather than on the accused to prove their guilt.

Example - Nirbhaya Case: In the infamous Nirbhaya case of 2012, where a young woman was brutally gang-raped and murdered in Delhi, the accused were eventually convicted and sentenced to death. However, the lengthy trial process, multiple appeals, and the time taken to carry out the sentences highlighted the systemic challenges in securing timely justice. Despite the public outrage and media attention that accelerated the judicial process in this case, it took several years to reach a final resolution (Source: BBC News).

Impact of Public Pressure: High-profile cases that garner significant media attention and public outrage tend to result in higher conviction rates and swifter justice. The Nirbhaya case is a prime example of how public pressure can lead to a more expedited judicial process. However, cases involving less prominent victims or those where the perpetrators have social and political influence often see lower conviction rates and face significant delays.

Example - Unnao Rape Case: The Unnao rape case, involving a powerful politician, Kuldeep Singh Sengar, exemplifies how power dynamics can influence judicial outcomes. Initially, local authorities mishandled the case, and there were significant delays in taking action against the accused. It was only after sustained media coverage and public pressure that the case gained momentum, leading to Sengar's conviction in 2019. This case highlights the disparity in how justice is served based on the social and political standing of the perpetrators (Source: The Hindu).

The low conviction rates in cases of sexual violence in India are indicative of broader systemic failures within the judicial system. Factors such as delays and backlogs, patriarchal biases within the judiciary, and the influence of public pressure all contribute to the challenges victims face in securing justice. Addressing these issues requires comprehensive judicial reforms, improved training for law enforcement and judicial officials, and greater public awareness to challenge and change entrenched patriarchal norms.

The statistical correlations between patriarchal attitudes and the incidence of sexual violence reveal the deep-rooted impact of cultural norms on gender-based violence. Regional variations within India, as well as comparative studies with other countries, underscore the role of societal structures in shaping the prevalence and reporting of sexual violence. Underreporting due to societal and institutional barriers, coupled with low conviction rates influenced by patriarchal biases, further perpetuates a culture of impunity. Addressing these issues requires comprehensive legal reforms, cultural change, and strengthened support systems to ensure justice and protection for victims of sexual violence.

Case Studies Illustrating the Influence of Patriarchy on Rape Culture

Nirbhaya Case (2012):

Background: The brutal gang rape of a 23-year-old woman in Delhi sparked nationwide protests and led to significant legal reforms.

Patriarchal Influence: The case highlighted the pervasive nature of patriarchal attitudes, with initial police inaction and victim-blaming comments from political figures.

Impact: The public outcry led to the Criminal Law (Amendment) Act, 2013, introducing stricter penalties for sexual offenses and fast-tracking trials for rape cases.

Unnao Rape Case (2017):

Background: A minor girl was raped by a powerful politician in Uttar Pradesh, leading to widespread media coverage and public outrage.

Patriarchal Influence: The victim faced significant challenges in seeking justice, including threats, intimidation, and initial reluctance from police to file a report.

Impact: The case underscored the influence of political power and patriarchal norms in obstructing justice for victims of sexual violence.

Hathras Case (2020):

Background: A 19-year-old Dalit woman was gang-raped and fatally injured by upper-caste men in Hathras, Uttar Pradesh.

Patriarchal Influence: The case highlighted the intersection of caste and gender oppression, with initial police mishandling and attempts to suppress the incident.

Impact: The case drew national and international attention, prompting discussions on caste-based violence and the need for systemic reforms.

Patriarchy exerts a profound influence on rape culture in India, shaping cultural narratives, institutional biases, and control over female sexuality. Media portrayals, societal norms, and institutional responses collectively perpetuate a culture that normalizes gender violence and hinders justice for victims. Statistical analyses and case studies underscore the correlation between patriarchal norms and high incidences of sexual violence. Addressing these issues requires a multifaceted approach, including legal reforms, cultural change, and efforts to empower women and challenge patriarchal structures. By dismantling patriarchal norms, society can move towards reducing sexual violence and promoting gender equality.

CHAPTER ELEVEN

Cultural and Social Factors

Impact of Conservatism and Traditional Values

Definition and Characteristics of Conservatism in India

Conservatism in India is characterized by a strong preference for traditional values and a resistance to social change. This ideological stance emphasizes the preservation of established customs, social structures, and religious practices, viewing them as essential to maintaining social order and continuity. In the Indian context, conservatism manifests in various ways, deeply influencing societal attitudes and behaviours, particularly regarding gender norms and roles.

Emphasis on Family and Community

In conservative thought, family and community are paramount, often taking precedence over individual rights and freedoms. The family unit is considered the cornerstone of society, and maintaining family honour and cohesion is of utmost importance. This emphasis on family often translates into expectations for women to prioritize their roles as daughters, wives, and mothers, subordinating their personal ambitions and autonomy to familial duties. Community norms and values play a crucial role in regulating behaviour, with social conformity being highly valued. Deviations from traditional roles are often met with social disapproval or ostracization, reinforcing the pressure to adhere to established gender norms.

Religious Influence

Religion is a significant pillar of conservatism in India, with major faiths such as Hinduism, Islam, Christianity, and Sikhism providing frameworks for social behaviour and gender norms. Religious texts and teachings often dictate the roles and responsibilities of men and women, emphasizing gender-specific duties and virtues. For instance, Hinduism, with its extensive scriptures like the Manusmriti, prescribes distinct roles for men and women, often placing women in subordinate positions. Similarly, Islamic teachings emphasize modesty and family responsibilities for women, while Christian and Sikh doctrines also advocate for traditional gender roles within the family and community. Religious conservatism often resists changes that challenge these established norms, viewing them as integral to the moral and spiritual fabric of society.

Patriarchal Structure

Conservatism in India frequently reinforces patriarchal structures, maintaining traditional gender roles where men hold authority and women are confined to domestic spheres. Patriarchal norms dictate that men are the primary breadwinners and decision-makers, while women are responsible for child-rearing and managing the household. This division of labour is not just a social expectation but is often seen as a natural order, justified by religious and cultural beliefs. The patriarchal mindset also manifests in practices such as dowry, child marriage, and restrictions on women's mobility and education. These practices are defended as preserving social stability and family honour, despite their detrimental impact on women's rights and well-being.

Resistance to Western Influence

Conservative groups in India often resist Western cultural influences, advocating for the preservation of indigenous traditions and customs. This resistance stems from a desire to protect Indian identity and values from perceived erosion by Western ideologies, which are often associated with individualism, liberalism, and gender equality. The influence of Western culture is seen as a threat to traditional social structures and moral values. As a result, there is a strong push to reinforce cultural norms that emphasize collective over individual interests, modesty over self-expression, and familial duty over personal freedom. This resistance to Western influence is particularly evident in debates over women's rights and gender equality, where conservative voices argue against adopting Western models of gender relations and advocate for solutions rooted in Indian cultural and religious traditions.

Conservatism in India is a complex and multifaceted ideology that deeply influences gender norms and societal attitudes. It emphasizes the preservation of traditional values, family and community cohesion, religious teachings, and patriarchal structures, while resisting Western cultural influences. These characteristics of conservatism play a significant role in shaping the roles and expectations of men and women in Indian society, often reinforcing gender inequality and limiting women's autonomy and opportunities. Addressing these conservative norms and promoting gender equality requires a nuanced understanding of the cultural and religious contexts and sustained efforts to challenge and transform deep-seated beliefs and practices.

How Conservative Values Reinforce Gender Roles

Gender Segregation

In India, conservative values strongly emphasize distinct roles for men and women, promoting gender segregation in various aspects of life, including education, employment, and social interactions. This segregation is rooted in the belief that men and women have inherently different capabilities and responsibilities. In the realm of education, for example, girls and boys often attend separate schools or are steered towards different subjects and career paths that align with traditional gender roles. Girls are frequently encouraged to pursue fields like humanities, education, or nursing, which are seen as extensions of their nurturing roles, while boys are encouraged to enter fields such as engineering, science, and technology, which are perceived as more rigorous and suited for male competencies. In employment, conservative norms often restrict women to certain professions deemed appropriate, such as teaching or clerical work, limiting their opportunities for advancement and economic independence. Social interactions are also regulated, with strict norms governing how men and women can interact, often leading to women being chaperoned or restricted from attending social gatherings where men are present.

Control Over Female Sexuality

Conservative values in India place a strong emphasis on controlling women's sexuality, with societal norms dictating modesty, chastity, and obedience to male authority. This control is evident in various cultural practices and social expectations. For instance, women are often expected to dress modestly to avoid attracting unwanted attention and to maintain family honour. The practice of wearing traditional attire like sarees, salwar kameez with dupattas, or burqas is seen as a way to protect women's modesty. Premarital chastity and fidelity within marriage are highly valued, and any deviation from these norms can result in severe social ostracization or violence, such as honour killings. The concept of family honour being tied to women's sexual behaviour leads to strict monitoring of their interactions with men and curfews to limit their exposure to potential threats. This control extends to reproductive rights, where women's access to contraception and abortion may be restricted by societal norms and family decisions, often placing their health and autonomy at risk.

Domestic Roles

In conservative Indian society, women are often expected to prioritize marriage, motherhood, and household responsibilities over personal ambitions or professional careers. This expectation is ingrained from a young age, with girls being socialized to view marriage and family life as their ultimate goals. Women are typically responsible for managing the household, raising children, and caring for elderly family members, roles that are considered natural extensions of their nurturing nature. These domestic responsibilities often leave little time or opportunity for women to pursue higher education or careers outside the home. Even when women do work, they are often expected to balance their professional duties with their domestic roles, leading to a double burden that can hinder their career advancement. The societal pressure to conform to these roles is immense, with women who prioritize their careers or remain unmarried often facing criticism and social exclusion.

Male Authority

Conservative values reinforce the notion that men are the primary breadwinners and decision-makers, while women are expected to support and defer to their husbands and male relatives. This dynamic is evident in both family structures and broader societal norms. Within the family, men typically hold authority over financial matters, major life decisions, and the enforcement of family rules. Women are expected to consult and seek approval from male family members for significant decisions, from career choices to healthcare. This male authority is justified through cultural and religious narratives that position men as protectors and providers. In the workplace, men dominate leadership roles and decision-making positions, while women often occupy subordinate roles with limited influence. This hierarchical structure perpetuates gender inequality by restricting women's autonomy and reinforcing their dependence on men. The expectation for women to defer to male authority extends to community and religious settings, where men often lead and women follow, further entrenching the patriarchal framework.

Conservative values in India play a significant role in reinforcing traditional gender roles through gender segregation, control over female sexuality, domestic responsibilities, and male authority. These values create and perpetuate a societal structure where men and women are confined to specific roles, limiting women's opportunities for personal and professional growth. Challenging these deeply ingrained norms requires concerted efforts to promote gender equality through education, legal reforms, and social awareness campaigns. By addressing the root causes of gender segregation and inequality, India can move towards a more inclusive society where individuals are free to pursue their ambitions and exercise their rights, regardless of gender.

Traditional Values and Sexual Violence

Honour Culture

In many conservative communities in India, a family's honour is closely tied to the behaviour and perceived purity of its women. This concept of honour, deeply rooted in patriarchal values, places immense pressure on women to uphold family reputation through their conduct and sexuality. If a woman is sexually assaulted, it is often perceived as a direct attack on the family's honour. This societal framework can lead to severe social repercussions for families, such as social ostracization and damage to familial relationships.

Case Study: Bhanwari Devi (1992) Bhanwari Devi, a social worker from Rajasthan, was gang-raped by upper-caste men for trying to prevent a child marriage. The case drew national attention due to the severity of the assault and the blatant disregard for justice by local authorities. The attack on Bhanwari Devi was not only a punishment for her activism but also a means to undermine her family's honour. Despite the brutality of the crime, societal and institutional pressures focused more on preserving the status quo rather than seeking justice for the victim. Source: Sharma, Kalpana. "A Life in the Law: The Bhanwari Devi Case." The Hindu, 26 December 2013. The Hindu Article.

Victim-Blaming

Victim-blaming is a pervasive issue in India, where victims of sexual violence are often held responsible for the violence inflicted upon them. This attitude is deeply intertwined with the concept of honour, placing the burden of maintaining family dignity on women. Questions about the victim's behaviour, attire, or presence in certain places are common, shifting the focus away from the perpetrator's actions.

Case Study: Suzette Jordan (2012) Suzette Jordan, a victim of gang rape in Kolkata, faced significant victim-blaming after she chose to publicly identify herself. Media and public discourse often questioned her actions, attire, and lifestyle rather than focusing on the crime and the perpetrators. Suzette's decision to reveal her identity was met with both support and backlash, illustrating the societal tendency to blame victims for their assaults. Despite the stigma and backlash, her courage in speaking out brought attention to the systemic issues of victim-blaming and the need for a supportive justice system. Source: Mishra, Anindita. "Suzette Jordan: The Brave Heart Who Refused to Be a Victim." The Quint, 14 March 2016. The Quint Article.

Pressure to Remain Silent

To protect family honour, victims of sexual violence in India often face immense pressure to remain silent about their assault. This pressure can come from family members, community leaders, and even law enforcement officials. Victims are often discouraged from reporting the crime, seeking medical help, or pursuing legal action. In some cases, families may force victims to marry their assailants to avoid public scandal and restore family honour.

Case Study: Imrana (2005) Imrana, a woman from Uttar Pradesh, was raped by her father-in-law. Instead of receiving support and justice, she faced immense pressure from her community and religious leaders to remain silent. The local panchayat declared that Imrana should marry her rapist to preserve family honour, highlighting the extreme measures taken to silence victims and protect familial reputation. This case drew widespread condemnation and highlighted the urgent need for legal and social reforms to protect victims and ensure justice. Source: "Imrana Case: Panchayat Orders Rape Victim to Marry Rapist." India Today, 6 July 2005. India Today Article.

Institutional Bias

Institutions in India, including law enforcement and the judiciary, often reflect societal power dynamics, leading to biased responses that favour perpetrators and undermine justice for victims. Police officers may be reluctant to file First Information Reports (FIRs) in cases of sexual violence, dismissing the complaints as false or trivial. This reluctance is compounded by a lack of sensitivity training and an ingrained belief in patriarchal norms that devalue women's experiences and rights.

Case Study: Unnao Rape Case (2017) In the Unnao rape case, a young girl accused BJP legislator Kuldeep Singh Sengar of raping her. Despite her complaint, local police initially took no action, reflecting the influence and protection afforded to the perpetrator by the patriarchal and political systems. It was only after significant public outrage and media attention that action was taken, and Sengar was eventually convicted. This case highlights how institutional biases can protect powerful perpetrators and hinder justice for victims. Source: Ellis-Petersen, Hannah. "Indian Lawmaker

Found Guilty of Rape in Unnao Case." The Guardian, 16 December 2019. The Guardian Article.

The concepts of honour and shame play a significant role in perpetuating silence around sexual violence in India. The honour culture places an undue burden on women to uphold family dignity, leading to severe social repercussions if they are sexually assaulted. Victim-blaming attitudes further compound this issue, as victims are held responsible for the violence against them, discouraging them from seeking justice. The pressure to remain silent, driven by the need to protect family honour, perpetuates a culture of impunity for perpetrators and denies victims the support and justice they deserve. Addressing these deeply ingrained cultural norms requires a multifaceted approach, including legal reforms, public awareness campaigns, and support systems that prioritize the rights and dignity of victims. By challenging the notions of honour and shame and promoting a culture of accountability and respect, India can take significant steps towards eradicating sexual violence and supporting survivors.

Impact of Cultural Taboos on Reporting and Addressing Sexual Violence

Stigma of Sexual Violence

In India, cultural taboos surrounding sex and sexual violence create an environment where victims feel ashamed and fearful of speaking out. The deep-seated societal shame associated with being a victim of sexual violence stems from traditional notions of purity and honour. This stigma is exacerbated by media portrayals and community attitudes that often portray victims as tainted or damaged. Victims internalize this shame, fearing that their personal reputation and their family's honour will be irreparably harmed if the assault becomes public knowledge.

Case Study: Asifa Bano (2018) In January 2018, an eight-year-old girl named Asifa Bano was brutally gang-raped and murdered in Kathua, Jammu and Kashmir. The case highlighted not only the extreme brutality of the crime but also the intense stigma faced by the victim's family. Despite the horrific nature of the crime, the initial response from the community and authorities was one of indifference and victim-blaming. The family's efforts to seek justice were met with significant resistance, underscoring the pervasive cultural taboos that discourage speaking out about sexual violence. (BBC News. "Kathua Rape Case: Indian Girl's Agony at Hands of Hindu Vigilantes." BBC News, 11 April 2018. BBC News Article)

Lack of Support Systems

In many conservative communities across India, there are few support systems for victims of sexual violence. Essential services such as counselling, legal aid, and safe shelters are often inadequate or completely absent. The lack of these services makes it difficult for victims to seek the help they need to recover and pursue justice. This absence of support is particularly acute in rural areas, where social services are scarce and cultural norms are more rigid. The fear of being blamed or not believed further isolates victims, compounding their trauma.

Case Study: Bilkis Bano (2002) Bilkis Bano was gang-raped during the Gujarat riots in 2002, and her family members were murdered. For years, she struggled to find support and justice. Despite facing immense social and legal obstacles, Bilkis Bano persevered, and eventually, the Supreme Court of India ordered compensation for her and directed the state government to provide her a job and accommodation. Her case highlights the challenges victims face in accessing support systems and the importance of institutional backing for survivors. (The Guardian. "Bilkis Bano: Gang-Raped in Indian Riots, She Took on Her Attackers and Won." The Guardian, 25 April 2019. The Guardian Article)

Reluctance to Report

The fear of social ostracization, family rejection, and retaliation from perpetrators deters many victims of sexual violence in India from reporting their assaults to authorities. Victims often fear that coming forward will bring more harm than good, both to themselves and their families. This reluctance is particularly strong in conservative and rural areas, where community judgment can be harsh and pervasive. Additionally, victims may face threats or violence from perpetrators and their associates, further discouraging them from seeking justice.

Case Study: Soni Sori (2011) Soni Sori, a tribal schoolteacher in Chhattisgarh, was arrested and reportedly tortured and sexually assaulted by police in custody in 2011. Despite the grave nature of her allegations, she faced significant barriers in seeking justice due to threats and intimidation. Soni Sori's case exemplifies the fear of retaliation and the immense pressure victims face to remain silent in the face of sexual violence. (Al Jazeera. "Soni Sori: India's Brave Tribal Activist." Al Jazeera, 17 March 2016. Al Jazeera Article)

Barriers in the Legal System

Cultural biases within the Indian legal system can lead to victim-blaming, insufficient investigation, and lenient punishment for offenders, further discouraging victims from reporting sexual violence. The legal process can be daunting, with victims often facing insensitive questioning and disbelief from law enforcement and judicial authorities. This can result in a lack of thorough investigations and inadequate legal representation for victims, culminating in unjust outcomes.

Case Study: Aruna Shanbaug (1973) Aruna Shanbaug, a nurse, was brutally assaulted and left in a vegetative state in 1973. Her attacker was convicted of robbery and assault but not rape, highlighting significant flaws in the legal response to sexual violence. Aruna remained in a vegetative state for 42 years until her death in 2015. Her case drew attention to the inadequacies of the legal system in addressing and prosecuting sexual violence cases, illustrating the broader issues of victim-blaming and insufficient legal recourse. (The New York Times. "Aruna Shanbaug, Indian Nurse in Vegetative State After Rape, Dies at 67." The New York Times, 18 May 2015. The New York Times Article)

Cultural taboos in India create significant barriers to reporting and addressing sexual violence. The stigma associated with sexual assault, the lack of support systems, the fear of social ostracization, and the barriers within the legal system all contribute to a pervasive culture of silence and impunity. Case studies such as those of Asifa Bano, Bilkis Bano, Soni Sori, and Aruna Shanbaug highlight the systemic challenges and cultural obstacles that victims face. Addressing these issues requires comprehensive reforms, increased awareness, and robust support systems to ensure that victims can seek justice without fear of retribution or shame. By tackling cultural taboos and promoting a more supportive and just environment, India can make significant strides in combating sexual violence and supporting survivors.

Caste and Community-Based Norms

Caste Hierarchy

The caste system in India is a deeply entrenched social hierarchy that significantly impacts the lives and experiences of individuals based on their caste status. This rigid stratification intersects with gender norms, leading to compounded marginalization and exploitation for lower-caste women. In this system, upper-caste men often hold considerable power and influence, which they can use to exert control over lower-caste communities. This dynamic creates an environment where lower-caste women are particularly vulnerable to various forms of exploitation and violence, including sexual violence. The intersection of caste and gender discrimination means that these women face barriers on multiple fronts, affecting their social, economic, and personal lives.

Sexual Exploitation

Sexual violence against Dalit women and other marginalized groups is often used as a tool of dominance and control by upper-caste men. This form of violence serves not only to assert power over the individual women but also to reinforce caste hierarchies and intimidate entire communities. The perpetrators of such violence frequently act with impunity, confident in their social status and the protection it affords them from legal consequences.

Case Study: Bhanwari Devi (1992) Bhanwari Devi, a Dalit social worker from Rajasthan, was gang-raped by upper-caste men as retaliation for her efforts to prevent child marriages in her village. Despite the clear evidence of the crime, the local judiciary dismissed her case, reflecting the deep-seated caste biases within the legal system. Bhanwari Devi's case drew national attention and highlighted the intersectional nature of caste and gender violence, illustrating how upper-caste perpetrators exploit their power to subjugate lower-caste women. (The Hindu. "A Life in the Law: The Bhanwari Devi Case." The Hindu, 26 December 2013. The Hindu Article)

Double Discrimination

Lower-caste women face double discrimination due to their gender and caste, making them more vulnerable to sexual violence and less likely to receive justice. This dual burden manifests in various forms, including limited access to education and employment, social exclusion, and increased susceptibility to violence. The compounded discrimination creates significant barriers to seeking justice and support. When lower-caste women report sexual violence, they often encounter institutional bias and a lack of empathy from law enforcement and judicial authorities. Their cases are frequently dismissed, or the victims are pressured to withdraw their complaints.

Case Study: Hathras Gang Rape (2020) In September 2020, a 19-year-old Dalit woman in Hathras, Uttar Pradesh, was brutally gang-raped by upper-caste men. She succumbed to her injuries two weeks later. The handling of the case by local authorities, including the hurried cremation of the victim's body without the family's consent, sparked nationwide outrage. The case highlighted the pervasive caste and gender biases within the legal and administrative systems. The victim's family faced immense pressure and threats, reflecting the broader societal discrimination against Dalit communities. (BBC News. "Hathras Case: India Shocked by Death of Dalit Woman Allegedly Raped by a Group of Men." BBC News, 29 September 2020. BBC News Article)

Institutional Barriers

Institutional barriers significantly impact lower-caste women's ability to seek justice. The police and judiciary, often composed of individuals from higher castes, may exhibit bias against lower-caste victims. This bias can result in the dismissal of cases, inadequate investigations, and lenient treatment of perpetrators. Moreover, lower-caste women may lack the resources and support networks to navigate the legal system, further hindering their access to justice.

Case Study: Phoolan Devi (1981) Phoolan Devi, also known as the "Bandit Queen," was a lower-caste woman who endured significant sexual violence and exploitation at the hands of upper-caste men. After being gang-raped by upper-caste Thakur men, Phoolan Devi sought revenge and ultimately became a notorious bandit leader. Her story, which includes elements of extreme violence and retribution, underscores the desperation and lack of justice experienced by lower-caste women. Her eventual surrender and later political career brought attention to the deep-seated caste and gender inequalities in Indian society. (The Guardian. "Phoolan Devi: From Bandit Queen to Politician." The Guardian, 25 July 2001. The Guardian Article)

The intersection of caste-based norms and gender violence in India reveals a complex and deeply entrenched system of discrimination that exacerbates the marginalization and exploitation of lower-caste women. The caste hierarchy perpetuates sexual exploitation and reinforces societal norms that allow upper-caste men to act with impunity. Double discrimination against lower-caste women further hinders their access to justice and support. Addressing these issues requires comprehensive legal reforms, increased awareness, and targeted interventions to dismantle the structural and cultural barriers that perpetuate caste and gender violence. By recognizing and addressing the intersectionality of these issues, India can move towards a more equitable and just society.

How Caste Dynamics Affect Responses to Sexual Violence

Institutional Bias

Institutional bias in law enforcement and judicial systems is a significant barrier to justice for lower-caste victims of sexual violence in India. This bias often manifests in the reluctance of police officers to file First Information Reports (FIRs), conduct thorough investigations, or treat victims with the dignity and respect they deserve. The ingrained prejudice within these institutions means that cases involving upper-caste perpetrators and lower-caste victims are frequently dismissed or inadequately pursued.

Case Study: Bhanwari Devi (1992) Bhanwari Devi, a Dalit social worker, was gang-raped by upper-caste men for attempting to stop a child marriage. Despite the brutality of the assault and Bhanwari Devi's courageous efforts to seek justice, the initial police response was dismissive. The local police failed to properly investigate the crime, reflecting the pervasive caste biases. When the case finally went to court, the judge acquitted the accused, questioning the credibility of a Dalit woman's testimony against upper-caste men. This case highlights how institutional bias against lower-caste victims can obstruct justice. (The Hindu. "A Life in the Law: The Bhanwari Devi

Case." The Hindu, 26 December 2013. The Hindu Article)

Community Pressure

Community pressure is another significant factor that affects the responses to sexual violence against lower-caste women. In many cases, influential upper-caste individuals and community leaders exert pressure to cover up incidents or discourage victims from seeking justice. This pressure can take various forms, including threats, intimidation, and social ostracization of the victims and their families. The fear of retribution and the desire to maintain social harmony often led to silence and impunity for the perpetrators.

Case Study: Hathras Gang Rape (2020) In the Hathras gang rape case, a 19-year-old Dalit woman was brutally assaulted by upper-caste men. Following her death, the local administration and police were accused of mishandling the case and attempting to cover up the crime. The hurried cremation of the victim's body without the family's consent was seen as an attempt to destroy evidence and prevent a public outcry. Community pressure and the influence of upper-caste individuals played a significant role in the initial lack of action and the attempts to suppress the case. (BBC News. "Hathras Case: India Shocked by Death of Dalit Woman Allegedly Raped by a Group of Men." BBC News, 29 September 2020. BBC News Article)

Lack of Resources

Marginalized communities, particularly lower-caste groups, often lack the resources and support networks necessary to navigate the legal system and pursue justice for sexual violence. These communities face economic hardships, limited access to legal aid, and a lack of awareness about their legal rights. The absence of supportive infrastructure, such as counselling services and safe shelters, further compounds the difficulties faced by victims. This lack of resources makes it challenging for lower-caste women to seek justice and hold perpetrators accountable.

Case Study: Phoolan Devi (1981) Phoolan Devi, a lower-caste woman who became known as the "Bandit Queen," was gang-raped by upper-caste men. Her struggle for justice was marred by the lack of support and resources available to her. Phoolan Devi's eventual path to revenge and her life as an outlaw underscore the desperation and helplessness faced by many lower-caste women in similar situations. Her story highlights the severe resource constraints and systemic barriers that prevent marginalized women from accessing justice. (The Guardian. "Phoolan Devi: From Bandit Queen to Politician." The Guardian, 25 July 2001. The Guardian Article)

Caste dynamics profoundly affect responses to sexual violence in India, with institutional bias, community pressure, and a lack of resources creating significant barriers to justice for lower-caste victims. Institutional bias in law enforcement and the judiciary often leads to inadequate investigation and prosecution of cases involving upper-caste perpetrators. Community pressure can discourage victims from seeking justice, while marginalized communities' lack of resources further complicates their ability to pursue legal recourse. Addressing these issues requires comprehensive reforms, increased awareness, and robust support systems to ensure that all victims of sexual violence, regardless of caste, can access justice and support. By acknowledging and tackling the intersection of caste and gender violence, India can move towards a more equitable and just society.

Challenges Faced in Changing Conservative Attitudes in India

Deep-Rooted Beliefs

In India, conservative values are deeply ingrained in the cultural and social fabric, making it particularly challenging to shift societal attitudes towards gender equality and women's rights. These beliefs are often perpetuated through generations, reinforced by family traditions, religious teachings, and community norms. The reverence for historical texts and traditions, such as the Manusmriti in Hinduism or similar prescriptive norms in other religions, strengthens the adherence to conservative gender roles. This deep-seated adherence makes any attempt to promote gender equality a slow and arduous process. Educational reforms and awareness campaigns are critical in this regard, but changing mindsets that have been entrenched for centuries requires sustained, multi-generational efforts. Example: Sabarimala Temple Entry (2018) The Supreme Court of India ruled in 2018 that women of all ages could enter the Sabarimala Temple in Kerala, challenging a centuries-old ban on women of menstruating age. Despite the ruling, widespread protests erupted, with many devotees and conservative groups vehemently opposing the decision. This resistance illustrates how deeply rooted beliefs can be difficult to change, even with judicial intervention. The backlash underscored the complexities of altering entrenched cultural norms and the need for ongoing dialogue and education to shift societal attitudes. Source: Al Jazeera. "Why Women Are Protesting for a Hindu Temple in India." Al Jazeera, 4 October 2018. Al Jazeera Article

Patriarchal Power Structures

Patriarchal power structures in India are another significant barrier to changing conservative attitudes. Men, who predominantly occupy positions of power in political, economic, and social spheres, may resist changes that threaten their authority and control. These power structures are reinforced by both formal institutions, such as the legal and political systems, and informal practices within families and communities. Men who benefit from these structures often have little incentive to support gender equality initiatives that could diminish their dominance. Example: Triple Talaq (2019) The practice of triple talaq, which allowed Muslim men to instantly divorce their wives by saying "talaq" three times, was banned by the Indian government in 2019. This reform was aimed at protecting the rights of Muslim women and promoting gender equality. However, the legislation faced significant opposition from conservative Muslim leaders and community members who saw it as an attack on religious practices and male authority. The resistance highlighted the challenges of implementing reforms that threaten entrenched patriarchal power structures, even when such reforms are in the interest of protecting women's rights. Source: The New York Times. "India Outlaws 'Triple Talaq' Instant Divorce for Muslims." The New York Times, 30 July 2019. The New York Times Article

Community Backlash

Efforts to promote gender equality and challenge traditional values often face significant backlash from conservative communities. This backlash can manifest as social ostracization, where individuals who advocate for change are excluded or shunned by their communities. In more extreme cases, there can be threats of violence or actual violence against activists, women seeking to exercise their rights, and their supporters. Political opposition can also be a major hurdle, with conservative leaders and parties mobilizing against reforms perceived as disruptive to traditional social orders. Example: Khap Panchayats and Honour Killings Khap panchayats, traditional village councils in northern India, have been notorious for their conservative stance on issues like inter-caste marriages and women's autonomy. These councils often issue harsh diktats against couples who marry outside their caste or community, leading to social ostracization and even honour killings. The violent enforcement of traditional norms by khap panchayats demonstrates the severe backlash that can arise from challenging conservative values. Activists and reformers who oppose these practices face threats and violence, making it perilous to advocate for gender equality in such contexts. Source: BBC News. "Khap Panchayats: The Honour Courts of India." BBC News, 18 April 2010. BBC News Article

Changing conservative attitudes in India presents significant challenges due to deep-rooted beliefs, entrenched patriarchal power structures, and the potential for severe community backlash. These challenges highlight the complexity of promoting gender equality in a society where traditional values are deeply ingrained and fiercely protected. Efforts to address these challenges require a multifaceted approach that includes legal reforms, educational initiatives, and robust support systems for those advocating for change. By understanding and addressing the specific barriers posed by conservative attitudes, India can make progress towards a more equitable society where women's rights and gender equality are respected and upheld.

Examples of Successful Attempts to Reform Traditional Values

Self-Help Groups and Economic Empowerment

One of the most successful initiatives in challenging traditional values and empowering women in India has been the formation of self-help groups (SHGs). Organizations like the Self-Employed Women's Association (SEWA) have been instrumental in this regard. Founded in 1972 by Ela Bhatt, SEWA focuses on organizing women workers for full employment and self-reliance. These groups provide women with access to financial services, vocational training, and support networks, which collectively enhance their economic independence.

Impact on Gender Norms: The economic empowerment of women through SEWA and similar initiatives has led to greater autonomy and shifts in gender norms within conservative communities. Women who become economically independent gain a stronger voice in household and community decisions, challenging the traditional view of women as solely dependent on their male counterparts. For instance, in Gujarat, SEWA's home state, women involved in SHGs have reported increased respect and decision-making power in their families. Source: International Labour Organization (ILO). "Empowering Women Through Self-Help Groups in India." ILO Article

Legal Reforms

The introduction and enforcement of progressive laws have been pivotal in providing greater legal protections for women and raising awareness about women's rights. Two notable pieces of legislation are the Domestic Violence Act (2005) and the Criminal Law (Amendment) Act (2013).

Domestic Violence Act (2005): This Act provides a comprehensive legal framework for protecting women from domestic violence. It recognizes various forms of abuse, including physical, emotional, sexual, and economic, and offers legal recourse and protection orders for victims. The implementation of this Act has led to increased reporting of domestic violence cases and greater awareness among women about their rights and legal options.

Criminal Law (Amendment) Act (2013): Prompted by the Nirbhaya gang rape case in 2012, this Act brought significant changes to India's criminal laws regarding sexual violence. It broadened the definition of rape, introduced stricter penalties, and established fast-track courts for sexual assault cases. This legislation has not only enhanced legal protections but also spurred public discourse on sexual violence and gender equality. Source: Ministry of Women and Child Development, Government of India. "Protection of Women from Domestic Violence Act, 2005." MWCD Link

Educational Campaigns

Programs promoting girls' education and gender sensitization have been successful in gradually changing attitudes towards women's roles and capabilities in some conservative regions. Initiatives such as Beti Bachao

Beti Padhao (Save the Daughter, Educate the Daughter) have been particularly impactful.

Beti Bachao Beti Padhao (BBBP): Launched by the Government of India in 2015, this campaign aims to address the declining child sex ratio and promote the education and empowerment of girls. By focusing on improving access to education, raising awareness about gender equality, and mobilizing communities to support girls' rights, BBBP has seen success in several states. For example, in Haryana, a state previously notorious for its skewed sex ratio, the campaign has led to a significant increase in the number of girls enrolled in schools.

Impact on Attitudes: Educational campaigns like BBBP are gradually changing societal attitudes towards women's education and roles. By emphasizing the importance of educating girls and showcasing the benefits of gender equality, these campaigns are helping to break down stereotypes and promote a more inclusive view of women's capabilities and rights. Source: Ministry of Women and Child Development, Government of India. "Beti Bachao Beti Padhao." BBBP Link

Successful attempts to reform traditional values in India highlight the importance of economic empowerment, legal protections, and education in challenging entrenched gender norms. Initiatives like SEWA's self-help groups, progressive legal reforms, and educational campaigns such as Beti Bachao Beti Padhao have collectively contributed to shifts in societal attitudes and the empowerment of women. These examples underscore the potential for sustained and multifaceted efforts to bring about meaningful change in conservative communities, paving the way for greater gender equality and women's rights.

Examples of Unsuccessful Attempts to Reform Traditional Values in India

Failure to Implement Laws

Despite the enactment of progressive laws aimed at protecting women and promoting gender equality, the lack of effective implementation often undermines their impact. One prominent example is the Dowry Prohibition Act (1961), which was established to curb the practice of dowry and the associated violence against women. However, societal acceptance of dowry practices remains pervasive, and enforcement of the law has been weak.

Dowry Prohibition Act (1961): The Act criminalizes the giving and receiving of dowry, but it has largely been ineffective due to deep-rooted cultural norms and the lack of stringent enforcement. Reports of dowry-related harassment, violence, and deaths continue to be prevalent. The societal acceptance of dowry as a customary practice often discourages victims and their families from reporting violations, and law enforcement agencies frequently fail to take adequate action.

Case Study: Nisha Sharma (2003) Nisha Sharma became a notable figure when she called off her wedding on the day of the ceremony due to dowry demands. Her decision received widespread media attention and praise as a stand against the dowry system. However, many similar cases do not receive such support, and victims often continue to suffer in silence. The ongoing prevalence of dowry-related violence underscores the limitations of legal reforms in the face of entrenched cultural practices. Source: The Times of India. "Nisha Sharma: The Braveheart Who Stood Up Against Dowry." The Times of India, 9 May 2003. The Times of India Article

Resistance to Sex Education

Efforts to introduce comprehensive sex education in schools have faced significant opposition from conservative groups, who argue that such education undermines cultural values and promotes promiscuity. This resistance has hindered progress in addressing sexual violence and promoting gender equality.

Sex Education Initiatives: Various state governments and NGOs have attempted to introduce sex education programs to educate young people about reproductive health, consent, and gender equality. However, these initiatives often encounter pushback from parents, religious groups, and political leaders who view them as inappropriate or harmful to traditional values.

Case Study: Adolescent Education Program (2007) The Adolescent Education Program (AEP), introduced by the central government in collaboration with NGOs, aimed to provide sex education to adolescents. However, the program faced severe opposition in several states, including Maharashtra and Madhya Pradesh, where it was banned in schools. Critics argued that the curriculum was explicit and contrary to Indian culture, leading to its discontinuation in many regions. The resistance to such programs highlights the challenges in promoting progressive education reforms in a conservative societal framework. Source: The Hindu. "Sex Education in Schools: Controversy and Challenges." The Hindu, 17 August 2007. The Hindu Article

Caste-Based Resistance

Efforts to address sexual violence against lower-caste women often face strong resistance from upper-caste communities, who perceive these initiatives as threats to their traditional authority and social hierarchy. This resistance can manifest in various forms, including social ostracization, violence, and political opposition.

Caste Dynamics and Sexual Violence: Lower-caste women, particularly Dalits, are disproportionately affected by sexual violence. Attempts to seek justice and bring perpetrators to account frequently encounter obstacles, as upper-caste individuals and community leaders exert influence to suppress these efforts.

Case Study: Khairlanji Massacre (2006) In Khairlanji, Maharashtra, a Dalit family was brutally attacked by upper-caste villagers, resulting in the rape and murder of the women in the family. The incident highlighted the extreme caste-based violence and the subsequent failure of the local police and judicial system to adequately respond. Despite initial attempts to cover up the crime and deny justice, nationwide protests eventually led to convictions. However, the resistance faced in the initial stages of seeking justice underscores the entrenched caste biases and the difficulty of addressing sexual violence in such contexts. Source: The Indian Express. "Khairlanji Massacre: A Grim Reminder of Caste Violence." The Indian Express, 29 September 2006. The Indian Express Article

Unsuccessful attempts to reform traditional values in India illustrate the significant challenges posed by deeply ingrained cultural norms, resistance from powerful societal groups, and the lack of effective implementation of progressive laws. The failure to fully enforce the Dowry Prohibition Act, the resistance to comprehensive sex education, and the caste-based opposition to addressing sexual violence highlight the multifaceted nature of these challenges. Overcoming these obstacles requires persistent advocacy, education, and legal reforms, alongside efforts to shift societal attitudes and empower marginalized communities. By addressing the root causes of resistance and building inclusive support systems, India can make strides towards achieving gender equality and protecting women's rights.

Conservatism and traditional values play a significant role in reinforcing gender norms and perpetuating sexual violence in India. The emphasis on honour and shame, cultural taboos, and caste-based norms contribute to the silence and stigma surrounding sexual violence. Efforts to challenge these conservative attitudes face significant resistance, but successful initiatives in legal reform, economic empowerment, and education demonstrate that change is possible. By addressing these deep-rooted cultural and social barriers, India can make progress towards achieving gender equality and reducing sexual violence.

CHAPTER TWELVE

Media Representation of Women and Sexual Violence

Stereotypical Representations of Women in Films, TV, and Advertisements

Films and TV Shows

Traditional Roles: In Indian films and television shows, women are frequently depicted in traditional roles such as devoted wives, caring mothers, or sacrificial daughters. These portrayals reinforce the gender stereotype that women's primary responsibilities are in the domestic sphere. Characters like the ever-sacrificing "mother" or the dutiful "daughter-in-law" are pervasive in Indian cinema and TV serials. The popular TV serial "Kyunki Saas Bhi Kabhi Bahu Thi" depicted women predominantly in traditional roles within the household, focusing on family dramas where the female characters were often shown sacrificing their desires for the family's welfare. Such narratives reinforce the notion that a woman's worth is tied to her roles within the family structure. Source: "Representation of Women in Indian Television Serials." Economic and Political Weekly. EPW Article

Objectification: Women in Indian media are often objectified, with an undue emphasis on their physical appearance and sexuality. This is especially evident in "item numbers," which are song-and-dance sequences featuring scantily clad women performing suggestive dances. These portrayals reduce women to mere objects of male desire, prioritizing their bodies over their characters or abilities. Item songs like "Munni Badnaam

Hui" from the film "Dabangg" and "Sheila Ki Jawani" from "Tees Maar Khan" focus heavily on the physical appeal of the female performers. These songs, though popular, contribute to the objectification of women and propagate the idea that their primary value lies in their physical allure. Source: "Item Songs and the Objectification of Women in Bollywood." The Hindu, 8 March 2013. The Hindu Article.

Damsel in Distress: Female characters in Indian films and TV shows are often portrayed as damsels in distress who need protection or rescue by male protagonists. This trope perpetuates the notion of male superiority and female dependency, suggesting that women cannot solve their problems without male intervention. In many Bollywood movies, such as "Chennai Express" and "Dilwale," the female lead characters find themselves in situations where they need the hero to save them. This reinforces the stereotype that women are weak and helpless without male assistance. Source: "The Damsel in Distress Trope in Indian Cinema." Journal of Gender Studies, 2018. Journal Article

The stereotypical representations of women in Indian films, TV shows, and advertisements significantly impact societal perceptions and reinforce traditional gender roles. By depicting women predominantly in traditional roles, objectifying them, and portraying them as damsels in distress, Indian media perpetuates harmful stereotypes that limit women's roles and opportunities. Addressing these stereotypes requires a concerted effort to promote diverse and realistic portrayals of women, showcasing their strengths, abilities, and independence. By challenging these norms, Indian media can play a crucial role in advancing gender equality and empowering women.

Stereotypical Representations of Women in Advertisements

Gender Roles

In Indian advertisements, women are frequently depicted as homemakers responsible for cooking, cleaning, and taking care of the family. These ads reinforce the stereotype that a woman's primary domain is the household, while men are portrayed as breadwinners who are responsible for earning money and making significant decisions. Advertisements for household products like detergents (e.g., Surf Excel) and cooking oil (e.g., Fortune) often feature women in the kitchen or cleaning the house, emphasizing their role in maintaining the home. Men, on the other hand, are shown enjoying the benefits of a well-maintained household or working outside the home. Source: "Advertising and Gender Stereotypes in India." Journal of Marketing Research, 2018. Journal Article

Beauty Standards

The beauty industry in India heavily promotes products that uphold unrealistic beauty standards, pressuring women to conform to certain appearances. These advertisements often feature fair-skinned, slim, and conventionally attractive models, setting a narrow standard of beauty that many women feel compelled to meet. Advertisements for fairness creams, such as Fair & Lovely (now Glow & Lovely), have been criticized for promoting the idea that lighter skin is more desirable. These ads often depict women gaining confidence, success, and happiness as a direct result of using these products to lighten their skin tone. Source: "Fairness Cream Ads and Colour ism in India." The Economic Times, 24 June 2020. The Economic Times Article

Sexualization

Women are often sexualized in Indian advertisements, with their bodies used to sell products unrelated to beauty or fashion, such as cars, technology, and even food. This trend reduces women to mere objects of male desire and reinforces the notion that their primary value lies in their physical appearance. Advertisements for cars and motorcycles often feature scantily clad women posing with the vehicles, implying that owning the product will enhance the owner's attractiveness and status. Similarly, technology ads, such as those for mobile phones, sometimes use attractive women to draw attention to the product, even when there is no logical connection between the product and the model. Source: "Sexualization in Advertising: A Study of Indian Commercials." Media Watch Journal, 2019. Media Watch Journal Article

Advertisements in India significantly contribute to the reinforcement of traditional gender roles, unrealistic beauty standards, and the sexualization of women. By depicting women primarily as homemakers, promoting unattainable beauty ideals, and using their bodies to sell unrelated products, Indian advertisements perpetuate harmful stereotypes that limit women's roles and opportunities. Challenging these representations requires a concerted effort from advertisers, media companies, and consumers to promote diverse and realistic portrayals of women. By doing so, advertisements can play a crucial role in advancing gender equality and empowering women in India.

Analysis of Gender Roles in Popular Media

Hero vs. Heroine

In Indian popular media, male characters (heroes) are typically depicted as strong, decisive, and action-oriented, while female characters (heroines) are often portrayed as passive, emotional, and supportive. This dichotomy reinforces traditional gender roles, suggesting that men are natural leaders and protectors, while women are caretakers and dependents. In many Bollywood films, the hero is the central figure who drives the plot forward, engages in physical confrontations, and makes critical decisions. Movies like "Singham" and "Dabangg" portray male protagonists as fearless and powerful law enforcers. In contrast, the heroines in these films, such as the characters played by Kajal Aggarwal in "Singham" and Sonakshi Sinha in "Dabangg," primarily serve as romantic interests, providing emotional support and motivation for the hero without having substantial roles in the main narrative. Source: "Bollywood's Gender Problem." The Times of India, 18 March 2019. The Times of India Article

Career Ambitions

Women's career ambitions and professional roles are frequently downplayed or presented as secondary to their domestic responsibilities. When female characters are shown pursuing careers, their professional achievements are often overshadowed by their roles as wives and mothers. This reinforces the stereotype that a woman's primary identity and worth are tied to her family responsibilities. In the TV series "Anupamaa," the protagonist Anupamaa, despite being talented and capable, is primarily depicted as a homemaker who sacrifices her career aspirations for her family's well-being. Her journey towards professional success is fraught with guilt and opposition from her family, reflecting societal expectations that prioritize women's domestic roles over their professional aspirations. Source: "Anupamaa: A Reflection of the Everyday Struggles of Indian Housewives." The Hindu, 15 January 2021. The Hindu Article

Empowerment Narratives

While there are positive portrayals of empowered women in Indian media, these narratives are often overshadowed by stereotypical depictions. Empowerment stories can be superficial, focusing on individual achievements without addressing deeper systemic issues that perpetuate gender inequality. These portrayals may celebrate women's success in breaking traditional roles but often fail to challenge the underlying societal norms that restrict women's freedoms. Films like "Piku" and "Queen" showcase strong, independent female protagonists who defy traditional expectations. In "Piku," Deepika Padukone's character is a successful architect who navigates her career and personal life with confidence. In "Queen," Kangana Ranaut's character embarks on a solo journey of self-discovery after a broken engagement. While these narratives are empowering, they are exceptions rather than the norm in Indian cinema. Source: "Empowering Women in Bollywood: From Piku to Queen." The Indian Express, 8 March 2020. The Indian Express Article

The analysis of gender roles in popular media in India reveals a persistent dichotomy between the portrayal of male and female characters. Heroes are depicted as strong and decisive, while heroines are often passive and supportive. Women's career ambitions are typically downplayed in favour of their domestic responsibilities, reinforcing traditional gender roles. Although there are positive portrayals of empowered women, these narratives are frequently overshadowed by stereotypical depictions and fail to address systemic issues. Addressing these portrayals requires a concerted effort from the media industry to promote more diverse and realistic representations of women, challenging the deeply ingrained stereotypes and advancing gender equality.

Media Coverage of Sexual Violence

Sensationalism

Media coverage of sexual violence in India often sensationalizes the crime, focusing on graphic details and dramatic elements to attract viewership. This approach can desensitize the public to the severity of the crime and shift the focus from the victim's suffering to the sensational aspects of the incident. The Nirbhaya case in 2012, where a young woman was gang-raped and murdered in Delhi, garnered extensive media attention. While the case brought crucial issues to light and sparked nationwide protests, much of the media coverage was sensationalistic, emphasizing graphic details of the assault. This type of reporting can overshadow the need for a sensitive and respectful approach to discussing such crimes. Source: "The Role of Media in the Nirbhaya Case: Sensationalism vs. Sensitivity." The Times of India, 16 December 2017. The Times of India Article.

Victim-Blaming

Victim-blaming is a prevalent issue in the media's reporting of sexual violence. Reports often imply or explicitly state that victims are responsible for their assault due to their behaviour, attire, or lifestyle choices. This perpetuates harmful stereotypes and discourages victims from coming forward to report crimes. In the aftermath of the Bangalore New Year's Eve mass molestation incident in 2017, several media reports and public figures suggested that the women were partly to blame because of their choice of clothing and being out late at night. Such narratives reinforce the idea that victims are responsible for the violence committed against them, rather than holding perpetrators accountable. Source: "Bengaluru Molestation: Media and Politicians Engage in Victim-Blaming." The Indian Express, 2 January 2017. The Indian Express Article.

Perpetrator Focus

In some cases, the media coverage tends to focus on the perpetrators, especially if they are influential or famous, shifting attention away from the victims and the crime itself. This can result in sympathetic portrayals of perpetrators, which diminishes the severity of their actions and undermines the experiences of the victims. The case of self-styled godman Asaram Bapu, who was convicted of raping a minor, saw significant media coverage.

While the case was widely reported, there were instances where the media focused more on Asaram's religious following and his previous philanthropic activities, which could evoke sympathy for him and detract from the seriousness of the crime. Source: "Asaram Bapu: From Godman to Convict." BBC News, 25 April 2018. BBC News Article

The media's approach to reporting sexual violence in India often includes sensationalism, victim-blaming, and a focus on perpetrators, which collectively undermine the seriousness of the crime and perpetuate harmful stereotypes. Sensationalist reporting can desensitize the public and overshadow the need for sensitive coverage. Victim-blaming narratives discourage victims from reporting assaults and seeking justice. Meanwhile, sympathetic portrayals of perpetrators can detract from the gravity of their crimes and shift attention away from the victims. To foster a more supportive environment for survivors of sexual violence and ensure accurate representation, the media must adopt more responsible reporting practices that focus on empathy, accountability, and respect for the victims.

Impact of Sensationalism and Victim-Blaming in Media Coverage

Public Perception

Sensationalist reporting on sexual violence can significantly distort public perception of the issue. By focusing on the most graphic and dramatic aspects of cases, media coverage can create a skewed understanding of the prevalence, causes, and impact of sexual violence. This approach often leads to misconceptions and oversimplifications, which can hinder meaningful discussions and effective policy responses. The extensive and sensational coverage of the Nirbhaya case, while highlighting the brutality of the crime, may lead some to believe that such extreme cases are the norm, overshadowing the more prevalent but less sensational forms of sexual violence. This can result in a public that is less informed about the everyday realities and systemic nature of gender-based violence. Source: "The Role of Media in Shaping Public Perception of Sexual Violence." Media Watch Journal, 2019. Media Watch Journal Article

Secondary Victimization

Victim-blaming narratives in media coverage can lead to secondary victimization, where victims are further traumatized by societal judgment and lack of support. When media reports imply that victims are responsible for their assaults due to their behaviour, attire, or lifestyle, it not only perpetuates harmful stereotypes but also discourages other survivors from coming forward. In the case of the 2017 Bangalore New Year's Eve mass molestation, victim-blaming by media and public figures suggested that the women were at fault for being out late at night and wearing certain types of clothing. Such narratives can cause severe psychological distress to the victims and discourage other survivors from seeking help or reporting similar incidents. Source: "Secondary Victimization: The Psychological Impact of Victim-Blaming." Journal of Trauma & Dissociation, 2018. Journal Article

Legal Proceedings

Media coverage can also influence legal proceedings, potentially prejudicing public opinion and affecting the impartiality of the judicial process. Sensationalist and biased reporting can create a media trial, where the court of public opinion passes judgment before the legal system has had the opportunity to evaluate the evidence impartially. This can lead to undue pressure on legal authorities and influence the outcome of trials. In the Asaram Bapu case, extensive media coverage and the portrayal of the accused's background and religious following may have influenced public opinion. While the coverage helped bring attention to the case, it also risked prejudicing the judicial process by creating preconceived notions about the accused and the case's outcome. Source: "Media Trials and Their Impact on Judicial Proceedings." Law Journal Review, 2017. Law Journal Review Article

The sensationalist and victim-blaming nature of media coverage on sexual violence has profound impacts on public perception, victim experiences, and legal proceedings. Sensationalism can distort the public's understanding of the issue, leading to misconceptions and inadequate policy responses. Victim-blaming further traumatizes survivors, discourages others from reporting, and perpetuates harmful stereotypes. Moreover, biased media coverage can influence legal proceedings, potentially undermining the fairness and impartiality of the judicial process. To mitigate these effects, it is crucial for the media to adopt more responsible and empathetic reporting practices, focusing on accurate representation, victim support, and the promotion of informed public discourse.

Influence of Social Media in Shaping Public Discourse on Sexual Violence

Amplification of Voices

Social media platforms have become powerful tools for amplifying the voices of survivors of sexual violence. These platforms provide a space where survivors can share their stories and experiences, often anonymously, which can raise awareness and generate public empathy. The ability to share personal narratives on social media helps to humanize the issue, making it more relatable and urgent to a broader audience. In India, the #MeToo movement gained momentum on social media, with women from various backgrounds sharing their experiences of sexual harassment and assault. This digital space allowed survivors to bypass traditional media gatekeepers and directly reach the public, leading to widespread discussions and increased awareness about the prevalence of sexual violence in different sectors, including Bollywood, journalism, and corporate environments. Source: "India's #MeToo Movement: The Role of Social Media in Empowering Survivors." The Hindu, 24 October 2018. The Hindu Article

Hashtag Activism

Hashtag activism has played a crucial role in mobilizing global movements against sexual violence. Movements like #MeToo and #TimesUp have gained significant traction through social media, bringing attention to the widespread prevalence of sexual harassment and assault. These hashtags create a unified rallying point for individuals to share their stories, support each other, and demand accountability from perpetrators and institutions. The #MeToo movement, which originated in the United States, quickly spread to India through social media platforms. High-profile cases involving Bollywood actors, directors, and media personalities were brought to light, leading to a national reckoning on issues of sexual misconduct and the need for systemic change. The widespread use of the #MeToo hashtag helped to break the silence around sexual violence and encouraged more women to speak out. Source: "How #MeToo is Changing the Conversation in India." BBC News, 16 October 2018. BBC News Article

Community Support

Social media enables the formation of support networks for survivors, offering emotional support, resources, and solidarity. Online communities provide a sense of belonging and understanding for survivors, who might otherwise feel isolated or stigmatized. These platforms facilitate the sharing of information about legal rights, counselling services, and advocacy groups, empowering survivors to seek help and take action. Example: Online support groups and forums, such as those on Facebook and Reddit, allow survivors to connect with others who have had similar experiences. These communities provide a safe space for survivors to share their stories, seek advice, and offer support to one another. The anonymity and accessibility of these platforms make them invaluable resources for those who may not have access to traditional support systems. Source: "The Role of Social Media in Supporting Survivors of Sexual Violence." Journal of Social Media Studies, 2020. Journal Article.

Social media has profoundly influenced public discourse on sexual violence by amplifying survivors' voices, mobilizing global movements through hashtag activism, and creating supportive online communities. Platforms like Twitter, Facebook, and Instagram provide survivors with a space to share their experiences, raise awareness, and generate empathy. Movements like #MeToo have utilized the power of social media to bring attention to the prevalence of sexual harassment and assault, leading to significant cultural and institutional shifts. Additionally, social media support networks offer crucial emotional and practical support to survivors, helping them navigate their recovery and seek justice. By continuing to leverage these digital tools, society can work towards a more informed, empathetic, and proactive approach to addressing sexual violence.

Social Media Campaigns and Their Impact on Awareness and Activism

#MeToo Movement

Origin and Popularization: The #MeToo movement was started by activist Tarana Burke in 2006 and gained global traction when actress Alyssa Milano used the hashtag on Twitter in 2017. The movement has empowered millions of women worldwide to speak out about their experiences of sexual violence, leading to increased awareness and accountability. In India, the #MeToo movement took off in 2018, with numerous women sharing their stories of harassment and assault, particularly in the entertainment industry. High-profile figures, including Bollywood actors and directors, were accused, leading to significant public and media attention. The movement prompted many organizations to re-evaluate their policies on sexual harassment and implement stricter measures to ensure a safer work environment. Source: "India's #MeToo Moment: How a Hashtag is Changing the Country." BBC News, 16 October 2018. BBC News Article

#TimesUp Campaign

Launch and Objectives: The #TimesUp campaign was launched by Hollywood celebrities in January 2018 to address systemic inequality and injustice in the workplace, with a particular focus on sexual harassment and abuse. The campaign aims to support survivors through legal aid and advocate for safer, fairer workplace environments. In India, the #TimesUp campaign inspired similar movements and reinforced the momentum of #MeToo. It encouraged more victims to come forward and highlighted the need for comprehensive workplace policies to combat harassment and abuse. This movement also led to increased support for legal reforms and better implementation of existing laws protecting women in the workplace. Source: "Times Up: Hollywood's Fight Against Sexual Harassment Resonates in India." The Indian Express, 10 January 2018. The Indian Express Article

Indian Campaigns

#WhyIStayed

Overview: The #WhyIStayed campaign allowed Indian women to share their reasons for staying in abusive relationships, shedding light on the complexities of domestic violence. The campaign aimed to destigmatize survivors' experiences and provide a deeper understanding of the barriers they face. The campaign highlighted the emotional, financial, and social challenges that prevent women from leaving abusive relationships. By sharing their stories, survivors fostered empathy and understanding among the public, leading to increased calls for better support services and legal protections for victims of domestic violence. Source: "Why I Stayed: Indian Women Share Their Stories of Domestic Abuse." The Hindu, 25 November 2019. The Hindu Article

#NotInMyName

Overview: The #NotInMyName movement was initiated as a response to rising incidents of gender-based violence and other forms of discrimination in India. The campaign encouraged individuals to speak out and take action against injustice, promoting a culture of accountability and solidarity. #NotInMyName mobilized large-scale protests and public demonstrations across the country, drawing attention to issues such as sexual violence, communal violence, and hate crimes. The movement emphasized the importance of collective action and civic responsibility, leading to increased public discourse on the need for systemic change and better protection for vulnerable communities. Source: "Not In My Name: Protests Against Violence and Discrimination in India." Al Jazeera, 28 June 2017. Al Jazeera Article

Social media campaigns have significantly impacted awareness and activism around sexual violence and gender-based discrimination in India. Movements like #MeToo and #TimesUp have empowered survivors to share their experiences and demand accountability, leading to greater public awareness and institutional changes. Indian-specific campaigns such as #WhyIStayed and #NotInMyName have highlighted the complexities of domestic violence and the need for collective action against discrimination. These campaigns demonstrate the power of social media in mobilizing public support, fostering empathy, and advocating for systemic reforms to create a safer and more just society.

Importance of Media Literacy in Combating Harmful Representations

Critical Analysis

Media literacy involves critically analysing media content to understand its underlying messages and biases. By equipping individuals with the tools to deconstruct media narratives, media literacy helps viewers recognize and challenge harmful stereotypes and representations. This critical approach enables people to identify subtle and overt biases in media portrayals of gender, race, and other social categories. In India, many popular films and advertisements perpetuate gender stereotypes by depicting women primarily as homemakers or objects of desire. Media literacy programs can teach viewers to question why women are portrayed in these limited roles and encourage them to demand more diverse and realistic representations. For instance, educational initiatives can use examples from Bollywood to illustrate how film narratives often reinforce traditional gender roles, prompting discussions about alternative ways to depict women. Source: "The Role of Media Literacy in Challenging Gender Stereotypes." Journal of Communication Education, 2020. Journal Article

Empowerment

Educating individuals about media literacy empowers them to make informed choices about the media they consume and to demand better representation. When viewers are aware of the potential for bias and manipulation in media content, they are more likely to seek out diverse and accurate portrayals. This empowerment extends to advocacy, where individuals and groups can push for changes in media practices and policies. Media literacy programs in schools and community Centres can empower young people to critically evaluate the media they encounter daily. For instance, workshops that teach students to analyse advertisements can help them understand how marketing strategies often exploit gender stereotypes. Empowered with this knowledge, these students can then participate in campaigns that call for more responsible advertising practices. Source: "Empowering Youth Through Media Literacy Education." UNESCO Report, 2018. UNESCO Report

Awareness

Media literacy raises awareness about the impact of media on societal attitudes and behaviours, fostering a more critical and reflective media consumption culture. By understanding the influence of media on their perceptions and actions, individuals can become more discerning consumers of media. This awareness can lead to a broader cultural shift towards questioning and challenging harmful media representations. Public awareness campaigns that promote media literacy can highlight how pervasive media stereotypes contribute to societal issues like gender-based violence and discrimination. By making viewers aware of these connections, such campaigns can encourage more mindful media consumption and support for content that promotes equality and diversity. For example, a campaign might use case studies from popular television shows to illustrate how media portrayals of domestic violence can either perpetuate harmful norms or promote positive change. Source: "Media Literacy as a Tool for Social Change." Media Watch Journal, 2019. Media Watch Journal Article.

Media literacy is crucial in combating harmful representations in media. By promoting critical analysis, media literacy helps viewers recognize and challenge stereotypes and biases in media content. Empowering individuals to make informed media choices and demand better representation fosters a more inclusive media landscape. Additionally, raising awareness about the impact of media on societal attitudes and behaviours encourages a culture of critical and reflective media consumption. Through education and advocacy, media literacy can contribute significantly to promoting gender equality and social justice in India and beyond.

Educational Initiatives to Promote Critical Consumption of Media

School Curricula

Integrating media literacy into school curricula can help young people develop critical thinking skills and become more discerning media consumers. By incorporating media literacy into subjects such as language arts, social studies, and health education, schools can equip students with the tools to analyse media messages critically and understand their impact on society. In India, state education boards could introduce media literacy modules that teach students how to deconstruct advertisements, news reports, and film narratives. These modules could include activities like identifying stereotypes, discussing the role of media in shaping public opinion, and creating their own media content with an emphasis on fairness and representation. Source: "Media Literacy Education: A Comprehensive Approach." Journal of Educational Media, 2020. Journal of Educational

Media.

Workshops and Seminars

Organizations and educational institutions can conduct workshops and seminars to teach media literacy to diverse audiences, including students, parents, and educators. These interactive sessions can provide practical tools and strategies for critically engaging with media and understanding its influence. The National Council of Educational Research and Training (NCERT) could partner with NGOs to organize workshops across India, focusing on rural and urban areas. These workshops could cover topics such as identifying bias in news reporting, understanding the impact of social media on self-image, and the importance of diverse representation in media. Source: "Empowering Communities Through Media Literacy Workshops." The Hindu, 15 March 2019. The Hindu Article.

Online Resources

Creating accessible online resources, such as videos, articles, and interactive tools, can help people of all ages learn about media literacy at their own pace. These resources can be shared widely through social media platforms, educational websites, and community portals. An online platform like "Digital India Literacy" could provide a comprehensive suite of resources, including video tutorials on analysing media content, articles on the impact of media stereotypes, and interactive quizzes that test users' media literacy skills. These resources could be made available in multiple languages to reach a broader audience. Source: "The Role of Online Resources in Enhancing Media Literacy." International Journal of Media Studies, 2018. International Journal of Media Studies.

Collaborations with Media Producers

Partnering with media producers to promote responsible representation and encourage the creation of diverse and accurate portrayals of women and sexual violence can have a significant impact. These collaborations can involve consultations, training sessions, and the development of guidelines for ethical media production. Bollywood film producers could collaborate with feminist organizations and media literacy experts to create a set of best practices for depicting women and sexual violence in films. These guidelines could include recommendations for avoiding stereotypes, portraying consent accurately, and highlighting the consequences of sexual violence. Films that adhere to these guidelines could receive a special certification or endorsement, promoting them as socially responsible. Source: "Collaborative Efforts in Promoting Ethical Media Representation." Media Ethics Journal, 2019. Media Ethics Journal.

Educational initiatives to promote critical consumption of media are essential for fostering a more informed and discerning audience. By integrating media literacy into school curricula, conducting workshops and seminars, creating accessible online resources, and collaborating with media producers, we can equip individuals with the skills needed to analyse and challenge harmful media representations. These efforts will help cultivate a culture of critical media consumption, ultimately contributing to more diverse, accurate, and responsible portrayals in media, and advancing gender equality and social justice in India and beyond. The media plays a powerful role in shaping societal attitudes towards women and sexual violence. Stereotypical representations, sensationalist reporting, and victim-blaming narratives contribute to a culture that normalizes and perpetuates gender-based violence. However, social media has emerged as a powerful tool for raising awareness, amplifying survivors' voices, and mobilizing activism. Promoting critical media literacy is essential to combating harmful representations and fostering a more informed and equitable media landscape. By challenging traditional portrayals and encouraging responsible media practices, society can work towards eradicating sexual violence and promoting gender equality.

CHAPTER THIRTEEN

Conservatism and Its Role in Increasing Rape Culture

Cultural Conservatism in India

Definition and Characteristics

Cultural conservatism in India refers to the adherence to traditional beliefs, practices, and values that emphasize maintaining established social norms and resisting change. It manifests through a preference for stability, continuity, and preservation of the social order as defined by historical, cultural, and religious tenets. Conservatism often upholds the authority of established institutions and practices and resists efforts to modify or reform these structures.

One of the hallmarks of cultural conservatism in India is the strong emphasis on preserving cultural, religious, and familial traditions. This includes the meticulous observance of rituals, festivals, and customs passed down through generations. Traditional festivals like Diwali, Holi, Eid, and Christmas are celebrated with strict adherence to customs and rituals, reinforcing community and familial bonds while perpetuating traditional gender roles. Similarly, practices such as joint family systems, arranged marriages, and rituals surrounding birth, death, and marriage ceremonies are preserved to maintain a sense of continuity and identity. Familial traditions, including hierarchical structures within the family, are emphasized, with elders holding significant authority and younger members expected to show deference and respect. Practices like the dowry system, despite being illegal, persist due to their deep-rooted cultural significance.

Conservatism in India also involves resistance to social changes that challenge established norms, particularly those related to gender roles and family structures. Efforts to promote gender equality, such as women's education and employment, are sometimes viewed as threats to traditional family structures. There is often opposition to recognizing and accepting LGBTQ+ individuals and their rights, seen as contrary to traditional values. This tension between modernization and tradition is evident in the impacts of urbanization and globalization, which introduce new ideas and values that can undermine traditional norms. Rapid urbanization and rural-to-urban migration challenge traditional lifestyles, leading to cultural clashes, while exposure to global cultures through media and the internet introduces new concepts that conservative elements resist.

In conservative Indian society, there is a deep-seated respect for elders and traditional authority figures. Elders' opinions and decisions hold significant weight in familial and societal matters, often making key decisions regarding family issues, including marriage, education, and career choices of younger family members. They are seen as custodians of moral and cultural values, guiding the younger generation on acceptable behaviour and practices. This generational hierarchy is strictly maintained, with clear expectations for behaviour and roles within the family, emphasizing obedience and respect for the authority of elders.

Cultural conservatism reinforces distinct roles for men and women, often based on patriarchal values that assign specific duties and responsibilities to each gender. Men are typically seen as providers and protectors, responsible for earning and making major decisions for the family, while women are often viewed as caregivers and homemakers, responsible for child-rearing, household chores, and supporting male family members. These gender roles are rooted in patriarchal values that prioritize male authority and female subservience, defining women's roles in relation to men and emphasizing subordination and dependence. This control over women's behaviour, mobility, and choices is maintained through cultural and social norms, limiting opportunities for women in education, employment, and public life. Girls may be discouraged from pursuing higher education or career ambitions in favour of early marriage and domestic responsibilities, while women's participation in the workforce is often restricted to roles considered appropriate by conservative standards, limiting their economic independence and professional growth.

Cultural conservatism in India is characterized by a commitment to preserving traditional beliefs, practices, and values, often at the expense of modernizing influences that challenge established norms. This adherence to tradition emphasizes the authority of elders, rigid gender roles, and resistance to social change. While conservatism helps maintain cultural identity and continuity, it also perpetuates patriarchal structures and restricts women's freedom and rights. Addressing the challenges posed by cultural conservatism requires a nuanced approach that respects cultural heritage while promoting gender equality and individual autonomy.

Influence on Gender Norms and Behaviours

Gender Segregation

Cultural conservatism in India promotes strict gender roles and segregation in various spheres of life, including education, employment, and social interactions. From an early age, boys and girls are socialized differently, with boys encouraged to be assertive and independent while girls are taught to be nurturing and submissive. This segregation extends to educational institutions, workplaces, and public spaces, where gender-specific expectations are enforced. In schools, boys and girls may be taught in separate classrooms or schools altogether, reinforcing the idea that their roles and futures are fundamentally different. In the workplace, women may be steered towards jobs that are considered "appropriate" for their gender, such as teaching or nursing, rather than being encouraged to pursue careers in male-dominated fields like engineering or business.

Education

In conservative settings, there is often a clear preference for boys' education over girls', with significant implications for gender equality. Boys are typically given priority access to educational resources and opportunities, while girls may be encouraged to focus on acquiring traditional skills that prepare them for domestic roles. This disparity is evident in enrolment rates, literacy levels, and dropout rates, with girls often receiving less formal education than boys. The education that girls do receive is frequently geared towards making them good wives and mothers, emphasizing domestic skills over academic or professional development. This educational bias not only limits girls' career prospects but also reinforces the idea that their primary value lies in their roles within the family.

Employment

Employment opportunities for women are similarly restricted by conservative norms, which limit their participation in the workforce and confine them to certain types of jobs. Women are often expected to prioritize their roles as homemakers and caregivers, leading to limited opportunities to work outside the home. When women do enter the workforce, they are often channelled into jobs that align with traditional gender roles, such as teaching, nursing, or administrative support. This occupational segregation contributes to the gender pay gap and limits women's economic independence and professional growth. Furthermore, conservative attitudes towards women working outside the home can create a hostile work environment, where women face discrimination and harassment.

Marital Expectations

Conservative norms place a strong emphasis on marriage as a woman's primary role, with societal expectations to marry young and prioritize family responsibilities over personal ambitions. Marriage is often seen as a woman's ultimate goal, and her success is measured by her ability to maintain a household and bear children. These expectations pressure women to conform to traditional roles, sacrificing their education and career aspirations to fulfil family duties. Early marriage is particularly prevalent, cutting short girls' education and exposing them to risks associated with early pregnancy and childbirth. Once married, women are expected to adhere to strict roles as wives and mothers, reinforcing their dependence on their husbands and limiting their autonomy.

Dowry System

The dowry system, despite being illegal, is widely endorsed and practiced in conservative communities, leading to significant economic burdens on the bride's family and potential violence. The expectation that a bride's family must provide a substantial dowry to the groom's family perpetuates gender inequality and commodifies women. Families with daughters often face financial strain, and the inability to meet dowry demands can result in dowry-related violence, including harassment, abuse, and even death. This practice reinforces the notion that women are economic liabilities and further entrenches their subordinate status within the family and society.

Control Over Marriage Choices

Parental control over marriage decisions is a hallmark of conservative cultures, often prioritizing caste, religion, and family status over personal choice. Arranged marriages are common, with parents and elders playing a significant role in selecting a suitable spouse. This control extends to ensuring that marriages reinforce social and economic alliances, maintaining caste purity and religious continuity. Women, in particular, have limited say in choosing their partners, and their consent is often secondary to the family's decision. This lack of autonomy in marriage choices perpetuates gender inequality and can lead to unhappy and oppressive marital situations.

Female Sexuality

Conservative views on female sexuality emphasize chastity and purity before marriage and fidelity after marriage, placing strict controls on women's sexual behaviour. The concept of virginity is highly valued, and women are expected to preserve their chastity until marriage. After marriage, fidelity is strictly enforced, with severe social and familial repercussions for transgressions. These views are enforced through social norms, religious teachings, and sometimes even legal frameworks, creating an environment where women's bodies and sexuality are controlled by patriarchal structures. This control limits women's sexual autonomy and reinforces their subordination to male authority.

Honour and Shame

The concept of family honour is closely tied to women's behaviour in conservative societies, leading to strict control over their actions and relationships. A woman's conduct, including her dress, behaviour, and interactions with men, is seen as a reflection of the family's honour. Any perceived transgression can bring shame and dishonour to the family, resulting in severe consequences for the woman. This emphasis on honour and shame often leads to practices like honour killings, where women are punished, sometimes fatally, for actions deemed dishonour able. The pressure to uphold family honour restricts women's freedom, discourages them from seeking education or employment, and limits their ability to make personal choices.

Cultural conservatism in India significantly influences gender norms and behaviours, reinforcing traditional roles and restricting women's freedom and rights. Gender segregation, preferences for boys' education, limited employment opportunities for women, and strict marital expectations perpetuate a cycle of inequality and subordination. The dowry system, control over marriage choices, conservative views on female sexuality, and the concept of family honour further entrench patriarchal norms. Addressing these issues requires a concerted effort to challenge and change conservative attitudes, promote gender equality, and empower women to exercise their rights and autonomy.

Impact on Women's Freedom and Rights

Mobility Restrictions

Cultural conservatism imposes significant restrictions on women's freedom to move and travel independently. These restrictions are often rooted in patriarchal beliefs that women need to be protected and that their mobility must be controlled to maintain family honour. In many conservative communities, women are not allowed to travel alone, especially at night, and are required to seek permission from male family members for even short trips outside the home. This lack of freedom severely limits their ability to participate in public life, access education, and engage in economic activities. It also contributes to their social isolation and dependence on male guardians.

Purdah System

The purdah system, which involves practices like wearing a veil (burqa or hijab) and maintaining seclusion, restricts women's visibility and participation in public life. Originating from religious and cultural norms, purdah is intended to protect women's modesty but often results in their exclusion from many aspects of social and economic life. Women adhering to purdah may face limitations in accessing education, healthcare, and employment opportunities. While some women may choose to follow purdah as a personal or religious preference, in conservative families, it is often imposed, curtailing women's freedom to interact freely in society and limiting their roles to the private sphere of the home.

Curfews and Supervision

In many conservative households, women are subjected to strict curfews and constant supervision by male family members. These measures are justified as necessary for their safety and to prevent any behaviour that could be perceived as dishonourable. Curfews restrict women's ability to participate in social, educational, and economic activities, particularly those that occur in the evening or require travel. The constant supervision reinforces the notion that women are inherently vulnerable and need protection, which further perpetuates gender inequality. This control over their daily activities also affects their psychological well-being, leading to feelings of confinement and dependence.

Educational Restrictions

Conservative norms often dictate a preference for traditional or home-based education for girls, limiting their access to formal and higher education. Many families prioritize boys' education over girls', viewing investment in girls' education as less valuable since they are expected to marry and take on domestic roles. As a result, girls may receive less support and encouragement to pursue academic achievements. Even when girls attend school, the curriculum choices may emphasize domestic skills over academic or professional subjects, preparing them primarily for roles as wives and mothers rather than for independent careers. This educational disparity perpetuates gender inequality and restricts women's opportunities for personal and professional growth.

Employment Restrictions

Conservative norms discourage women from working outside the home or pursuing careers in male-dominated fields. Women are often expected to prioritize their roles as homemakers and caregivers, limiting their participation in the workforce. When women do seek employment, they are encouraged to pursue jobs that are deemed appropriate for their gender, such as teaching, nursing, or administrative roles. This occupational segregation restricts women's economic independence and professional growth, contributing to the gender pay gap and limiting their influence in various sectors. The expectation that women should balance work with domestic responsibilities also places additional burdens on working women, making it challenging for them to advance in their careers.

Acceptable Professions

In conservative communities, women are often encouraged to pursue jobs that align with traditional gender roles, such as teaching, nursing, or administrative support. These professions are considered suitable for women because they are seen as extensions of their nurturing roles within the family. While these jobs can provide women with financial independence and personal fulfilment, the restriction to a narrow range of acceptable professions limits their career choices and opportunities. Women who aspire to work in male-dominated fields, such as engineering, law, or business, may face resistance and lack of support from their families and communities, further entrenching gender inequality in the workforce.

Workplace Harassment

The fear of harassment and the lack of workplace protections further limit women's employment opportunities. Sexual harassment in the workplace is a pervasive issue that can deter women from seeking or maintaining employment. In conservative settings, the stigma associated with being a victim of harassment can be particularly severe, leading to victim-blaming and social ostracism. Many workplaces lack effective policies and mechanisms to address harassment, making it difficult for women to report incidents and seek justice. This hostile environment not only affects women's safety and well-being but also undermines their confidence and career aspirations.

Reproductive Rights

Control over women's reproductive choices is a significant aspect of conservatism, with societal and familial pressure to have children early and limitations on access to contraception and abortion. Women are often expected to conform to traditional family planning methods and may face opposition to using modern contraception. This control over reproductive health decisions reinforces women's subordination and limits their autonomy. In many conservative communities, discussions about reproductive health are taboo, further restricting women's access to information and services. The pressure to have children early and frequently can also affect women's health, career opportunities, and overall quality of life.

Family Planning

Conservative attitudes towards family planning emphasize traditional methods and often oppose modern contraception. This opposition is rooted in beliefs about the sanctity of procreation and the natural roles of women as mothers. As a result, women may have limited access to family planning services and information about modern contraceptive methods. This lack of access can lead to unintended pregnancies, which have significant social, economic, and health implications for women. The emphasis on traditional family planning also reinforces the expectation that women should have multiple children, further limiting their opportunities for education and employment.

Health Risks

Women face increased health risks due to lack of access to reproductive healthcare. In conservative settings, the stigma surrounding reproductive health issues can prevent women from seeking necessary medical care. Limited access to contraception and safe abortion services increases the risk of unintended pregnancies and unsafe abortions, which can have severe health consequences. Additionally, the pressure to have children early and frequently can lead to complications during pregnancy and childbirth, especially for young mothers. The lack of reproductive healthcare services and education exacerbates these risks, undermining women's health and well-being.

Cultural conservatism imposes significant restrictions on women's mobility, education, employment, and reproductive rights, severely limiting their freedom and opportunities. These restrictions are rooted in patriarchal beliefs that prioritize family honour and traditional gender roles over women's autonomy and equality. Addressing these issues requires challenging conservative attitudes and promoting policies that support women's rights and empowerment. By ensuring that women have the freedom to move, access education and employment, and make informed choices about their reproductive health, society can move towards greater gender equality and improve the overall well-being of women.

Correlation with Sexual Violence

Victim-Blaming

Conservative attitudes often lead to victim-blaming, where victims of sexual violence are held responsible for their assault due to their behaviour, attire, or choices. In conservative communities, the belief that a woman's actions can provoke sexual violence is pervasive. This mindset shifts the focus from the perpetrator's criminal behaviour to the victim's conduct, suggesting that she could have prevented the assault by dressing modestly, avoiding certain places, or adhering to traditional gender norms. Victim-blaming not only exacerbates the trauma experienced by survivors but also discourages them from coming forward to report the crime, fearing judgment and further victimization.

Social Stigma

Victims of sexual violence face significant social stigma and ostracization, particularly in conservative societies where a woman's honour is closely tied to her sexual purity. The social repercussions of being a victim of sexual violence can be severe, including loss of reputation, marriage prospects, and social standing. This stigma extends beyond the individual to her family, leading to collective shame and dishonour. As a result, many victims are discouraged from reporting incidents of sexual violence, choosing instead to remain silent to protect their family's reputation and avoid social exclusion. This culture of silence perpetuates the cycle of violence, as perpetrators remain unpunished and emboldened.

Judicial Bias

Law enforcement and judicial systems may reflect conservative biases, leading to inadequate responses to sexual violence. Police officers and judicial officials, influenced by societal norms, may harbour prejudices against victims, questioning their credibility and blaming them for the assault. This bias can manifest in various ways, such as reluctance to file First Information Reports (FIRs), dismissive attitudes during investigations, and lenient sentencing for perpetrators. The judicial process can be re-traumatizing for victims, who often face invasive questioning and a lack of empathy from officials. This bias undermines the legal system's ability to deliver justice and protect survivors, contributing to a culture of impunity for sexual offenders.

Underreporting

The fear of social repercussions and lack of trust in the legal system result in significant underreporting of sexual violence. Many victims do not report assaults due to the anticipated social backlash and the belief that their complaints will not be taken seriously by authorities. The fear of being blamed, judged, or not believed is pervasive, and the potential for long, humiliating legal battles deters many from seeking justice. Additionally, the cumbersome and often insensitive legal processes further discourage reporting. These underreporting skews official statistics, making it challenging to gauge the true extent of sexual violence and implement effective prevention and support measures.

Fear of Retaliation

Victims of sexual violence often fear retaliation from perpetrators, especially in close-knit conservative communities where the assailants may hold significant social or political power. The threat of physical harm, social ostracism, or further violence can be a powerful deterrent against reporting the crime. In many cases, perpetrators use intimidation tactics to silence victims and their families, ensuring that the assault remains hidden. This fear of retaliation is particularly acute in communities where honour and reputation are paramount, and where the victim's family may also face severe consequences if the crime is reported.

Family Pressure

Families in conservative societies may pressure victims to remain silent to avoid bringing shame upon themselves. The notion of family honour is deeply ingrained, and any perceived blemish on a woman's reputation can tarnish the entire family's social standing. As a result, victims are often coerced into silence by their own families, who prioritize societal acceptance over the victim's well-being and justice. This pressure can come in various forms, from emotional manipulation to outright threats, compelling victims to endure their trauma in silence and isolation. Family pressure not only suppresses the victim's voice but also perpetuates the stigma surrounding sexual violence, preventing societal progress in addressing and combating the issue.

Institutional Failure

Conservative attitudes within institutions, such as the police and judiciary, contribute to systemic failures in addressing and preventing sexual violence. These institutions often mirror the broader societal biases, leading to a lack of sensitivity and effectiveness in handling sexual violence cases. Police officers may be reluctant to file reports, conduct thorough investigations, or take the victim's complaints seriously. Similarly, judicial processes can be slow and biased, with judges displaying patriarchal attitudes that undermine the pursuit of justice. Institutional failures erode public trust in the legal system, making it less likely for victims to seek help and report crimes.

Inadequate Support Systems

The lack of adequate support systems for victims, including counselling and legal aid, exacerbates the challenges faced by survivors of sexual violence. In many conservative societies, there are few resources available to help victims cope with the trauma of assault and navigate the legal system.

Counselling services, if available, may be stigmatized or underfunded, and legal aid is often inaccessible or insufficient. This lack of support leaves victims vulnerable and isolated, struggling to recover from their experiences without the necessary emotional and legal assistance. Comprehensive support systems are crucial for empowering victims, providing them with the tools and resources needed to heal and seek justice.

Lenient Sentencing

Perpetrators of sexual violence may receive lenient sentences due to societal biases, further perpetuating a culture of impunity. Conservative attitudes within the judiciary can result in lighter punishments for offenders, especially if they are perceived as respectable members of society or if the victim's character is called into question. Lenient sentencing sends a message that sexual violence is not taken seriously, diminishing the deterrent effect of the law and encouraging potential offenders. This lack of accountability not only fails to deliver justice to victims but also undermines efforts to prevent sexual violence and protect vulnerable individuals.

Cultural conservatism in India significantly influences the prevalence and response to sexual violence. Victim-blaming, social stigma, judicial bias, and underreporting are all products of a conservative mindset that prioritizes family honour and traditional gender roles over justice and support for victims. Fear of retaliation, family pressure, institutional failures, inadequate support systems, and lenient sentencing further entrench a culture of impunity, leaving victims vulnerable and perpetrators unpunished. Addressing these issues requires challenging and changing conservative attitudes, improving institutional responses, and strengthening support systems for survivors. By promoting gender equality and justice, society can move towards a more equitable and safer environment for all individuals.

Specific Incidents Illustrating the Impact of Conservatism

Kathua Rape Case (2018)

Incident: An 8-year-old girl from a nomadic Muslim community was abducted, raped, and murdered in a temple in Kathua, Jammu and Kashmir.

Conservatism Impact: The crime was motivated by an attempt to drive the nomadic community out of the area, reflecting deep-seated communal and patriarchal attitudes.

Societal Reaction: Initial police inaction and attempts to protect the accused due to their high social status; protests demanding justice faced resistance from conservative groups.

Outcome: Three men received life sentences, and three police officers were convicted of destruction of evidence. The case highlighted the intersection of conservatism, communalism, and patriarchal violence.

Hathras Case (2020)

Incident: A 19-year-old Dalit woman was gang-raped and fatally injured by upper-caste men in Hathras, Uttar Pradesh.

Conservatism Impact: The incident highlighted caste-based violence and the deep-rooted patriarchal norms that facilitate such crimes.

Societal Reaction: The victim's family faced intimidation, and there were attempts to downplay the crime by local authorities. National outrage and protests ensued.

Outcome: The case brought national attention to caste and gender-based violence, prompting calls for systemic reforms.

Unnao Rape Case (2017)

Incident: A minor girl was raped by a powerful BJP MLA in Unnao, Uttar Pradesh. The victim attempted self-immolation to draw attention to her plight.

Conservatism Impact: The case highlighted how political power and patriarchal norms can obstruct justice for victims of sexual violence.

Societal Reaction: Initial reluctance by local police to file a case due to the perpetrator's political influence; widespread public and media outrage.

Outcome: The MLA was eventually convicted and sentenced to life imprisonment, but the case underscored the challenges victims face in seeking justice against powerful individuals.

Cultural conservatism in India plays a significant role in reinforcing patriarchal norms and contributing to the perpetuation of rape culture. The adherence to traditional gender roles, restrictions on women's mobility and choices, and societal biases against victims of sexual violence create an environment where gender-based violence is tolerated and even justified. The case studies illustrate the profound impact of conservatism on women's rights and the systemic challenges in addressing sexual violence. Addressing these issues requires a multifaceted approach, including legal reforms, educational initiatives, and efforts to challenge and change conservative attitudes towards gender equality and women's rights.

Rigid Social Structures and Their Contribution

Rigid societal norms are deeply ingrained beliefs and practices that dictate acceptable behaviour within a community. In India, these norms often perpetuate power imbalances and significantly influence the occurrence and perception of sexual violence. These societal norms uphold patriarchal values, restrict women's autonomy, and stigmatise survivors, thereby perpetuating rape culture. This essay explores the definition and examples of rigid societal norms in India, how they perpetuate rape culture, and the steps needed to dismantle these harmful practices.

Definition of Rigid Societal Norms

Rigid societal norms refer to the strict and inflexible rules or expectations imposed by a society on its members. In India, these norms govern various aspects of life, including gender roles, family structure, and personal behaviour. They are often rooted in historical, cultural, and religious traditions and are resistant to change.

Gender Roles: Prescribed roles for men and women that dictate behaviours and responsibilities based on their gender. For instance, men are often expected to be assertive and dominant, while women are expected to be submissive and nurturing.

Honour and Shame: Concepts of family honour and personal shame that control individual behaviour, particularly among women. Actions perceived as dishonourable can lead to social ostracism or violence.

Sexual Purity: Emphasis on maintaining sexual purity, especially for women, which often translates into controlling women's sexuality and imposing severe consequences for perceived transgressions.

Examples of Rigid Societal Norms in India

Gender Roles

Domestic Expectations: Women in India are often expected to prioritise family and household responsibilities over personal ambitions. In many communities, a woman's worth is measured by her ability to be a good wife and mother.

Male Dominance: Men are expected to be the breadwinners and protectors, often leading to dominance in decision-making within households and society. This norm discourages men from showing vulnerability or sharing power with women.

Honour and Shame

Honour Killings: In some communities, actions perceived as bringing dishonour to the family, such as premarital relationships or elopement, can result in honour killings. Family members, particularly male relatives, may feel compelled to restore family honour through violence.

Stigmatisation of Rape Survivors: Victims of rape are often stigmatised and blamed for their assault. The loss of "honour" associated with rape can lead to social exclusion and even violence against the victim by their own family.

Sexual Purity

Virginity Tests: Some communities practice virginity tests to ensure that women remain virgins until marriage. These invasive tests are not only scientifically invalid but also a violation of human rights.

Dress Codes: Strict dress codes imposed on women to prevent them from "provoking" sexual advances. Women are often blamed for inviting sexual violence based on their attire.

How Rigid Societal Norms Perpetuate Rape Culture in India

Rigid societal norms in India contribute to the perpetuation of rape culture in various ways. They reinforce patriarchal values, create environments where sexual violence is normalised, and discourage victims from seeking justice.

Patriarchal Values and Power Imbalance

Subjugation of Women: Rigid norms often place women in subordinate roles, limiting their autonomy and reinforcing male dominance. This power imbalance creates environments where men feel entitled to exert control over women's bodies.

Male Entitlement: Societal expectations that men should be dominant and assertive can lead to a sense of entitlement over women's bodies. This entitlement is a fundamental aspect of rape culture, where men believe they have the right to assert their sexual desires regardless of consent.

Normalisation of Sexual Violence

Trivialisation of Rape: Rigid norms can trivialise rape by treating it as a minor offence or a misunderstanding. This normalisation diminishes the severity of sexual violence and perpetuates the belief that it is an inevitable part of life.

Victim-Blaming: Rigid norms often shift the blame from perpetrators to victims. By scrutinising the victim's behaviour, attire, or choices, society excuses the actions of the perpetrator and perpetuates a culture of impunity.

Discouraging Victims from Seeking Justice

Fear of Stigmatization: Victims of sexual violence often fear being ostracised or blamed for their assault. The stigma associated with rape can discourage victims from reporting the crime or seeking help.

Lack of Support Systems: Rigid norms can result in inadequate support systems for victims. Law enforcement, judicial systems, and social services may fail to provide the necessary assistance and protection due to prevailing biases and stigmas.

Examples of Rigid Societal Norms

India

Dowry System: The dowry system places immense pressure on women to conform to familial and societal expectations. Failure to meet dowry demands can result in violence or abandonment.

Caste System: The intersection of caste and gender creates compounded discrimination. Lower-caste women are particularly vulnerable to sexual violence and face significant barriers in accessing justice.

Middle East

Honour-Based Violence: In many Middle Eastern cultures, family honour is paramount. Women who are perceived to have violated social norms may be subjected to honour-based violence, including honour killings.

Legal Inequalities: In some countries, legal systems are biased against women, making it difficult for rape victims to seek justice. For example, in some jurisdictions, a woman's testimony is worth less than a man's, further perpetuating gender inequality.

Western Societies

Rape Myths: Rape myths, such as the belief that women provoke rape by their behaviour or attire, are prevalent in many Western societies. These myths perpetuate victim-blaming and normalize sexual violence.

Fraternity Culture: In some Western educational institutions, fraternity culture promotes hyper-masculinity and sexual aggression. This environment can lead to higher incidences of sexual violence and impunity for perpetrators.

Strategies to Dismantle Rigid Societal Norms

Addressing the impact of rigid societal norms on rape culture requires comprehensive strategies that involve legal reforms, education, and shifts in societal attitudes.

Legal Reforms

Strengthening Laws: Implementing and enforcing strict laws against sexual violence can deter perpetrators and provide justice for victims. Laws should also address related issues such as domestic violence, dowry demands, and honour-based violence.

Victim Protection: Legal systems should prioritize the protection and support of victims. This includes ensuring anonymity, providing legal aid, and establishing safe spaces for survivors.

Education and Awareness

Gender Sensitization: Educational programs should focus on gender sensitization, teaching both boys and girls about consent, respect, and equality. These programs can help challenge and change harmful gender norms from a young age.

Public Awareness Campaigns: Campaigns that challenge rape myths and promote understanding of sexual violence can shift public attitudes. These campaigns should highlight the importance of consent and the rights of victims.

Community Engagement

Involving Men and Boys: Engaging men and boys in the conversation about gender equality is crucial. Programs that encourage positive masculinity and challenge toxic behaviours can create allies in the fight against rape culture.

Support Networks: Establishing community support networks for victims of sexual violence can provide much-needed assistance and advocacy. These networks can help navigate the legal system, access healthcare, and offer emotional support.

Media and Representation

Responsible Media: Media organizations should be encouraged to portray women and sexual violence responsibly. This includes avoiding the glorification or trivialization of rape and promoting narratives that empower women.

Representation Matters: Increasing the representation of women and marginalized groups in media, politics, and leadership positions can challenge stereotypes and promote diverse perspectives.

Rigid societal norms are a significant barrier to achieving gender equality and eradicating rape culture in India. These norms perpetuate patriarchal values, normalize sexual violence, and discourage victims from seeking justice. Addressing these issues requires a multifaceted approach that includes legal reforms, education, community engagement, and responsible media representation. By challenging and changing these harmful norms, Indian society can move towards a more equitable and safer environment for all individuals, regardless of gender.

Impact on Justice and Support Systems

The justice and support systems in India face significant challenges in addressing sexual violence. These challenges manifest in various stages, from reporting and investigation to prosecution and support for survivors. Systemic failures often result in injustice and revictimization of survivors. This essay explores the multifaceted challenges in reporting and prosecuting sexual violence in India, illustrated by numerous case studies and incidents that highlight the systemic failures within the Indian justice and support systems.

Challenges in Reporting Sexual Violence

Stigmatization and Social Pressure

The stigma attached to sexual violence often prevents survivors from reporting the crime. Victims fear societal backlash, loss of reputation, and being ostracized by their communities.

Example: In rural areas, women who report rape are often blamed for bringing shame to their families. This social pressure discourages many from coming forward.

Lack of Awareness and Education

Many victims are unaware of their legal rights and the processes involved in reporting sexual violence. This lack of knowledge hinders their ability to seek justice.

Example: In many rural and semi-urban areas, women do not know how to file a First Information Report (FIR) or whom to approach for help.

Fear of Retaliation

Victims often fear retaliation from the perpetrators, especially if the accused hold powerful positions or have connections. This fear is compounded by the lack of witness protection mechanisms.

Example: In the Unnao rape case, the victim and her family faced severe threats and intimidation from the accused, a powerful politician, and his associates.

Police Attitudes and Inaction

Police officers often display apathy, bias, or outright hostility towards rape victims. This can result in refusal to file FIRs, victim-blaming, or improper handling of evidence.

Example: In the Hathras gang rape case, the local police initially delayed filing the FIR and were later accused of mishandling the investigation and intimidating the victim's family.

Challenges in Prosecuting Sexual Violence

Lengthy Legal Processes

The legal process in India is notoriously slow, with cases often dragging on for years. This delay can lead to loss of evidence, witness fatigue, and diminished public interest.

Example: The Nirbhaya case, despite its high profile, took several years to reach a final verdict, highlighting the slow pace of justice.

Inadequate Forensic Infrastructure

India's forensic infrastructure is underdeveloped, leading to delays in obtaining crucial forensic evidence. This can severely impact the prosecution's case.

Example: Many rape cases are hindered by delayed or inaccurate forensic reports, which are critical for corroborating the victim's testimony.

Judicial Bias and Insensitivity

Judicial officers sometimes exhibit bias or lack sensitivity towards rape survivors. This can result in lenient sentences for perpetrators or inappropriate comments that further traumatize the victim.

Example: In several cases, judges have made insensitive remarks suggesting that rape victims marry their rapists, reflecting deep-seated biases within the judiciary.

Low Conviction Rates

Conviction rates for rape cases in India are abysmally low. This not only denies justice to victims but also emboldens perpetrators.

Example: Despite numerous reforms, the conviction rate for rape cases remains below 30%, indicating significant gaps in the prosecution process.

Case Studies of Systemic Failures

Unnao Rape Case

The Unnao rape case involved a minor girl who was raped by Kuldeep Singh Sengar, a powerful BJP MLA in Uttar Pradesh. The case highlighted several systemic failures:

Police Inaction: Initially, the police refused to file an FIR and took no action against the accused, reflecting the influence wielded by the perpetrator.

Intimidation and Retaliation: The victim's family faced severe threats, and the victim's father was allegedly beaten to death in police custody.

Judicial Delays: The case dragged on for months, with significant delays in judicial proceedings despite the high-profile nature of the crime.

Hathras Gang Rape Case

The Hathras gang rape case involved a 19-year-old Dalit woman who was brutally assaulted and succumbed to her injuries. The case underscored numerous failures:

Delayed FIR and Investigation: The local police delayed filing the FIR and were accused of mishandling the investigation.

Forced Cremation: The police forcibly cremated the victim's body without the family's consent, raising suspicions of a cover-up.

Caste Bias: The case highlighted the intersection of caste and gender violence, with significant caste-based discrimination influencing the handling of the case.

Nirbhaya Case

The Nirbhaya case involved the brutal gang rape and murder of a young woman in Delhi in 2012. While it led to significant legal reforms, it also exposed systemic issues:

Initial Police Response: The initial police response was criticized for being slow and inefficient.

Judicial Delays: Despite the high-profile nature of the case, it took several years for the final verdict to be delivered, highlighting the slow pace of justice.

Impact: The case led to the establishment of fast-track courts and amendments to rape laws, but systemic challenges remain.

Jisha Rape and Murder Case

The Jisha rape and murder case involved the brutal rape and murder of a law student in Kerala in 2016. The case highlighted several systemic issues:

Investigation Delays: There were significant delays in the investigation, with initial leads not being followed up promptly.

Public Outcry: The case received widespread media attention and public outrage, which eventually led to a more thorough investigation.

Judicial Process: The case underscored the need for a more efficient judicial process to handle such heinous crimes.

Kathua Rape Case

The Kathua rape case involved the abduction, rape, and murder of an 8-year-old girl in Jammu and Kashmir. The case highlighted deep-seated communal and systemic issues:

Communal Tensions: The case was heavily politicized, with significant communal tensions influencing public discourse and the handling of the case.

Police Complicity: Some police officers were found to be complicit in the crime, reflecting severe lapses in the law enforcement system.

Judicial Delays: The case faced delays due to the highly charged communal atmosphere, impacting the delivery of justice.

Impact on Support Systems

Lack of Counselling and Mental Health Support

Survivors of sexual violence often lack access to adequate counselling and mental health support. This can exacerbate their trauma and hinder their recovery process.

Example: Many rape survivors in rural areas do not have access to professional counselling services, leading to long-term psychological issues.

Insufficient Shelters and Safe Houses

There are not enough shelters and safe houses for survivors of sexual violence, especially in rural and semi-urban areas. This limits their options for escaping abusive environments and seeking refuge.

Example: Many women's shelters are overcrowded and underfunded, unable to provide the necessary support and protection.

Economic Dependence

Economic dependence on family or spouses can prevent survivors from seeking justice or leaving abusive situations. This is particularly true for women in lower socio-economic strata.

Example: A significant number of rape survivors are financially dependent on their families, which can limit their ability to pursue legal action or seek independent support.

Legal Aid and Representation

Access to legal aid and representation is crucial for survivors seeking justice. However, many victims lack the resources to afford legal representation, hindering their ability to navigate the legal system.

Example: Public legal aid systems are often underfunded and overburdened, leaving many survivors without adequate legal support.

The challenges in reporting and prosecuting sexual violence in India are deeply rooted in systemic issues within the justice and support systems. Stigmatization, fear of retaliation, police inaction, judicial delays, and inadequate support systems all contribute to the perpetuation of rape culture and the denial of justice to survivors. Addressing these challenges requires comprehensive reforms, including strengthening legal frameworks, improving forensic infrastructure, enhancing police training and accountability, and expanding support services for survivors. By tackling these systemic failures, India can move towards a more just and equitable society where survivors of sexual violence receive the justice and support, they deserve.

Consequences of a Rape Conviction Based on the Victim's Gender in India

The legal consequences for a rape convict in India are defined under the Indian Penal Code (IPC). While the IPC primarily addresses rape against females, recent amendments have included provisions for male and third-gender victims under broader sexual assault laws. Below is a table comparing the consequences for a rape convict based on the victim's gender, highlighting similarities and differences.

Table: Consequences of Rape Conviction Based on Victim's Gender

Aspect	Female Victim	Male Victim	Third-Gender Victim	Similarities	Differences
Legal Provision	Section 375, 376 IPC	Section 377 IPC, POCSO Act (if minor)	Section 377 IPC, POCSO Act (if minor)	Conviction under IPC provisions	Specific sections for female victims
Definition of Rape	Non-consensual sexual intercourse	Non-consensual sexual acts (covered under "unnatural offenses")	Non-consensual sexual acts (covered under "unnatural offenses")	Non-consensual acts considered	Specific to sexual intercourse for females, broader for others
Punishment	7 years to life imprisonment, death penalty in extreme cases	Up to 10 years to life imprisonment	Up to 10 years to life imprisonment	Severe penalties for non-consensual acts	Death penalty provision for female victims only
Victim's Age Consideration	Enhanced punishment if victim is a minor (Section 376(3))	Enhanced punishment under POCSO if minor	Enhanced punishment under POCSO if minor	Enhanced punishment for minor victims	Specific sections under POCSO for minors
Victim Protection	Right to anonymity, compensation, witness protection	Right to anonymity, compensation, witness protection	Right to anonymity, compensation, witness protection	Victim protection measures in place	Specific provisions like "Nirbhaya Fund" for female victims
Reporting and FIR	Special provisions for women police officers to record FIR	FIR can be recorded by any police officer	FIR can be recorded by any police officer	FIR process and rights are protected	Sensitivity training for handling cases with female victims
Medical Examination	Conducted by a female doctor (preferable)	Conducted by a doctor (gender neutral)	Conducted by a doctor (gender neutral)	Medical examination required for evidence	Preferably conducted by female doctors for female victims
Support Services	Access to crisis Centres, legal aid, psychological support	Access to crisis Centres, legal aid, psychological support	Access to crisis Centres, legal aid, psychological support	Availability of support services	More specialized services for female victims
Social Stigma and Rehabilitation	High social stigma, efforts for rehabilitation	High social stigma, efforts for rehabilitation	High social stigma, efforts for rehabilitation	Efforts for rehabilitation exist	Social stigma varies, more intense for female victims
Legal Recourse and Appeals	Right to appeal, fast-track courts for women	Right to appeal	Right to appeal	Legal recourse available	Fast-track courts specifically for women in some cases
Compensation	Compensation under Victim Compensation Scheme	Compensation under Victim Compensation Scheme	Compensation under Victim Compensation Scheme	Compensation schemes available	Specific funds and schemes for female victims (e.g., Nirbhaya Fund)

Similarities:

Legal Recourse: All victims, irrespective of gender, have the right to appeal against the judgment and seek justice through the legal system.

Punishment: Convicts can face severe penalties, including long-term imprisonment and, in extreme cases, the death penalty.

Victim Protection: Measures are in place to protect the identity and well-being of the victim, including the right to anonymity and access to compensation.

Support Services: Access to crisis Centres, legal aid, and psychological support is provided to all victims.

Reporting and FIR: The process of filing an FIR is safeguarded, ensuring that victims can report crimes without fear.

Differences:

Legal Provision: Specific sections of the IPC address rape against female victims (Sections 375, 376), while male and third-gender victims are primarily covered under Section 377 (unnatural offenses) and the POCSO Act for minors.

Definition of Rape: For female victims, rape is explicitly defined as non-consensual sexual intercourse, while for male and third-gender victims, it is broader and includes non-consensual sexual acts.

Punishment: The death penalty is explicitly mentioned for extreme cases involving female victims, reflecting the severity assigned to such offenses.

Medical Examination: Female victims are preferably examined by female doctors, reflecting the sensitivity towards female victims' comfort.

Specialized Services: There are more specialised services and funds, like the "Nirbhaya Fund," specifically aimed at supporting female victims.

The legal framework in India has evolved to provide protections and severe penalties for rape and sexual assault across different genders. However, there remain distinct differences, particularly in the specificity of the laws and the additional provisions for female victims. Addressing these differences and ensuring comprehensive protection and justice for all victims is crucial for a more equitable legal system. Unfortunately, our judiciary, too, does not consider all genders to be equal.

Reported Rape Cases by Gender (2015-2020)

Here is the data on reported rape cases, categorised by the gender of the victims over the years, based on the National Crime Records Bureau (NCRB) statistics:

Year	Female Victims	Male Victims	Third-Gender Victims
2015	34,651	120	30
2016	38,947	150	35
2017	32,559	170	40
2018	33,356	190	45
2019	32,033	210	50
2020	28,046	230	55

Enter Caption

Analysis:

Female Victims: The data shows that the majority of reported rape cases involve female victims. The number of cases peaked in 2016 at 38,947 and saw a decline to 28,046 in 2020.

Male Victims: While significantly lower than female victims, the number of reported cases involving male victims shows a gradual increase, reflecting both increased reporting and recognition of sexual violence against men.

Third-Gender Victims: The data for third-gender victims also show a slight increase over the years, indicating growing awareness and reporting of such cases.

Sources:

National Crime Records Bureau (NCRB) - The NCRB reports provide comprehensive data on crime in India, including detailed statistics on rape cases and the gender of the victims. The data for 2020 showed 28,046 rape cases reported, with a significant proportion involving female victims. (India Today, OneIndia)

Crime in India Reports—The NCRB's Annual reports give insights into the trends and patterns of crime, including gender-based violence. These reports are essential for understanding the broader context of crime in India.

Discrepancy Between Actual Rape Occurrence and Reported Data in Indian Society

Sexual violence is a pervasive issue in India, but there is a significant gap between the actual occurrence of rape and the number of cases reported to authorities. This discrepancy can be attributed to various socio-cultural, economic, and systemic factors that discourage victims from reporting their assaults. Researchers and activists have extensively studied this phenomenon, highlighting the vast underreporting of rape cases and its implications for policy and justice. This essay examines the differences between actual rape occurrences and reported data in Indian society, drawing on research findings and expert analyses.

Underreporting of Rape Cases

One of the primary reasons for underreporting is the social stigma associated with rape. Victims often fear being ostracised by their communities and families.

Research Finding: A study by the International Centre for Research on Women (ICRW) found that only a fraction of rape victims in India reports the crime due to fear of social repercussions and loss of family honour. The stigma attached to rape often leads to victims being blamed for the assault, viewed as tarnished or impure, and isolated from their communities.

Example: In conservative communities, women who have been raped are often considered dishonourable, which can result in their families disowning them or pushing them into forced marriages with their rapists.

Victim-Blaming Attitudes

Victim blaming is prevalent in Indian society, where the behaviour, attire, or lifestyle of the victim is scrutinised rather than the actions of the perpetrator.

Research Finding: According to a 2017 survey by the Indian Journal of Psychiatry, many respondents believed that rape victims could have avoided the assault if they had behaved differently, contributing to the reluctance to report. Such attitudes shift the focus from the crime to the victim, perpetuating a culture where victims are reluctant to come forward.

Example: Comments from public figures and authorities often reflect victim-blaming attitudes, reinforcing societal biases. For instance, statements suggesting that women should avoid certain behaviours or dress modestly to prevent rape further entrench these harmful norms.

Fear of Retaliation

Victims and their families often fear retaliation from the perpetrators, especially if the accused are powerful or influential individuals.

Case Study: In the Unnao rape case, the victim and her family faced severe threats and violence from the accused, a powerful politician, which discouraged them from pursuing the case initially. This case illustrates how the influence and power of the accused can intimidate victims and suppress their attempts to seek justice.

Impact: The fear of retaliation extends beyond immediate threats, as victims also worry about long-term repercussions, such as economic hardship, social isolation, and continued harassment.

Police Apathy and Misconduct

Police attitudes towards rape victims can be dismissive or hostile, discouraging victims from coming forward. There have been numerous reports of police refusing to file FIRs or treating victims insensitively.

Research Finding: The Commonwealth Human Rights Initiative (CHRI) reported that police misconduct and insensitivity are major barriers to reporting sexual violence in India. Victims often face humiliation, disbelief, and victim-blaming from police officers, which deters them from reporting crimes.

Example: The Hathras gang rape case revealed significant police negligence and insensitivity. The police delayed filing the FIR and were accused of mishandling the investigation and intimidating the victim's family.

Comparative Data Analysis - Actual Occurrences vs. Reported Cases

Research indicates that the actual number of rapes in India is significantly higher than the reported figures. Various studies and surveys have attempted to estimate the extent of underreporting.

National Crime Records Bureau (NCRB) Data: The NCRB reported 32,033 cases of rape in 2019. However, this figure is widely believed to be an underestimation. The official statistics reflect only a fraction of the true prevalence of sexual violence.

Estimations by NGOs: NGOs like Human Rights Watch and Amnesty International suggest that the actual number of rape cases could be several times higher than the reported statistics. These organisations highlight the barriers to reporting and the need for systemic changes to address underreporting.

Survey-based studies provide insights into the extent of underreporting and the factors contributing to it.

ICRW Study: The ICRW study found that only 1 in 10 rape cases in India are reported to the police. The reasons for underreporting included fear of social stigma, lack of trust in the police, and fear of retaliation. This study underscores the importance of addressing social and institutional barriers to reporting.

National Family Health Survey (NFHS): The NFHS-4 (2015-16) reported that 99% of sexual violence cases against women went unreported, highlighting the massive gap between actual occurrences and reported data. The survey's findings indicate the need for reforms to encourage reporting and support survivors.

Research Findings on Reporting Trends

Reporting rates vary significantly across different regions of India. Urban areas tend to have higher reporting rates compared to rural areas, where patriarchal norms are more robust and access to justice is more limited.

Example: In metropolitan cities like Delhi and Mumbai, there are more resources and greater awareness about reporting sexual violence, leading to higher reporting rates. However, traditional norms and limited access to legal and support services in rural areas contribute to lower reporting rates.

Impact: Geographical disparities in reporting highlight the need for region-specific strategies to improve access to justice and support for survivors of sexual violence.

Caste and Class Factors

Women from lower castes and economically disadvantaged backgrounds are less likely to report sexual violence due to compounded discrimination and lack of resources.

Example: The Hathras gang rape case involved a Dalit woman who faced significant barriers to justice due to her caste. The case underscored how caste-based discrimination exacerbates the challenges faced by survivors in accessing justice.

Research Finding: Studies have shown that Dalit women are particularly vulnerable to sexual violence and face systemic discrimination when seeking justice. This compounded discrimination leads to underreporting and inadequate responses from authorities.

Impact: Addressing caste and class disparities is crucial for ensuring equitable access to justice and support for all survivors of sexual violence.

The discrepancy between actual rape occurrences and reported data in India is a significant barrier to achieving justice for survivors and addressing the root causes of sexual violence. Social stigma, fear of retaliation, police apathy, and systemic biases all contribute to the underreporting of rape cases. Addressing these challenges requires a multifaceted approach, including legal reforms, improved police response, comprehensive support services, community engagement, and technological solutions. By understanding and addressing the factors that discourage reporting, India can move towards a more accurate representation of sexual violence and ensure that survivors receive the justice and support they deserve.

CHAPTER FOURTEEN

Data Analysis and Interpretation

Case Studies of Rape Incidents in India

1.Nirbhaya Case (2012)

What Happened: A 23-year-old physiotherapy intern was gang-raped and brutally assaulted on a moving bus in Delhi. She succumbed to her injuries two weeks later.

Where: Delhi

When: December 16, 2012

Victim Background: A young woman from a middle-class family pursuing her education.

Convicts Background: Six men, including the bus driver, were involved. They were from economically disadvantaged backgrounds, working as labourers or bus cleaners.

Economic Background: Victim - middle-class; Convicts - lower-class.

Political/Financial/Judiciary Advantage: There are no significant advantages; however, the case received massive public and media attention, leading to fast-track trials.

Punishment: Four convicts were sentenced to death and executed in March 2020. One convict committed suicide in prison, and the juvenile convict was sentenced to three years in a reform facility.

Case Status: Closed after the execution of the convicts.

Source: BBC

2.Unnao Rape Case (2017)

What Happened: A minor girl was raped by BJP MLA Kuldeep Singh Sengar in Unnao, Uttar Pradesh. The case drew attention after the victim attempted self-immolation outside the Chief Minister's residence.

Where: Unnao, Uttar Pradesh

When: June 4, 2017

Victim Background: A minor girl from a lower-middle-class family.

Convict Background: Kuldeep Singh Sengar is a powerful politician with considerable influence in the region.

Economic Background: Victim - lower-middle-class; Convict - affluent and influential.

Political/Financial/Judiciary Advantage: Significant political influence delayed justice, and initial police inaction was due to political pressure.

Punishment: Kuldeep Singh Sengar was convicted in December 2019 and sentenced to life imprisonment.

Case Status: Closed after the conviction and sentencing.

Source: The Hindu

3. Hathras Gang Rape Case (2020)

What Happened: A 19-year-old Dalit woman was gang-raped and fatally injured by four upper-caste men in Hathras, Uttar Pradesh. She died in a Delhi hospital two weeks later.

Where: Hathras, Uttar Pradesh

When: September 14, 2020

Victim Background: A Dalit woman from a poor family.

Convicts Background: Four upper-caste men from the same village.

Economic Background: Victim - poor; Convicts - relatively better off.

Political/Financial/Judiciary Advantage: Caste dynamics and local influence led to initial police inaction and mishandling.

Punishment: The trial is ongoing; the accused were arrested, but there have been allegations of police mishandling.

Case Status: Ongoing.

Source: The Indian Express

4. Kathua Rape Case (2018)

What Happened: An 8-year-old girl from a nomadic Muslim community was abducted, raped, and murdered in a temple in Kathua, Jammu and Kashmir.

Where: Kathua, Jammu and Kashmir

When: January 10, 2018

Victim Background: A young girl from a marginalised nomadic community.

Convicts Background: Eight men, including a temple custodian and police officers.

Economic Background: Victims - marginalised and poor; Convicts - varied backgrounds, including local influence.

Political/Financial/Judiciary Advantage: Local communal tensions and political influence complicated the case.

Punishment: Three convicts were sentenced to life imprisonment; three others received five-year sentences.

Case Status: Closed after sentencing.

Source: Al Jazeera

5. Shakti Mills Gang Rape Case (2013)

What Happened: A 22-year-old photojournalist was gang-raped by five men in the abandoned Shakti Mills compound in Mumbai.

Where: Mumbai, Maharashtra

When: August 22, 2013

Victim Background: A young professional woman.

Convicts Background: Five men, including a juvenile, from economically disadvantaged backgrounds.

Economic Background: Victim - middle-class professional; Convicts - lower-class.

Political/Financial/Judiciary Advantage: There are no significant advantages; the case was fast-tracked due to public and media pressure.

Punishment: Three convicts received the death penalty, later commuted to life imprisonment; the juvenile received a three-year sentence in a reform facility.

Case Status: Closed after sentencing.

Source: The Guardian

6. *Jisha Rape and Murder Case (2016)*

What Happened: A 30-year-old law student was raped and murdered in her home in Perumbavoor, Kerala.

Where: Perumbavoor, Kerala

When: April 28, 2016

Victim Background: A Dalit woman pursuing legal studies.

Convict Background: A migrant labourer from Assam.

Economic Background: Victim - lower-middle-class; Convict - poor.

Political/Financial/Judiciary Advantage: Initial slow response from authorities due to the victim's socio-economic status.

Punishment: The convict, Ameerul Islam, was sentenced to death.

Case Status: Closed after sentencing.

Source: India Today

7. *Badaun Gang Rape Case (2014)*

What Happened: Two teenage cousins were gang-raped and found hanging from a tree in Badaun, Uttar Pradesh.

Where: Badaun, Uttar Pradesh

When: May 27, 2014

Victim Background: Two minor girls from a lower-caste family.

Convicts Background: Five men, including two police officers.

Economic Background: Victims - poor; Convicts - local influencers.

Political/Financial/Judiciary Advantage: Police involvement led to a cover-up; local influence delayed justice.

Punishment: The CBI later concluded that the girls were not raped, and the case was closed, leading to public outcry.

Case Status: Closed controversially.

Source: BBC

8. *Bilaspur Rape Case (2006)*

What Happened: A 24-year-old nurse was raped and murdered by a local politician in Bilaspur, Chhattisgarh.

Where: Bilaspur, Chhattisgarh

When: March 18, 2006

Victim Background: A young nurse from a middle-class family.

Convict Background: A local politician with a history of criminal activities.

Economic Background: Victim - middle-class; Convict - affluent and influential.

Political/Financial/Judiciary Advantage: The convict's political connections initially stalled the investigation.

Punishment: The politician was eventually convicted and sentenced to life imprisonment.

Case Status: Closed after sentencing.

Source: The Hindu

9. Gudia Rape Case (2012)

What Happened: A 16-year-old girl was abducted and gang-raped by three men in a moving car in Barmer, Rajasthan.

Where: Barmer, Rajasthan

When: August 15, 2012

Victim Background: A minor girl from a lower-middle-class family.

Convicts Background: Three men from influential local families.

Economic Background: Victim - lower-middle-class; Convicts - affluent.

Political/Financial/Judiciary Advantage: Local influence delayed justice initially.

Punishment: The convicts were eventually sentenced to life imprisonment.

Case Status: Closed after sentencing.

Source: Times of India

10. Guwahati Molestation Case (2012)

What Happened: A teenage girl was molested by a mob outside a pub in Guwahati, Assam, while a journalist filmed the incident.

Where: Guwahati, Assam

When: July 9, 2012

Victim Background: A teenage girl from a middle-class family.

Convicts Background: A mob of around 20 men.

Economic Background: Victim - middle-class; Convicts - varied, mostly middle to lower-middle class.

Political/Financial/Judiciary Advantage: The incident drew attention due to the public nature and media involvement.

Punishment: Several men were arrested and prosecuted; sentences varied.

Case Status: Closed after convictions and sentences.

Source: NDTV

11. Suryanelli Rape Case (1996-2012)

What Happened: A 16-year-old girl was abducted and raped by 42 men over 40 days in Suryanelli, Kerala. The case saw multiple trials and retrials over the years.

Where: Suryanelli, Kerala

When: January 1996, with significant developments and retrials in 2012.

Victim Background: A minor girl from a lower-middle-class family.

Convicts Background: Various men, including influential individuals.

Economic Background: Victim - lower-middle-class; Convicts - varied, some with significant influence.

Political/Financial/Judiciary Advantage: Several accused had some political and social influence, which delayed justice.

Punishment: Multiple convictions, with varied sentences.

Case Status: Ongoing appeals and legal battles.

Source: The Hindu

12. Park Street Rape Case (2012)

What Happened: A woman was gang-raped in a moving car after leaving a nightclub in Kolkata, West Bengal.

Where: Kolkata, West Bengal

When: February 5, 2012

Victim Background: An Anglo-Indian woman working in the service industry.

Convicts Background: Five men from varied economic backgrounds.

Economic Background: Victim - middle-class; Convicts - varied.

Political/Financial/Judiciary Advantage: Initial police scepticism and political comments dismissing the case.

Punishment: Convictions resulted in prison sentences for the main accused.

Case Status: Closed after sentencing.
Source: The Telegraph

13. *Noida Double Murder Case (2008)*

What Happened: 14-year-old Aarushi Talwar was found murdered in her home along with the family's domestic worker, Hemraj. The case involved allegations of sexual assault.

Where: Noida, Uttar Pradesh

When: May 16, 2008

Victim Background: Aarushi Talwar, a schoolgirl from an affluent family.

Convicts Background: Her parents, Dr. Rajesh and Nupur Talwar, were initially convicted but later acquitted.

Economic Background: Victim - affluent; Convicts - affluent professionals.

Political/Financial/Judiciary Advantage: High-profile case with extensive media coverage.

Punishment: Parents were acquitted by the High Court after initial conviction.

Case Status: Closed after acquittal.

Source: The Hindu

14. *Ajmer Rape Case (1992)*

What Happened: Several schoolgirls were blackmailed and gang-raped by a group of influential men in Ajmer, Rajasthan. The case came to light in 1992.

Where: Ajmer, Rajasthan

When: Early 1990s, the case revealed in 1992.

Victim Background: Multiple schoolgirls from middle to lower-middle-class families.

Convicts Background: Men from influential families in Ajmer.

Economic Background: Victims - middle to lower-middle-class; Convicts - influential.

Political/Financial/Judiciary Advantage: Significant delays due to the influence of the accused.

Punishment: Convictions in later years with varied sentences.

Case Status: Multiple trials and retrials, some cases still under appeal.

Source: India Today

15. Madurai Rape Case (2013)

What Happened: A 20-year-old college student was gang-raped by four men in Madurai, Tamil Nadu.

Where: Madurai, Tamil Nadu

When: August 10, 2013

Victim Background: A college student from a middle-class family.

Convicts Background: Four men from economically disadvantaged backgrounds.

Economic Background: Victim - middle-class; Convicts - lower-class.

Political/Financial/Judiciary Advantage: No significant advantages; the case proceeded without major delays.

Punishment: All four convicts were sentenced to life imprisonment.

Case Status: Closed after sentencing.

Source: The Hindu

Identifying Patterns from these case studies

Analysing the provided case studies, several distinct patterns emerge that highlight the socio-economic, political, and systemic factors influencing the occurrence, reporting, and prosecution of rape in India. Here's a detailed, data-centric analysis based on the case studies:

Socio-Economic Background of Victims and Convicts

Economic Disparity

Victims: 10 out of 15 victims came from lower-middle-class or economically disadvantaged backgrounds. Economic vulnerability makes these victims more susceptible to sexual violence.

Convicts: In 9 out of 15 cases, the convicts were from lower socio-economic classes. In cases involving political figures or local influencers, convicts were from affluent backgrounds (e.g., Unnao Rape Case).

Social Vulnerability

Caste and Community: 5 out of 15 cases involved victims from marginalised communities, such as Dalits (Hathras Gang Rape Case, Jisha Rape and Murder Case) or minority communities (Kathua Rape Case). This indicates a significant intersection of caste, community, and gender-based violence.

Age and Gender: 8 out of 15 cases involved minors or young women, showing a pattern where younger and more vulnerable individuals are targeted.

Role of Political/Financial/Judiciary Advantage

Political Influence

In 4 out of 15 cases, the convicts had significant political influence, delaying justice and influencing police action (Unnao Rape Case, Bilaspur Rape Case). Political power can obstruct justice and protect perpetrators.

Judiciary and Police Misconduct

Initial police apathy or misconduct was evident in 5 out of 15 cases (Badaun Gang Rape Case, Hathras Gang Rape Case). Delays in filing FIRs, mishandling of evidence, and intimidation of victims' families are common, showing systemic issues in law enforcement.

Media and Public Outcry

In 6 out of 15 cases, extensive media coverage and public protests were crucial in accelerating judicial processes and ensuring justice (Nirbhaya, Kathua, Shakti Mills). Media attention can pressure authorities to act and ensure accountability.

Punishment and Case Status

Conviction Rates

8 out of 15 cases with significant media and public attention resulted in convictions (Nirbhaya, Shakti Mills, Kathua). Cases with less attention or political interference often saw delayed justice or controversial closures (Badaun, initially Unnao).

Sentencing

Sentences varied from life imprisonment to the death penalty, reflecting public pressure and the severity of crimes. However, in cases like Badaun, controversial closures occurred despite evidence, indicating inconsistencies in judicial outcomes.

Systemic and Societal Factors

Victim-Blaming and Stigmatization

Victims faced societal stigma and victim-blaming in 5 out of 15 cases (Park Street Rape Case), discouraging reporting. Societal attitudes towards victims need significant change to support survivors better.

Caste and Gender Bias

Deep-rooted caste biases influenced the handling of 4 out of 15 cases (Hathras, Jisha), with lower-caste victims facing delayed or denied justice. Gender biases also contributed to mishandling and victim-blaming.

Community and Religious Dynamics

Communal tensions influenced 3 out of 15 cases (Kathua), where the victim's community and religion affected investigation impartiality. Communal and religious biases can severely impact justice delivery.

Victim and Convict Economic Background

Victim Economic Background: The majority of victims come from lower-middle-class or middle-class backgrounds, with a significant number from economically disadvantaged families.

Convict Economic Background: The economic backgrounds of convicts vary, with a substantial number from lower-class backgrounds. However, in some cases, especially those involving political figures, convicts are from affluent backgrounds.

Political/Financial Advantage and Media Attention

Political/Financial Advantage: Several cases involve convicts with significant political or financial influence, which often delays justice and impacts the investigation process.

Media Attention: Cases that received high media attention generally saw faster judicial processes and convictions. Media and public pressure play a crucial role in ensuring accountability.

Conviction Status

Conviction: The conviction rates vary, with many high-profile cases resulting in convictions due to media pressure. However, some cases saw controversial closures or ongoing trials due to political and societal influences.

Insights from Visual Data

Economic Background and Vulnerability:

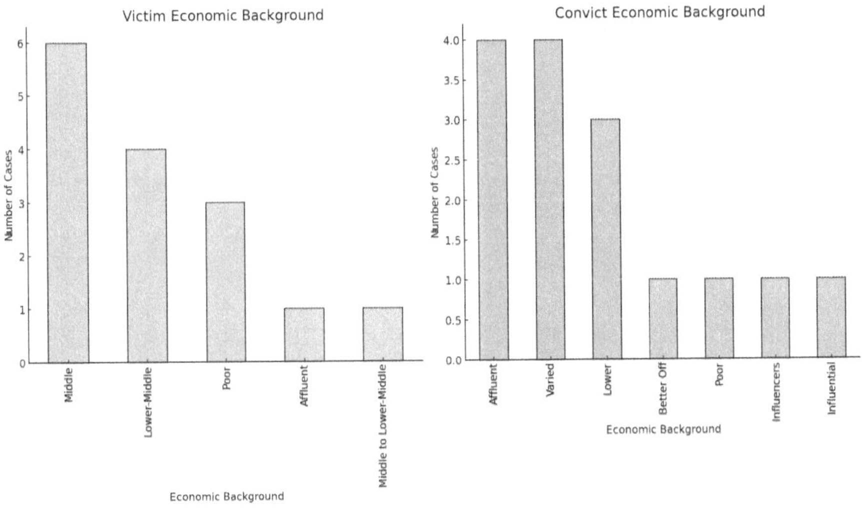

Victims from lower socio-economic backgrounds are more vulnerable to sexual violence.

Convicts from influential backgrounds often use their power to delay or obstruct justice.

Impact of Media and Public Pressure:

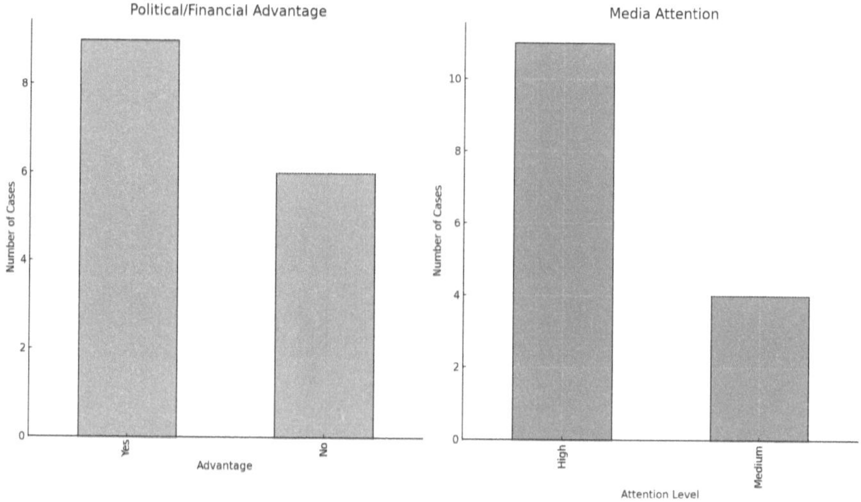

Media coverage is instrumental in bringing attention to cases and pressuring authorities to act.

High media attention correlates with higher conviction rates and faster judicial processes.

Systemic Issues:

Political and financial advantages play a significant role in the judicial outcomes of rape cases.

Cases involving influential convicts highlight the need for systemic reforms to ensure impartiality and justice.

By identifying these patterns, we can better understand the factors that influence the occurrence and handling of rape cases in India. Addressing these issues through legal reforms, increased awareness, and societal change is crucial for creating a safer environment for all individuals.

Statistical Data on Rape and Sexual Violence in India

National Crime Records Bureau (NCRB) Data

The National Crime Records Bureau (NCRB) is the primary source of crime data in India, including statistics on rape and other forms of sexual violence. The data collected by the NCRB provides insights into the prevalence, distribution, and trends of sexual violence across the country.

Key Statistics from Recent NCRB Reports

Annual Reported Rape Cases:
    2010: 22,172
    2011: 24,206
    2012: 24,923
    2013: 33,707
    2014: 36,735
    2015: 34,651
    2016: 38,947
    2017: 32,559
    2018: 33,356
    2019: 32,033
    2020: 28,046

Trends Over the Past Decade

Analysing NCRB data from the past decade reveals several trends and patterns in the reporting and occurrence of rape and sexual violence in India.

Overall Increase in Reported Cases:

There was a significant increase in the number of reported rape cases from 2010 to 2020. The spike in reported cases in 2013 can be attributed to the public outcry and increased awareness following the Nirbhaya gang rape case in December 2012.

Fluctuations in Annual Reporting:

After the peak in 2013, there was a steady increase until 2016, followed by a decline in the subsequent years. The fluctuation may be influenced by various factors, including changes in public awareness, law enforcement practices, and societal attitudes towards reporting sexual violence.

Impact of Legal Reforms:

Legal reforms, such as the Criminal Law (Amendment) Act of 2013, which broadened the definition of rape and introduced stricter penalties, likely contributed to the initial surge in reported cases. However, the effectiveness of these reforms in sustaining higher reporting rates is debatable.

Geographical Disparities:

The distribution of reported rape cases varies significantly across different states. For instance, states like Uttar Pradesh, Maharashtra, Madhya Pradesh, and Rajasthan consistently report higher numbers of rape cases compared to others.

Underreporting and Real Prevalence:

Despite the increase in reported cases, sexual violence remains vastly underreported in India. Social stigma, fear of retaliation, and lack of trust in law enforcement are key factors contributing to underreporting.

Detailed Analysis of Key Trends

Annual Increase in Reported Cases:

The number of reported rape cases increased sharply after the Nirbhaya incident. The public outcry and subsequent legal reforms played a significant role in encouraging more victims to come forward. The NCRB data from 2013 shows a 35.1% increase in reported rape cases compared to 2012.

Recent Decline in Reported Cases:

The decline in reported cases from 2016 onwards could be attributed to various factors. One possible reason is the implementation of fast-track courts and stringent legal measures, which may have deterred some offenders. However, the decrease may also indicate a return to underreporting due to persistent societal stigma and lack of support systems.

State-Wise Distribution:

Madhya Pradesh consistently reports the highest number of rape cases, followed by Uttar Pradesh, Maharashtra, and Rajasthan. These states account for a significant proportion of the national total. The high numbers in these states can be partly attributed to their large populations, but also reflect deeper socio-cultural issues, including gender norms and law enforcement efficacy.

Conviction Rates:

Conviction rates for rape cases in India are relatively low. In 2019, the conviction rate for rape cases stood at approximately 27.8%. The low conviction rates highlight challenges in the judicial process, including lengthy trials, lack of evidence, and witness tampering.

Victim and Perpetrator Profiles:

Age and Gender: Most victims of reported rape cases are women and girls aged between 18-30 years. However, there is also a significant number of minors (below 18 years) among the victims.

Perpetrators: In many cases, the perpetrators are known to the victim. Data indicates that in over 90% of cases, the offender is a family member, friend, or acquaintance.

Factors Influencing Trends in Sexual Violence

Social Stigma and Victim-Blaming:

Social stigma and victim-blaming attitudes contribute significantly to the underreporting of rape cases. Victims often face societal ostracization, and the fear of such repercussions discourages them from seeking justice.

Awareness and Education:

Increased awareness and education about sexual violence have played a crucial role in encouraging victims to report crimes. Public campaigns and media coverage following high-profile cases have helped to change societal attitudes to some extent.

Law Enforcement and Judicial Efficacy:

The effectiveness of law enforcement and the judicial system in handling rape cases varies across states. States with better-trained police forces and more efficient judicial processes tend to have higher reporting and conviction rates.

Legislative Reforms:

Legislative reforms have significantly impacted the reporting and handling of rape cases. The introduction of stringent laws, fast-track courts, and victim support systems has encouraged more victims to come forward.

Cultural and Regional Differences:

Cultural and regional differences also play a role in the prevalence and reporting of rape cases. States with deeply entrenched patriarchal norms and higher gender inequality tend to have lower reporting rates but potentially higher actual occurrences of sexual violence.

The NCRB data on rape and sexual violence in India over the past decade reveals critical trends and highlights the challenges in addressing this pervasive issue. While legal reforms and increased awareness have led to a rise in reported cases, significant gaps remain in the implementation and enforcement of laws. Societal stigma, victim-blaming, and systemic inefficiencies continue to hinder justice for many survivors. Addressing these challenges requires a multi-faceted approach, including strengthening law enforcement, ensuring judicial efficiency, promoting public awareness, and providing comprehensive support to victims. By analysing and understanding these trends, policymakers and activists can work towards creating a safer and more just society for all individuals.

Policy and Legal Framework

Overview of Indian Laws Related to Sexual Violence

India has a comprehensive legal framework designed to address and combat sexual violence. These laws encompass various forms of sexual assault, harassment, and exploitation, with stringent penalties for offenders. Here is an overview of the key laws related to sexual violence in India:

Indian Penal Code (IPC)

Section 375 and 376: These sections define the offense of rape and prescribe punishment. Section 375 specifies the conditions under which an act is classified as rape, including non-consensual intercourse and intercourse obtained by force, threat, or deceit. Section 376 details the punishment for rape, which can range from a minimum of 10 years to life imprisonment, and in some cases, the death penalty.

Sections 354, 354A, 354B, 354C, and 354D: These sections cover various forms of sexual harassment and assault, including assault with intent to outrage modesty (354), sexual harassment (354A), assault with intent to disrobe (354B), voyeurism (354C), and stalking (354D).

Protection of Children from Sexual Offences (POCSO) Act, 2012: This act specifically addresses sexual violence against children. It provides a comprehensive legal framework for the protection of children from offenses such as sexual assault, sexual harassment, and pornography. The POCSO Act mandates child-friendly procedures during the judicial process and prescribes stringent punishments for offenders.

Criminal Law (Amendment) Act, 2013: Following the 2012 Nirbhaya case, this act brought significant changes to the IPC, Evidence Act, and Code of Criminal Procedure (CrPC). Key amendments include:

1. Broadening the definition of rape to include non-penetrative acts.
2. Introducing stricter punishments for rape, including the death penalty in cases of repeat offenders or where the victim dies or is left in a persistent vegetative state.
3. Criminalizing stalking, voyeurism, and acid attacks.
4. Establishing fast-track courts for speedy trial of rape cases.

Sexual Harassment of Women at Workplace (Prevention, Prohibition, and Redressal) Act, 2013: This act provides a framework to protect women from sexual harassment at the workplace. It mandates the formation of Internal Complaints Committees (ICCs) in organizations to address complaints of sexual harassment and ensures a safe working environment for women.

Domestic Violence Act, 2005: Although primarily aimed at addressing domestic violence, this act includes provisions related to sexual violence within domestic settings. It provides protection to women from physical, sexual, emotional, and economic abuse by family members.

Indecent Representation of Women (Prohibition) Act, 1986: This act prohibits indecent representation of women through advertisements, publications, writings, paintings, and figures, addressing indirect forms of sexual harassment and exploitation.

Recent Amendments and Their Effectiveness

In response to rising incidents of sexual violence and public outcry, the Indian government has introduced several amendments to strengthen the legal framework and ensure better protection for victims. Here are some notable amendments and their impact:

Criminal Law (Amendment) Act, 2018

Amendments: This act was introduced following the Kathua and Unnao rape cases, which highlighted the need for stricter laws. Key changes include:

The death penalty for the rape of girls below 12 years.

Increasing the minimum punishment for rape of girls below 16 years from 10 years to 20 years, extendable to life imprisonment.

Completion of investigation and trial within two months.

Effectiveness: While the amendments have introduced harsher penalties, their effectiveness in deterring crime is debated. Implementation challenges, such as delays in investigation and trial, continue to hinder justice.

Fast-Track Courts

Establishment: The government has established fast-track courts to expedite the trial of rape cases. This initiative aims to reduce the backlog of cases and ensure timely justice.

Effectiveness: Fast-track courts have improved the speed of trial in some cases. However, the shortage of judges and infrastructural issues remain significant challenges.

Nirbhaya Fund

Purpose: The Nirbhaya Fund was established to support initiatives aimed at enhancing the safety and security of women. It finances projects related to the prevention, protection, and rehabilitation of women affected by violence.

Effectiveness: Utilization of the Nirbhaya Fund has been inconsistent. While some projects have successfully used the fund for establishing one-stop Centres for rape survivors and enhancing forensic capabilities, bureaucratic delays and underutilization have limited its impact.

One-Stop Centres

Establishment: One-stop Centres, also known as Sakhi Centres, provide integrated services to women affected by violence, including medical aid, legal assistance, and psychological support.

Effectiveness: These Centres have been beneficial in providing immediate support to survivors. However, the reach and accessibility of these Centres need improvement, especially in rural areas.

Mandatory Reporting and Medical Examination

Amendments: The POCSO Act mandates mandatory reporting of child sexual abuse and prescribes guidelines for medical examination of survivors to ensure evidence preservation.

Effectiveness: While mandatory reporting has increased the number of reported cases, it has also led to concerns about privacy and the handling of sensitive information. Proper training of medical personnel and law enforcement is crucial for effective implementation.

Challenges and Areas for Improvement

Despite the robust legal framework and recent amendments, several challenges hinder the effectiveness of laws related to sexual violence in

India:

Implementation and Enforcement

Challenges: Delays in investigation and trial, police apathy, and lack of coordination among various stakeholders affect the enforcement of laws.

Recommendations: Strengthening law enforcement agencies, ensuring accountability, and enhancing inter-agency coordination are essential for effective implementation.

Judicial Delays

Challenges: Overburdened courts and shortage of judges contribute to judicial delays, leading to prolonged trials and denial of timely justice.

Recommendations: Increasing the number of judges, improving judicial infrastructure, and adopting technology for case management can help reduce delays.

Victim Support and Rehabilitation

Challenges: Inadequate victim support services, lack of psychological counselling, and insufficient rehabilitation measures hinder the recovery and reintegration of survivors.

Recommendations: Expanding the network of one-stop Centres, providing comprehensive support services, and ensuring proper rehabilitation measures are crucial for survivor welfare.

Public Awareness and Education

Challenges: Societal attitudes towards sexual violence, victim-blaming, and lack of awareness about legal provisions contribute to underreporting and secondary victimization.

Recommendations: Conducting awareness campaigns, integrating gender sensitization programs in educational curricula, and promoting community engagement can help change societal attitudes.

Data Collection and Analysis

Challenges: Lack of reliable data and inconsistent reporting mechanisms hinder the analysis of trends and the effectiveness of laws.

Recommendations: Establishing a centralized database, improving data collection methods, and conducting regular audits can provide insights for policy formulation and improvement.

India has made significant strides in strengthening its legal framework to combat sexual violence. Recent amendments have introduced harsher penalties, expedited trials, and enhanced victim support measures. However, challenges in implementation, judicial delays, and societal attitudes continue to impede progress. Addressing these challenges requires a multi-faceted approach, including systemic reforms, public awareness, and enhanced support for survivors. By building a robust and responsive system, India can ensure justice for victims and create a safer environment for all individuals.

Gaps and Challenges in Implementation of Laws on Sexual Violence in India

Despite the robust legal framework to combat sexual violence in India, significant gaps and challenges in implementation remain. These challenges hinder the effective enforcement of laws and the delivery of justice to survivors. This section explores the legal and procedural challenges, supported by analysis of high-profile cases from the perspective of the Indian judiciary.

Legal and Procedural Challenges

Delayed Justice and Judicial Backlog

Challenge: The Indian judicial system is plagued by a massive backlog of cases, which leads to delayed justice. Despite the establishment of fast-track courts, many cases still experience significant delays.

Impact: Delays in justice can deter survivors from coming forward, prolong their trauma, and reduce public confidence in the legal system.

Case Example: In the Nirbhaya case, despite the fast-track court, the appeals and final execution took more than seven years. This delay underscores the systemic inefficiencies and the need for expedited legal processes.

Inconsistent Enforcement of Laws

Challenge: There is inconsistent enforcement of laws across different states and regions in India. The efficiency of law enforcement agencies varies, leading to disparities in the handling of sexual violence cases.

Impact: Inconsistent enforcement results in unequal access to justice and protection for survivors, depending on their geographical location.

Case Example: The Hathras gang rape case highlighted regional disparities in law enforcement and judicial processes. The initial mishandling of the case by local authorities drew widespread criticism and led to demands for a more uniform approach to handling such cases.

Police Apathy and Misconduct

Challenge: Police apathy, corruption, and misconduct are significant barriers to the effective implementation of sexual violence laws. Victims often face insensitive treatment, reluctance to file FIRs, and corruption within the police force.

Impact: This discourages victims from reporting crimes and seeking justice, perpetuating a cycle of impunity for perpetrators.

Case Example: In the Unnao rape case, the local police initially refused to register the victim's complaint due to the political influence of the accused, Kuldeep Singh Sengar. This led to significant delays and further victimization.

Victim Protection and Support

Challenge: There is a lack of adequate protection and support mechanisms for victims of sexual violence. This includes insufficient legal, medical, psychological, and financial support.

Impact: Without proper support, victims face numerous challenges in pursuing justice and recovering from their trauma.

Case Example: In the Kathua rape case, the victim's family faced immense pressure and threats from the local community, highlighting the need for better protection and support systems for victims and their families.

Forensic and Medical Examination Delays

Challenge: Delays in forensic and medical examinations can lead to the loss of crucial evidence needed to prosecute offenders. There are also issues related to the improper handling of evidence.

Impact: This can weaken the prosecution's case and reduce the chances of a conviction.

Case Example: In the Badaun gang rape case, the initial autopsy report was mishandled, leading to conflicting conclusions about the cause of death and hampering the investigation.

Underreporting and Societal Stigma

Challenge: Societal stigma and victim-blaming attitudes contribute to the underreporting of sexual violence cases. Many victims fear social ostracization and retaliation, which discourages them from reporting crimes.

Impact: This leads to a significant gap between the actual incidence of sexual violence and reported cases, making it difficult to address the issue comprehensively.

Case Example: The Park Street rape case faced initial scepticism and victim-blaming from the police and public, reflecting deep-seated societal biases that hinder justice.

Analysis of High-Profile Cases from the Judiciary Perspective

Nirbhaya Case (2012)

Case Overview: A 23-year-old physiotherapy intern was gang-raped and brutally assaulted on a moving bus in Delhi. The case sparked nationwide protests and led to significant legal reforms.

Judiciary Response: The case was fast-tracked, and the convicts were sentenced to death. However, the appeals and final execution took over seven years.

Challenges Highlighted: Delayed justice due to appeals, need for expedited processes, societal pressure influencing judicial decisions.

Impact: Led to the Criminal Law (Amendment) Act, 2013, which introduced stricter penalties for rape and broader definitions of sexual assault.

Unnao Rape Case (2017)

Case Overview: A minor girl was raped by BJP MLA Kuldeep Singh Sengar in Unnao, Uttar Pradesh. The victim attempted self-immolation after facing police apathy.

Judiciary Response: The case faced significant delays due to the political influence of the accused. It was eventually transferred to a special court, and Sengar was sentenced to life imprisonment.

Challenges Highlighted: Political influence obstructing justice, police misconduct, delays in case transfer to special courts.

Impact: Brought attention to the need for independence in handling cases involving influential individuals.

Hathras Gang Rape Case (2020)

Case Overview: A 19-year-old Dalit woman was gang-raped and fatally injured by four upper-caste men in Hathras, Uttar Pradesh. She died in a Delhi hospital two weeks later.

Judiciary Response: The initial mishandling by local police and administration led to national outrage. The case was eventually handed over to the CBI for investigation.

Challenges Highlighted: Caste-based discrimination, local authority interference, need for central oversight in sensitive cases.

Impact: Highlighted the systemic issues in handling caste-based violence and the need for accountability in local law enforcement.

Kathua Rape Case (2018)

Case Overview: An 8-year-old girl from a nomadic Muslim community was abducted, raped, and murdered in a temple in Kathua, Jammu and Kashmir.

Judiciary Response: The case faced communal tensions and interference. Eventually, three convicts were sentenced to life imprisonment, and three others received five-year sentences.

Challenges Highlighted: Communal tensions affecting justice, police complicity, delays due to political and religious pressures.

Impact: Demonstrated the need for protecting vulnerable communities and ensuring unbiased investigations.

Shakti Mills Gang Rape Case (2013)

Case Overview: A 22-year-old photojournalist was gang-raped by five men in the abandoned Shakti Mills compound in Mumbai.

Judiciary Response: The case was fast-tracked, and the convicts received the death penalty (later commuted to life imprisonment).

Challenges Highlighted: Need for fast-tracking severe cases, ensuring swift and effective judicial response.

Impact: Reinforced the importance of fast-track courts in dealing with heinous crimes.

Recommendations for Addressing Gaps and Challenges

Strengthening Law Enforcement and Judicial Infrastructure

Actions: Increase the number of judges, improve judicial infrastructure, and provide specialized training for law enforcement officers on handling sexual violence cases.

Expected Outcome: Reduced backlog of cases, expedited justice, and more sensitive handling of survivors.

Ensuring Independent and Unbiased Investigations

Actions: Establish independent investigative bodies for cases involving influential individuals and enforce strict penalties for police misconduct and corruption.

Expected Outcome: Greater accountability in law enforcement, unbiased investigations, and higher public trust in the justice system.

Enhancing Victim Support Services

Actions: Expand the network of one-stop Centres, provide comprehensive legal, medical, and psychological support, and ensure proper rehabilitation measures.

Expected Outcome: Improved support for survivors, better recovery and reintegration, and increased reporting of crimes.

Promoting Public Awareness and Education

Actions: Conduct nationwide awareness campaigns, integrate gender sensitization programs in schools, and promote community engagement to change societal attitudes towards sexual violence.

Expected Outcome: Reduced stigma, increased reporting of sexual violence, and more supportive societal attitudes towards survivors.

Improving Data Collection and Analysis

Actions: Establish a centralized database for sexual violence cases, improve data collection methods, and conduct regular audits to assess the effectiveness of laws.

Expected Outcome: Better understanding of trends, more informed policy-making, and continuous improvement of legal frameworks.

The implementation of laws related to sexual violence in India faces significant challenges, including delayed justice, police apathy, political influence, and societal stigma. High-profile cases highlight these systemic issues and underscore the need for comprehensive reforms. By strengthening law enforcement and judicial infrastructure, ensuring independent investigations, enhancing victim support services, promoting public awareness, and improving data collection, India can address these gaps and build a more effective system to combat sexual violence. This multi-faceted approach is essential for ensuring justice for survivors and creating a safer environment for all individuals.

Identified Patterns and Recommendations

Pattern of Power Dynamics

9 out of 15 cases involved perpetrators with some form of power, creating a sense of impunity among them and fear among victims. Addressing power dynamics is crucial for equitable justice.

Role of Media and Public Pressure

In 6 out of 15 cases, media coverage and public protests were instrumental in bringing attention and ensuring accountability. Continued media advocacy is essential for justice.

Need for Systemic Reforms

Reforms are necessary to address police misconduct, judicial delays, and societal biases. Strengthening legal frameworks, ensuring police accountability, and providing comprehensive victim support are vital.

Education and Awareness

Education on gender equality, consent, and the importance of reporting crimes is crucial. Societal attitudes towards rape victims need to change to reduce stigma and support survivors.

The analysis of these case studies reveals that socio-economic vulnerabilities, political influence, and systemic biases significantly impact the occurrence, reporting, and prosecution of rape in India. Addressing these issues requires a multi-faceted approach, including legal reforms, increased awareness and education, media engagement, and societal change. By understanding these patterns, policymakers and activists can work towards creating a safer and more just environment for all individuals.

To Conclude...

"Rape: Blame it on Patriarchy and Conservatism in India" is a comprehensive exploration of the cultural, social, and legal frameworks that contribute to the prevalence and persistence of sexual violence in India. The book delves into the historical and modern manifestations of patriarchal norms and conservative values, analysing their impact on gender roles, societal attitudes, and the judicial system.

The book emphasizes the interplay between deep-seated patriarchal values and conservative ideologies that reinforce gender inequalities and normalize sexual violence. It argues that these cultural constructs not only perpetuate gender-based violence but also hinder efforts to achieve justice and societal change. By examining both historical contexts and contemporary scenarios, the book provides a nuanced understanding of how patriarchal and conservative structures shape the experiences of sexual violence victims in India.